Using Interactive Video in Education

Penelope Semrau

California State University, Los Angeles

Barbara A. Boyer

California State University, Los Angeles

Allyn and Bacon

Boston   London   Toronto   Sydney   Tokyo   Singapore

This book is dedicated to my mother, Victoria Semrau.

Series Editor: Nancy Forsyth
Editorial Assistant: Christine Nelson
Cover Administrator: Linda Dickinson
Manufacturing Buyer: Megan Cochran
Signing Representative: Dede Saelens
Editorial-Production Service: TKM Productions
Text Designer: Suzanne Pescatore
Cover Designer: Suzanne Harbison

Copyright © 1994 by Allyn and Bacon
A Division of Paramount Publishing
160 Gould Street
Needham Heights, Massachusetts 02194

Library of Congress Cataloging-in-Publication Data

Semrau, Penelope.
    Using interactive video in education / Penelope Semrau, Barbara A.
Boyer.
      p.   cm.
    Includes bibliographical references (p.) and index.
    ISBN 0-205-15257-0
    1. Interactive video--United States. 2. Teaching--Aids and
devices. I. Boyer, Barbara A. II. Title.
LB1028.75.S46 1993
371.3'34--dc20   93-23444

Printed in the United States of America

10 9 8 7 6 5 4 3 2 1   98 97 96 95 94 93

Contents

Preface

The purpose of *Using Interactive Video in Education* is to introduce pre-service and in-service educators to the use of videodiscs in the classroom. Chapter 1 starts off with an overview of the technology, emphasizing its strengths, classroom uses, levels of interactivity, and an explanation of the CAV and CLV formats. The chapter ends with a discussion on emerging technologies such as MPC, DVI, QuickTime, and CD-I. Chapter 2 provides some excellent lesson plans, using popular commercial videodiscs such as Bio Sci II, GTV: A Geographic Perspective on American History, Interactive NOVA: Animal Pathfinders, The National Gallery of Art, and Vincent van Gogh Revisited. These lessons can serve as models in inventing your own lessons and integrating videodiscs. These lessons emphasize cooperative learning strategies, interdisciplinary activities, and evaluation of both process and product. Chapter 3, which covers the evaluation of interactive video, is rooted in current research theories. The chapter can be used to evaluate interactive video programs as well as to serve as a guide in developing your own evaluation instruments. Chapters 4 and 5 introduce authoring tools with step-by-step hands-on activities for creating interactive video programs. These chapters also compare the strengths and features of various popular authoring tools for the Apple and Macintosh computers and MS/PC-DOS computers. In conclusion, Chapter 6 describes the processes in making a videodisc. The chapter is filled with photographs illustrating the various activities and tasks such as developing a treatment, script, flowchart, and storyboard. Even though many educators may not actually make their own videodisc, the chapter explains this procedure.

Every chapter begins with objectives of what will be covered and ends with suggested learning extensions. Several useful appendices include sources for purchasing videodiscs, sources for mastering videodiscs, associations and conferences on interactive video, and a listing of authoring tools.

Using Interactive Video in Education is full of figures and photographs that illustrate the concepts and technologies discussed. There is an excellent balance of theory and hands-on applications.

Acknowledgments

There are so many helpful people who contributed to the completion of this book who we would like to acknowledge and thank. First, we would like to express our appreciation to Nancy Forsyth of Allyn and Bacon for her direction and encouragement during the writing of this book. We would like to thank our sales representative Dede Saelens; the editorial staff at Allyn and Bacon, in particular Christine Nelson; the reviewers of the manuscript, Paul Jones (Towson State University), David McMullen (Bradley University), and Vicky Sharp; (California State University, Northridge) and the staff at TKM Productions. All contributed to the quality of the book.

We highly value the input of Jeri Wilson and Curtis Wong, previously of The Voyager Company and now at Continuum Productions Corp.; and Lisa Badgett, art teacher at Southwest Academy in San Marino, California, who read, tested, and advised us on the content while the manuscript was being developed. We are also appreciative of Russell Young, lab technician at California State University, for setting up the necessary software and hardware for use in writing this text. And we wish to thank Ken Urbina, previously of Hillside Elementary School (Los Angeles Unified School District) and currently the principal of Atwater Elementary School, who was generous with his time and videodiscs in the preparation of this text.

We want to thank the companies that sent photographs for use in this book: Apple Computer Inc., Broderbund Software, Edmark Corp., Electronic Vision Inc., Hoffman Educational Systems, Intelligent Resources Integrated Systems, NewTek Inc., Optical Data Corp., Optical Disc Corp., Philips International, Pioneer Communications, Roger Wagner Publishing, Sony Corp., Tandy Corp., Techware Corp., and 3M Optical Recording.

We also wish to acknowledge Betty Tong, Shirley Liu, and Silvia Martinez, students of Diane Munson at Garfield Elementary School in Alhambra, California; who created the "Creepy Critters" in Chapter 4; Bob Mohl and Margo Nanny of Aurora Media, who created the treatment, script, storyboard, and computer screens in Chapter 6; and Stan Carstensen and Bill Stellmacher of California State University, who created some of the photography.

Most importantly, we sincerely appreciate the generous support of the following individuals who supplied the interactive multimedia products used in preparing the content:

Dawn Albertson of Broderbund Software
Teri Sturla of LucasArts Entertainment
Sarah Clarke of National Geographic
Mark Stollar of Scholastic Software
Jeri Wilson and Curtis Wong of The Voyager Company
Heidi Nietert, Joan Cash, and Terry Palasz of Videodiscovery, Inc.

Finally, we want to express our appreciation to Dr. Allen Mori, Dean of the School of Education at California State University–Los Angeles, who created the educational technology labs for our students' use, which was used extensively in the writing of this book.

1

Introduction to Videodiscs in the Classroom

Chapter Objectives

After completing this chapter, you will be able to:

- ❏ *Describe the features of a videodisc compared to a 1/2" VHS videotape.*
- ❏ *Explain what* interactivity *means.*
- ❏ *Identify the differences between levels 1 and 3.*
- ❏ *Explain what a CAV and a CLV videodisc is.*
- ❏ *Give examples of how videodiscs could be used in a classroom by teachers and students.*
- ❏ *List some emerging technologies to watch for in the future.*

Introduction

The first videodisc was demonstrated to the world in December 1972 (Optical Data Corporation, 1991, Module 6.5). Since then, over 2,200 titles have emerged for educational use, with science, health, and social science being the most popular subject areas (Emerging Technology Consultants, 1992, p. 1). In such areas as art, music, and foreign language, videodiscs have also been widely used. Videodiscs are one of the most innovative and exciting media to enter into education. For a listing of companies specializing in videodiscs for use in the classroom, please refer to Appendix A.

Increased Use of Videodiscs in Education

The use of videodiscs in classroom instruction is increasing every year and promises to revolutionize what will happen in the classroom of tomorrow. In 1991, a nationwide survey was conducted with more than 40,000 schools. Survey results noted that 7,500 schools were presently using videodiscs and 2,400 schools planned to increase their videodisc purchases (*Electronic Learning*, October 1991, p. 6). Another survey revealed that 43 percent of the technology coordinators polled from 332 school districts currently use videodiscs (*AmigaNews*, 1991, p. 1). On August 20, 1990, the Florida education commissioner announced that Florida would be purchasing videodisc players with barcode readers for each of the state's 2,500 K–12 public schools (*Instruction Delivery Systems*, November/December 1990, p. 30). And, in 1990, the San Juan Capistrano Unified School District in California bought 180 videodisc players to teach science to grades 4 through 6 (*Multimedia & Videodisc Monitor*, January 1991, p. 28). It is clear that teachers are welcoming this new technology in great numbers.

In some states, teachers are adopting videodiscs as their choice of textbook. In November 1990, the Texas Textbook Committee unanimously recommended the statewide adoption of Windows on Science for its 1,056 school districts (*Multimedia & Videodisc Monitor*, February 1991, p. 5). Windows on Science by Optical Data Corporation is a series of 11 videodiscs, 6,000 pages of teacher lesson guides, student hands-on activities, and correlated printed readers. Each videodisc is narrated

FIGURE 1-1   Key scientific concepts come alive with Optical Data's Windows on Science—a popular videodisc-based elementary science curriculum for grades 1 through 6. Photo courtesy of Optical Data Corporation.

in English and Spanish on separate audio tracks. Windows on Science is being used in elementary science instruction grades 1 through 6 (*Tech Trends*, 1990, p. 5). This was the first videodisc program to be adopted by a state as its textbook choice. Figure 1-1 displays the Windows on Science videodisc product.

As another example, the Virginia Beach School District, which is Virginia's second largest school district with more than 58,000 K–8 students, purchased 64 sets of Windows on Science. Betsy Thigpen, principal of Williams Elementary School in the Virginia Beach School District, stated, "Videodiscs are the textbooks of the future" (*Tech Trends*, 1991, p. 5). Videodiscs go beyond traditional texts by providing students access to video, stills, animation, and multiple branching and navigation tools. Optical Data claims that more than 7,500 schools nationwide are using its videodiscs in daily classroom instruction (Optical Data Corporation, 1991).

Videodiscs in the Classroom

Over the years, teachers have used lectures, movies, books, audio recordings, computers, and hands-on activities as a way to teach. Videodiscs let the teacher combine these various media. With a videodisc, a teacher has access to movies, text, and audio, all from the same source—a shiny, plastic disc. Figure 1-2 shows two 12" plastic videodiscs. Coupled with a computer, the teacher has the ultimate control over the

FIGURE 1-2   12" videodiscs. Photo courtesy of Pioneer Communications of America.

playback of the videodisc and can play back selected videos from the videodisc in any desired order. Thus, the teacher has control over the learning environment.

Recently, teachers have started to supplement their lectures with videodisc presentations. Instead of using slides, science teachers can now use videodiscs to show images of plankton, biomes, and mammals. Science videodiscs allow students to view basic science experiments that traditionally have been considered too expensive, too dangerous, or too time consuming to perform in the classroom. Scientific videodiscs are quickly eliminating huge filing cabinets that store thousands of biological slides that can bend, fall apart, deteriorate, or get shown upside down. Some of these include Bio Sci II by Videodiscovery Inc., which is geared toward high school science; Interactive NOVA: Animal Pathfinders by Scholastic Software, which focuses on the natural sciences for grades 5 through 12; and Windows on Science by Optical Data Corporation. Figure 1–3 illustrates the use of Bio Sci II for a class presentation. For a listing where you can obtain videodiscs, please refer to Appendix A.

Using a videodisc in the art classroom, students can compare artworks created during a specific time period and in a particular style, such as the nineteenth century and the Impressionist period. A single videodisc can contain the magnificent collection of the National Gallery of Art, as well as a motion-pictured guided tour through the museum and a history of the Gallery's origins. Use of interactive video in the

FIGURE 1–3   A teacher supplementing a class lecture with visuals from the Bio Sci II Videodisc by Videodiscovery, Inc. Used by permission of Videodiscovery, Inc., Seattle, WA., publishers of interactive video for science education.

classroom helps students visualize concepts and ideas while increasing the student and teacher interaction. Additionally, students are now using videodiscs to enhance their own class presentations with visuals selected from a videodisc.

What Is a Videodisc?

The Technical Aspects of a Videodisc

In your everyday conversations, you have probably already heard of the term *videodisc*. Sometimes it is called *laserdisc*. Both terms are used interchangeably to refer to video on disc. A videodisc is a flat, metallic-looking plastic disc. It looks like a shiny 331/3 rpm (revolutions per minute) phonograph record album. Its mirror-like surface has a purpose—to reflect the light of the laser beam, which is the device used to read the information off the disc. A laser beam is also the method used to record originally the information on a videodisc when its manufactured. In encoding information on the videodisc, the laser beam etches a spiral of circles into the metallicized coating on the disc. (Refer to Chapter 6 for an overview of how to make a videodisc.) If you look at the surface of the disc under a microscope, as in Figure 1–4, you would see millions of microscopic pits that have been etched into the surface. Each pit measures about 0.5 micron in diameter. The pits represent the video and audio information.

FIGURE 1–4   A microscopic view of a videodisc showing its pits. Photo courtesy of 3M Prerecorded Optical Media.

Playback of a Videodisc

During playback, a low-powered laser beam housed inside the video-disc player bounces off the pits on the surface of the videodisc, which in turn sends back signals. These signals are played back as visuals and audio on your video monitor. Both sides of a videodisc can be used.

A videodisc is not a recordable medium like a computer diskette. Although it is possible to record on a videodisc using a specialized videodisc recorder, most educational users probably will not be doing this due to the expenses involved. A special videodisc recorder, such as the Pioneer VDR-V1000 is a rewritable videodisc recorder. (Refer to Figure 1–5.) A recorder differs from the kind of videodisc player that is used in the classroom.

Generally, the kind of videodiscs used by teachers are commercially produced and cannot be altered or re-recorded on. Although advancements are being made toward a reasonably priced record/playback machine, today's videodisc player as used in the classroom is only for the playback of a videodisc and not for recording. Videodiscs come in two sizes—8" and 12", with 12" being the more popular of the two in education.

Analog and Digital Information

Information can be of two types—digital (as used by computers) and analog (as used for VHS videotapes and videodiscs). Analog information is continuous and changing, whereas digital information is discrete. Some types of analog information include time, temperature, and

FIGURE 1–5   The VDR-V1000 by Pioneer is a rewritable videodisc recorder. Photo courtesy of Pioneer Communications of America.

speed. As an example, time is not an exact, discrete number because it is continuously changing. As soon as we tell the time, it has already changed to a different time. It is continually changing; it is never static. A videotape is also recorded continuously in time. The video and audio are moving, changing, and being recorded in time. Digital data, or numbers, are what a computer uses. In particular, a computer uses binary data—bits and bytes. Measurement of the width of a table top is also expressed in digital data, which are precise, static, and unchanging.

Think of a videodisc as video on disc. Like a VHS tape, a videodisc contains both video and audio information. A videodisc can also contain digital code, although this use is uncommon. For example, a videodisc that has programming code on it can act like software to control a computer. Because interactive video companies are continually upgrading their software, it is more economical to put the software on a diskette than a videodisc. Every time the software is changed, a new videodisc would have to be mastered—and this is more expensive than duplicating computer diskettes. Videodiscs encoded with programming code are rarely used in education today. This feature is used mostly in military and industrial applications.

Two or More Audio Tracks

Although a videodisc is capable of offering four audio tracks, the use of two tracks is more common. A videodisc can have two analog and two digital audio tracks. Until recently, most videodisc players were capable of playing only analog audio. Thus, two audio tracks are more typical.

Some companies are using the two tracks for bilingual education, placing English on one track and a second language on the other. Normally, a videodisc can contain more than 20 hours of audio; however, with the new audio compression techniques, it can now hold 150 hours of audio per side.

Videodiscs Compared to VHS Tapes

Perhaps you have already seen a videodisc—many video rental stores are selling and renting videodiscs at reasonable prices. Like videotape, a videodisc is multimedia containing sound, video, computer animations, and stills. A *still* is a nonmoving picture like a screen of text, a map, a photograph, or one frame from a motion video. In addition to the multimedia feature, a videodisc offers random access, high-quality visuals, capability for interactivity and barcoding, and two or more audio tracks.

Videodisc technology offers the opportunity to access individual frames, chapters, or time code within seconds and with perfect accuracy. On the other hand, a VCR has some capability to do this, but this can be a slow and frustrating experience for anyone who has tried to rewind a tape to replay a specific scene. Generally, in rewinding the tape, you may go too far back and pass the desired frame. Then, when you fast forward to it, you might end up going past the scene.

A videodisc is able to maintain the high quality of its visuals and audio even after repeated use, unlike a videotape, which will show signs of deterioration, loss of original colors, and a reduction in sound clarity.

Unlike the deterioration that occurs on a videotape from using the VCR for freeze framing, this does not happen with a videodisc because nothing touches the surface of the videodisc except for a laser beam. *Freeze framing* is when a particular frame in a motion video is frozen in time. The motion video is stopped on a particular frame, which is then displayed as a still for a period of time.

It is difficult to predict the shelf life of videodiscs, but one can accurately say that they easily can last more than 20 years. This is based on the fact that videodiscs have been around since the 1970s and there hasn't been any deterioration in these videodiscs.

One drawback to commercially produced videodiscs is that they are a playback-only media and cannot be recorded on. Although it is possible to record on a videodisc, it is not practical at this time due to the expense. Unlike other media, a videodisc is usually recorded at the manufacturing site and is not altered. To play back a videodisc, most of us will use videodisc "players" rather than expensive "recorders." VCRs, on the other hand, are quite popular because they can be used for both play back as well as recording. Expensive specialized recordable videodisc players range in price from $19,000 to $49,000. Figure 1–5 displays the rewritable videodisc recorder—the VDR-V1000 by Pioneer.

Random Access

Videodiscs offer *random access*, which is the ability to select and display any single frame from the 54,000 available on one side of the videodisc within seconds. Obviously, this is not a feature of VHS videotapes. With this feature, a teacher may select which frames in which sequence to show to a class. The videodisc does not have to be played back in a linear order starting from frame 1 through frame 54,000. Stills can be played back in any order desired. A videodisc is unlike a videotape, which is played back in a linear fashion running continuously from the beginning to the end. Random access allows the teacher to select any frame instantly without having to rewind or fast forward the tape.

Interactivity

Teachers say they like the interactive qualities available with the use of software and a videodisc. *Interactive video* means that the teacher or student can control the selection, order, and pacing of information being presented from the videodisc by making choices at a computer. Interactivity emphasizes the difference between the strict linear and nonlinear playback of videodiscs. *Linear playback* means that the videodisc is played continuously from beginning to end. Viewing a videotape and looking at slides in a slide carousel from slide 1 to slide 100 are both examples of linear playback. Although it is possible to fast forward a videotape in search of a particular visual, this can be cumbersome and time consuming. The interactivity that is possible with a videodisc and software is what makes it so appealing for education and significantly different from using a videotape.

Interactive video also means that while one full-motion video is being displayed on the video monitor, the teacher could also display definitions for terms on the computer screen that are directly related to the same topic in the video. For example, Diane Douglas, a health teacher at John I. Leonard High School in West Palm Beach, Florida, commented on the interactive qualities of an AIDS videodisc that is being used throughout the state of Florida, "When the map of the United States comes up, the students are curious as to which states have the highest and lowest number of AIDS deaths.... Of course, they first want to know about Florida." Douglas simply slides an arrow on the computer screen to Florida and clicks once to bring up the mortality rate of AIDS in Florida (Holzberg, 1991, p. 15). Use of a computer gives the teacher more flexibility and ease of control over the videodiscs. Most teachers who have worked with videodiscs in the classroom prefer using them with a computer.

To Get Started

To start using videodiscs in your classroom, at a minimum you would need a video monitor, a videodisc player, and a videodisc. Using this system configuration, you would operate the videodisc player in the same way that you operate your home VCR, using either the buttons on the front panel of the videodisc player or a hand-held remote control. Figure 1–6 displays a close-up of a remote control unit by Pioneer. For more control and interactivity, a microcomputer would be added to your basic configuration. Later in this chapter, the types of equipment are discussed (see Components of Interactive Video Systems).

Common Videodisc Formats and Levels of Interactivity

Videodisc Formats

Videodiscs can be pressed in two formats: CAV and CLV.

CLV Constant linear velocity (CLV) is also called *extended play*. CLV discs are intended for continuous viewing. A typical application of a CLV disc is for movies. A 12" CLV disc can store up to 60 minutes of motion video, and an 8" CLV disc can play up to 20 minutes of motion video per side of disc.

FIGURE 1–6   A hand-held remote control unit can be used to view specific frames from a videodisc. Photo courtesy of Pioneer Communications of America.

A CLV disc is chapter and time addressable rather than frame addressable. A CLV disc can be prerecorded with chapter stops numbering from 0 to 79. Chapters are a way of grouping similar information together, like chapters in a textbook. Chapter stops are encoded points put on the disc during mastering. The user can jump around to selected chapter stops by entering the desired chapter number into a hand-held remote control. The videodisc player will jump to the selected chapter and start playing from there until the next chapter stop is encountered, and then the playback stops. A CLV disc is most similar to a VCR tape in that it is time coded. Like a videotape, one can search through a CLV videodisc using time references, such as 15 minutes and 10 seconds.

All frames containing video and audio information on a CLV disc are of the same length, as shown in Figure 1–7. At the outer edge of the CLV disc, several frames occupy a single rotation, whereas only one frame will occupy a single rotation near the inner edge. Generally, a frame is less than one complete rotation, except near the center, where it is a complete rotation. The speed at which a CLV revolves inside the videodisc player varies to account for the varying number of frames per rotation stored on a disc. When the laser beam is at the inner rim, the videodisc revolves at 1,800 rpm, whereas the videodisc spins at 600 rpm when the laser is at the outer edge.

A CLV disc is also similar to a videotape in that it is meant to be viewed continuously from beginning to end. Some popular movies that have appeared at theaters are now being offered for home viewing as CLV videodiscs. If the CLV videodisc is stopped, the still picture displayed on the monitor will appear jittery and not quite in focus. There-

FIGURE 1–7   Each frame on a CLV videodisc is the same length. It takes more frames to occupy a single rotation at the outer edge of the disc than toward the center. (Alessi, S. M., & Trollip, S. R. (1991). *Computer-based instruction: Methods and development.* Englewood Cliffs, NJ: Prentice Hall. Reprinted by permission.)

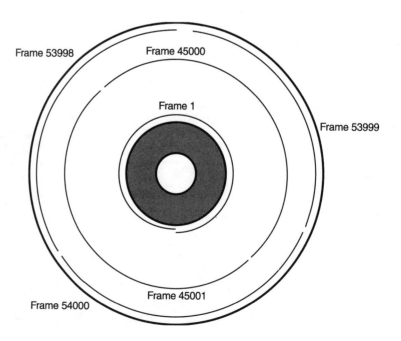

fore, because the quality of displaying a still is so poor, a CLV is not capable of actual freeze framing.

CLV videodiscs can be stopped, played forward or reverse, scanned forward or reverse, searched for a particular chapter or time code, and played with audio channel one on/off, with audio channel two on/off, and with both audio channels on/off. Since you cannot freeze frame stills from a CLV, you also cannot step forward or step reverse a frame.

CAV Constant angular velocity (CAV) is also called *standard play.* Constant angular velocity refers to the fact that the videodisc is revolving at a constant rate of 1800 rpm inside the videodisc player.

If you want random access to individual frames, then choose a CAV format. Each of the 54,000 frames on one side of a disc is frame addressable with picture-perfect clarity. Imagine having the ability to search among 54,000 still pictures for that special one and then to have it displayed within a few seconds.

Each video frame on a CAV disc is equal to one concentric track of information on the disc, as illustrated in Figure 1–8. One side of a 12" CAV videodisc can hold up to 54,000 frames, which are etched into the surface of the videodisc like 54,000 individual concentric tracks. The center-most track is frame 1 and the outer most is frame 54,000. If placed under a microscope, each track would appear as millions of

FIGURE 1–8   Each frame on a CAV disc is one complete rotation of the disc. The information in an outer frame, such as frame 50,000, takes up one complete rotation, just like an inner frame. Thus, the information in frame 50,000 is more spread out. (Alessi, S. M., & Trollip, S. R. (1991). *Computer-based instruction: Methods and development.* Englewood Cliffs, NJ: Prentice Hall. Reprinted by permission.)

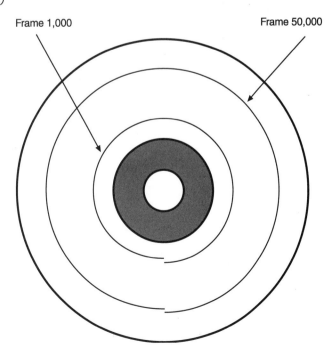

Frame 1,000   Frame 50,000

minute pits. One side of an 8" CAV disc holds up to 14 minutes of video, 25,200 still frames, or any combination of the two. The playing of a videodisc starts from the center. Each complete rotation of the disc results in one video frame. CAV videodiscs rotate at a constant speed of 30 rotations per second. This speed matches the speed of 30 frames per second at which video is played back. The information is spread out more along the track at frame 54,000. A CAV disc can contain up to 30 minutes of full-motion video per side.

A CAV videodisc creates the illusion of motion video by rapidly displaying a series of frames. The motion video is produced in the same way that a "flipbook" creates animation by rapidly flipping through the pages where each sequential page shows a bird flying away. A videodisc displays motion at the rate of 30 frames per second. Thus, 54,000 frames will equal 30 minutes of motion video. A full-motion video can be accompanied with the playback of audio, whereas a still cannot. A still is more like a freeze frame, and when the visual is frozen, so is the audio.

A CAV disc is capable of being played forward/reverse, played in slow motion forward/reverse, played in fast motion forward/reverse, stepped one frame forward/reverse, searched for a particular frame or chapter, scanned forward/reverse, and played with audio channel one on/off, with audio channel two on/off, and with both audio channels on/off. A CAV disc can also be encoded during the manufacturing, with chapter stops ranging in numbers from 0 to 79 on one side.

Features and Strengths

CAV and CLV videodiscs have the following features and strengths:

- Both CAV and CLV discs can contain full-motion video as well as up to four audio tracks—two analog and two digital.

- Both CAV and CLV discs have a higher resolution for visuals than that of a videotape.

- Both CAV and CLV discs can be searched by chapters. Content on a disc is broken into chapters, as in a textbook. To go to Chapter 6, for example, you simply key this chapter into the remote control and instantly the videodisc starts playing from there.

- Both CAV and CLV discs offers random access—that is, you can specify the ordering of the playback. The search and display time is precise and done in typically less than three seconds.

- Both CAV and CLV discs are very durable because their surfaces are coated with a protective plastic. The visuals and audio on a videodisc will not deteriorate, fade, or wear down with repeated use, nor will freeze framing deteriorate the visuals.

- Both CAV and CLV discs can be used with a barcode reader.

- A CAV disc is frame addressable. Any of the 54,000 frames on a single side of a 12" CAV disc can be selected and displayed within seconds.

- A CAV disc is interactive when controlled with software on a computer. A teacher can make choices at the computer regarding which frames to display and which audio track to hear, such as the Spanish version.

- A CLV disc can be searched by time. Simply key the desired time code in terms of minutes and seconds into the remote control and the videodisc will start playing from there.

Levels of Interactivity with Videodiscs

Due to the differences between videodisc players, the degrees of interactivity that a user can have with a videodisc varies. The various degrees of interactivity are referred to as *levels of interactivity*. *Levels* refer to the way that the videodisc is used. There are five levels of varying interactivity—levels 0, 1, 2, 3, and 4. The most common levels used in education are levels 1 and 3. Level 4 is still in development and will be defined more clearly over the next few years.

Level 0   Level 0 refers to the continuous, linear playback of a videodisc from beginning to end without interruption. You would place the videodisc into the player and start playing it from the beginning continuously through to the end. Most CLV discs are of the level 0 type. Basically, a level 0 disc is used in the same way as a videotape. Today, many popular videos are available also as level 0 discs.

Level 1   A level 1 videodisc is designed to be controlled by the user using a hand-held remote control, by pressing buttons on the front panel of the videodisc player, or using a barcode reader. (Barcodes are discussed later in this chapter.) Figure 1–9 shows a user controlling a level 1 videodisc with a hand-held remote control. A level 1 disc is played back in a nonlinear manner. CAV discs are typically level 1 discs where each one of the 54,000 frames per side is frame addressable. Windows on Science, a videodisc series for K–6 science instruction, is a good example of level 1 interactivity. Selections from the Windows on Science videodiscs are controlled manually by pressing the keys on a remote control. A level 1 disc usually contains both still frames and full-motion video sequences. Interspersed between the motion video clips in the Windows on Science videodiscs are stills. These stills are displayed as a list of questions for discussing the content that was just viewed in the motion video.

Example level 1 players include the Pioneer LD-V2000 and the Philips CDV-400. A level 1 player does not have an RS-232C port, therefore it cannot be interfaced to a computer. But a higher level 3 videodisc player can be used interchangeably as both a level 1 and 3 player.

Most teachers first starting with videodiscs prefer to work with level 1 discs. As they become more experienced, they say they prefer level 3 videodiscs, which provide for more interactivity. Level 1 is the most popular educational use of videodiscs today.

Level 2   A level 2 disc is encoded with programming code that controls the playback of the videodisc. A level 2 disc requires a special industrial level 2 videodisc player with a built-in microprocessor to execute the program code on the disc. This programming code, called *digital dumps*, is put on the disc when it is originally manufactured. When the videodisc is played back, the program code is dumped into the memory of the microprocessor. The program code is then read and interpreted by the microprocessor to control the starting, stopping, and playback of the

FIGURE 1-9   A user controlling a level 1 videodisc with a hand-held remote control.

videodisc. This smart videodisc player is a substitute for an external controlling computer system because it does the job of a computer. Level 2 videodiscs are not usually found in schools. Typically, level 2 discs are found in public kiosks at airports, large stores, and special events like the Olympics. Some videodisc players can be used for both levels 2 and 3, such as the Pioneer LD-V6000A and Sony LDP-2000.

Level 3   A level 3 videodisc is controlled by the user making choices with software at a computer. A level 3 disc requires the use of a computer. Level 3 videodiscs are usually accompanied by software customized to the contents in the videodiscs. The software is loaded into the computer. The software serves as a means to retrieve information from the disc, as well as to store responses from the student or teacher. By interacting with the software, the student or teacher can select which videodisc sequences to view and in what order. It is possible for a student to see frame 1 immediately followed by frame 100. The student simply makes a choice from a selection presented on the computer screen where each choice is keyed to a different frame number in the videodisc. The software acts as a driver for the videodisc player, calling up the desired frames. The selected frame will be presented on the video monitor. The software can also diagnose the user's input and display videodisc sequences appropriate to the student's learning style. The interactive qualities of a level 3 videodisc program clearly differentiate it from such linear media as videotapes.

Everything that can be done with a level 1 disc can also be done with a level 3 disc. Additionally, a level 3 videodisc gives the teacher or student greater flexibility, interactivity, and control with the use of a computer. Level 3 videodiscs with ancillary software include GTV: A Geographic Perspective on American History by the National Geographic Society, which is videodisc product developed for social studies classes in grades 5 through 12; The Voyager Company's Vincent van Gogh Revisited for classes teaching art history, art criticism, and aesthetics; Scholastic's Interactive NOVA: Animal Pathfinders for science instruction in grades 5 and up; and Videodiscovery's Bio Sci II for science instruction in high school classes. Chapter 2 describes lessons for using these videodiscs in the classroom.

You can also make your own level 3 software to accompany a CAV videodisc. An *authoring tool* is a specialized program that allows nonprogrammers (such as teachers) to develop their own customized software to go with a videodisc. There are more than 80 different authoring tools for every computer imaginable. Appendix C provides a comprehensive listing of the various authoring tools. The most popular ones are The Voyager Company's Videodisc ToolKit and IBM's LinkWay for the MS/PC-DOS computer and The Voyager Company's Videodisc ToolKit for the Macintosh. Chapters 4 and 5 provide an introduction to authoring tools.

A level 3 videodisc player has an RS-232C port in the back of it where a cable can be directly plugged into it, thereby connecting it to the computer. Figure 1–10 shows the back of a Pioneer LD-V4200 videodisc player. An RS-232C cable is the standard serial interface between a computer and its peripherals, such as a videodisc player. Through the RS-232C serial communications cable, the videodisc player receives commands from the computer and returns information regarding its status to the computer.

A level 3 videodisc player gives the user flexibility because both level 3 and level 1 videodiscs can be used on the same player, whereas a level 1 videodisc player can never be converted to a level 3 player because it lacks an RS-232C port. Pioneer's LD-V2200, CLD-V2400, LD-V4200, and LD-V4400, and Sony's MDP-1100 and LDP-1450 are all examples of level 3 players. Figure 1–11 shows a level 3 setup using the Sony LDP-1450. The Pioneer CLD-V2400, as shown in Figure 1–12, is a multidisc player capable of playing digital CD audiodiscs as well as videodiscs.

Level 4   Level 4 interactivity includes all the features obtainable at level 3, plus any new features that may be added on in the future. Level 4 features may mean using a videodisc player with a variety of other hardware components, such as using several videodisc players at the same time, attaching a CD-ROM player to the videodisc player setup, or using other peripheral devices with the videodisc player such as temperature sensors, steering wheels, or a CPR training system.

Special level 4 videodisc players are required for level 4 discs. These have only recently started to appear. Level 4 applications are too expensive today for educational uses and are used almost exclusively by the military.

FIGURE 1-10   The back of a Pioneer LD-V4200 videodisc player. The RS-232C interface connector is the standard interface between a computer and a videodisc player. Photo courtesy of Pioneer Communications of America.

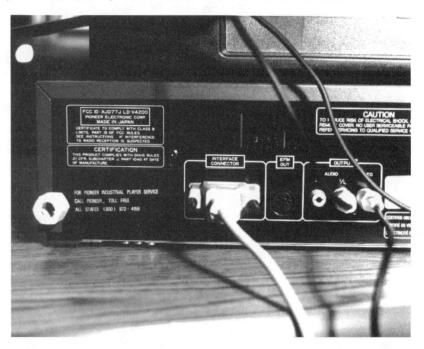

FIGURE 1-11   The Sony LDP-1450 set up for level 3 interactivity. Photograph courtesy of Sony Corporation.

FIGURE 1-12   The Pioneer CLD-V2400 LaserDisc Player is a level 3 player. Photo courtesy of Pioneer Communications of America.

Repurposing a Videodisc

Repurposing means taking an ordinary CAV videodisc that is designed for one purpose and using it for another. For example, if you created your own software to control the playback of a Windows on Science videodisc, this would be considered a repurposing of the disc. Using a software authoring tool, you can create your own customized software application to repurpose the videodisc. Teachers can do this by using authoring tools like HyperCard or LinkWay. Chapter 4 provides an introduction to authoring tools plus a hands-on exercise using the HyperCard and ToolKit authoring tools on the Macintosh. For the MS/PC-DOS user, Chapter 5 describes various authoring tools for the MS/PC-DOS computer. In addition, Chapter 5 provides a hands-on exercise for using LinkWay and ToolBook with ToolKit on the MS/PC-DOS computer.

By repurposing a disc, you are creating software customized to the needs of your classroom as well as drawing on the professionally created slides and full-motion video already contained in the videodisc. Also, you can insert feedback to your students that reflects your personality and the kind of help that you would like your students to receive. Some teachers have even digitized their own voice on the Macintosh for audio feedback that is truly personalized.

Most educational level 3 videodisc products offer built-in ways to develop your own customized slide shows. Educational products, such as Interactive NOVA: Animal Pathfinders, GTV: A Geographic Perspective on American History, and Vincent van Gogh Revisited, allow the user to select specific frames and motion video clips and put them in a special software file called a slide show. This is all done with simple point and click mouse actions. At any time, visuals can be added to and deleted from the file, and the sequence of how the visuals are played back can be changed. The time that each visual is displayed can be either manually selected with a click on the mouse or set to a predetermined time (such as three seconds). In Figure 1-13, GTV is being used to create a slide show. Teachers find that creating their own slide shows is easy to do and meets the needs of their classroom. Using a built-in program eliminates the need to learn an authoring tool.

FIGURE 1-13   Creating a customized slide show with GTV: A Geographic Perspective on American History by National Geographic Society/LucasArts Entertainment Company.

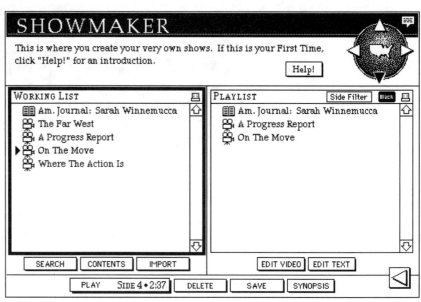

Chapters 3 and 4 cover repurposing with hands-on exercises with the following authoring tools: HyperCard and ToolKit for the Macintosh, LinkWay, and ToolBook and ToolKit for the MS/PC-DOS computer.

Barcode

Barcoding is the markings you see on many of the products you buy in grocery stores. A barcode is a series of narrow stripes of black and white, as depicted in Figure 1–14. In the grocery business, this barcode is called a *universal price code*, or UPC. Each UPC, or barcode, is synchronized to an individual brand-name product, price, and other information. When you check out, the clerk at the cash register scans the barcode printed on the side of the product across a barcode reader. Immediately the price associated with the scanned product is displayed on the cash register terminal.

FIGURE 1-14   A barcode representing a frame number on a CAV videodisc.

Van Gogh

|||||||||| |||| ||| || ||||||| ||

frame 1524

This same type of barcoding is being used today with videodiscs. Educational videodiscs are supplemented with books filled with thousands of barcodes. It may surprise you that 61 percent of the K–12 videodiscs are already accompanied by barcoded instructional materials (Emerging Technology Consultants, 1992, p. 12). Many textbook companies are beginning to correlate their texts with videodiscs by putting barcodes inside the texts. Each barcode in the book refers to a different frame out of a possible 54,000 frames on one side of a CAV videodisc.

To use barcoding, simply wave the pen-shaped barcode reader over the desired barcode to select a frame from the videodisc. Figure 1–15 illustrates how this is done. The selected frame will appear instantly on the video monitor.

A barcode reader acts like a remote control, except that you do not have to key in the frame numbers—you just scan in the frame number. The basic operations of the videodisc player, such as "play video" and "stop" can be controlled with the barcode reader by scanning the barcode that is associated with this action.

There are a variety of barcode readers. Figures 1–16 and 1–17 show two barcode readers available from Pioneer. Most teachers enjoy using barcode readers because they are easier to use than remote controls. Companies such as Videodiscovery, Houghton Mifflin, Silver Burdett &

FIGURE 1–15   Using a barcode reader to scan over a barcode to select a video frame. Used by permission of Videodiscovery, Inc., Seattle, WA., publishers of interactive video for science education.

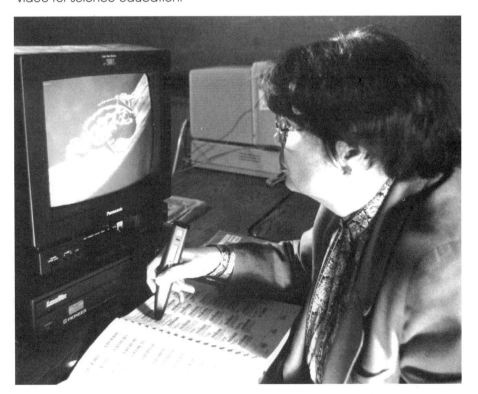

FIGURE 1-16   A close-up of a barcode reader available from Pioneer. Photo courtesy of Pioneer Communications of America.

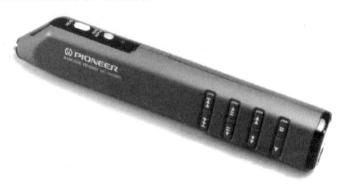

Ginn, and Hoffman Educational Systems are indexing entire contents of their videodiscs and providing books full of barcodes along with the videodiscs. Houghton Mifflin has begun distributing American History, a videodisc barcoded to its popular American History textbook series. The American History videodisc contains more than 2,490 still images as well as 28 minutes of full-motion video. The American History disc can be accessed either with a barcode reader or a remote control.

Hoffman Educational Systems publishes Laser Learning–a barcoded reading program with 18 videodiscs designed for grades 4 through 6. Laser Learning applies the whole-language approach based on content-rich lessons in literature, science, social studies, history, and the arts. Silver Burdett & Ginn have made available three Science Horizons Videodiscs for use with their textbooks in earth, life, and physical science for grades 3 through 6. These discs are correlated to the teacher's

FIGURE 1-17   Another type of barcode reader from Pioneer. The user simply lays it over the barcode instead of scanning the barcode. Many users find this type easier to use. Photo courtesy of Pioneer Communications of America.

guide. The teacher's guide provides barcodes for specific motion video clips and stills as barcode stickers. These stickers can be pasted into the teacher's own lesson plans to customize them. Another scientific videodisc that comes with a book full of barcodes indexed to the various topics on the disc is Bio Sci II for high school science courses.

Barcoding Software

For those of you who want to create your own barcodes, there is barcoding software that you can use with your computer. Using the Pioneer Bar'n'coder software on the Macintosh, teachers can select which stills and motion video clips they want to access from the videodisc. The software automatically generates the appropriate barcodes and prints them using either a dot-matrix or laser printer. Although they can be printed out on standard computer paper, they work best if they are printed onto adhesive-backed address labels. Then they can be easily peeled off and pasted into daily lesson plans for truly customized instruction. During class instruction, the teacher simply scans the barcodes in the lesson plan to control the videodisc player.

With barcode software, barcodes can be generated and then copied and pasted into other documents. They can be pasted into such word-processing and desktop publishing files as lesson plans, quizzes, student worksheets, as well as other learning resource materials.

Barcoding software, such as the LaserBarcode Tool Kit software by Pioneer, is available for IBM PCs and compatibles. BarCode Maker by Creative Laser Concepts is also available for a variety of computers, including IBM and compatibles, Apple II, and Macintosh.

Components of an Interactive Video System

The number of videodisc players in schools continues to escalate annually. Just look at the facts:

- A 1987 study noted that about half of the 100,000 videodisc systems being used in the United States for nonconsumer use were for training and educational applications (Miller, 1987).

- A 1989 study reported that 6 percent of K–12 schools nationwide had at least one videodisc player (Bruder, 1989, p. 28).

- A 1990 article noted that the number of videodisc players for nonconsumer use increased to approximately 150,000. Of these, it was estimated that some 30,000 were in education (Pollack, 1990, p. 14).

- A 1991 report noted that of the 35,000 videodisc players in the K–12 schools, 90 percent were manufactured by Pioneer (*Electronic Learning*, March 1991, p. 8). Although Pioneer has maintained the greatest market share of videodisc players sold in the United States, Sony's sales are rapidly increasing.

To get started working with videodisc technology, what exactly does a teacher need?

Minimum Setup: A Videodisc Player and Standard Television Set

The most basic configuration consists of a videodisc player hooked up to a monitor or standard TV (see Figure 1–18). Some players will accept a standard TV in place of a monitor. The video image is of a higher quality when used with a color video monitor. With the videodisc player, you can control the playback of the videodisc by simply pressing the buttons in the control panel on the front of the videodisc player. The videodisc can be played forward, stopped, and stepped forward/reverse.

An example of a level 1 player is the LD-V2000, which can be used with an ordinary TV. The LD-V2000 can access a selected frame out of 54,000 on one side of a videodisc in less than eight seconds. The speed of accessing the desired frame is called the *access time*. Generally, the more expensive the player, the faster the access time. A limitation to a level 1 player is that it can never be hooked up to a computer. The LD-V2000 is barcode compatible and includes a wireless hand-held remote control. Panasonic's answer to level 1 playback is the LX-120, which comes with a battery-powered hand-held remote control. The LX-120 can be connected to a standard television and is also barcode compatible.

The minimum equipment requirements needed to get started with level 1 CAV videodiscs include the following:

FIGURE 1–18   The minimum hardware configuration for a level 1 videodisc application includes a videodisc player, a monitor, and perhaps a remote control. Used by permission of Videodiscovery, Inc., Seattle, WA., publishers of interactive video for science education.

Level 1 Setup
- Pioneer LD-V2000 or Panasonic LX-120
- Television set or monitor
- CAV videodisc
- Optional: Barcode reader or remote control

Interactive Video Setup: Videodisc Player, Monitor, and Computer

Level 3 interactivity allows the user to control the playback of the videodisc with a computer. The basic configuration for level 3 interactivity consists of a level 3 videodisc player, monitor, and computer. Figure 1–19 illustrates the basic configuration for level 3 use.

Any personal computer, such as the IBM PS/2, Macintosh Performa 400, or Apple IIGS, can be interfaced to a level 3 videodisc player with a connecting cable going from the RS-232C port in the back of the videodisc player to the computer. An advantage to having a level 3 player is that it can also be used as a level 1 stand-alone player. Examples of level 3 players by Pioneer are the LD-V4200, LD-V4400, LD-V2400, and LD-V2200. The LD-V4400 replaces the LD-V4200 since Pioneer has discontinued manufacturing the LD-V4200. A benefit of the Pioneer LD-V2200 is that is can also be connected to a standard TV. Not all players are able to do this—many need to be connected to a video

FIGURE 1–19   The basic hardware configuration for a level 3 videodisc application consists of a computer, videodisc player, and monitor.

monitor. A comparable level 3 model by Sony is the MDP-1100 player. The MDP-1100 comes standard with a remote control, is barcode ready, and can be used with a standard TV. A more expensive videodisc player by Sony is the LDP-1450. Level 3 players generally provide for remote control and barcode reading.

The search access time on the Pioneer LD-V4200 and LD-V4400 is faster than the LD-V2200 or LD-V2400 players. Most players have an average access time of 2 to 3.5 seconds. The access time of the Sony LDP-1450 is less than 2 seconds. The faster the access time, the more expensive is the player.

Whole-Class Instruction

For whole-class instruction, an LCD (liquid crystal display) projection panel would come in handy to project what is on your computer screen to a large screen. As shown in Figure 1–20, the LCD panel sits on top of an ordinary overhead transparency projector. It acts as another monitor by displaying whatever appears on the computer screen. A cable connects the LCD to the computer. The overhead projector projects the visuals displayed in the LCD to the large screen in the same way that it projects the information from a plastic transparency. nView Corporation markets a variety of LCDs for different computers.

To complete your setup, you would hook a large Sony 21" (or larger) monitor to the videodisc player to display the video information. The

---

FIGURE 1–20   LCD panels are great for whole-class instruction. The LCD sits on top of an ordinary overhead transparency projector and displays the exact image shown on the computer screen. (P. Merrill et al. (1992). *Computers in education* (2nd ed., p. 45). Boston: Allyn and Bacon. Reprinted by permission.)

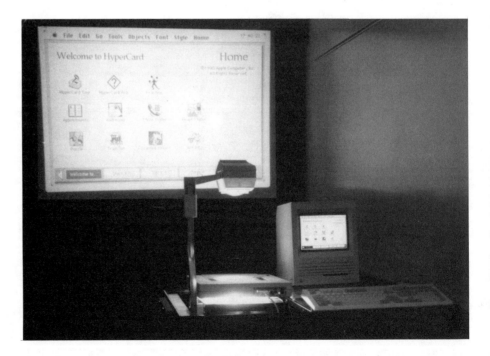

audio is played back using the speakers in the video monitor.

The minimum equipment requirements needed to work with interactive video at level 3 include the following:

Level 3 Setup
• Pioneer LD-V4400 or Sony LDP-1450
• Sony color monitor (the larger the better)
• Macintosh LC or IBM PS/2 computer
• RS-232C cable
• CAV videodisc
• Level 3 software to support the CAV videodisc
• Optional: Barcode reader and a wireless remote control

Educational Features of Videodiscs

Videodiscs Offer a Rich Base of Various Audiovisual Information

Videodiscs offer an exciting array of multimedia all in one package. One videodisc can contain full-motion color videos, stills (i.e., photographs, graphic illustrations, maps), computer-generated animations, title screens, and two or more audio tracks.

With the continuing high student dropout rate, perhaps educators need to start looking at alternative methods of delivering instruction. Recent use of videodiscs in the classroom has shown some very positive results. In fact, students have shown significantly more positive attitudes toward learning from interactive video than from other methods of instruction (Cushall, Harvey, & Brovey, 1987, p. 2). In addition to being a multimedia source, videodiscs are also a multisensory educational tool. Students who are predominantly visual learners will appreciate a videodisc for its graphics, full-motion videos, maps, photographs, and diagrams. Auditory learners will learn from a videodisc by focusing on the various sound effects, narration, and music, or in bilingual education where one track can be heard in Spanish and the other in English.

Videodiscs Provide In-Depth Information

Used in conjunction with software, a videodisc is a visual database that can be searched for selected visual/audio information. For example, a fourth-grader who is using a videodisc discovers that the spotted owl is an endangered species. Curious about what other endangered species exist, the student double clicks with the mouse on the word *endangered* that appears on the computer screen. Instantly, a list of other endangered animals, such as the sea otter, African white tiger, and killer whale, appear on the computer screen. The student clicks once on the words *sea otter* to see a visual instantly displayed on the video monitor. The software is used by the student to display individual frames from the videodisc. After reading through the textual information presented on the computer screen about the sea otter, the student discovers that the one thing she does not understand is the term *biome*. The student double clicks on the word *biome* and is presented with a world map that illustrates various locations of biomes. A definition of *biome* also appears on the computer screen, as well as a listing of the various biomes. By clicking on one of the biomes, such as desert, a series of various desert pictures are displayed on the video monitor. Use of a videodisc by students fosters critical thinking by allowing the learners to look at the information in a variety of formats, to be able to compare and contrast various kinds of information, to analyze and evaluate the information, and ultimately to use the information in a different context.

The databasing features of interactive video mean that a student or teacher can jump around amongst the various kinds of information in the videodisc and software in a nonlinear, nonsequential manner. Most of us probably think in a nonlinear style by association, making links between various kinds of ideas and feelings. The use of interactive video in the classroom lends itself to this kind of nonsequential, nonlinear yet highly productive associative learning.

Videodiscs Offer High-Quality Video

The quality and sharpness of a visual displayed on a television is measured by the number of lines of horizontal resolution—the more the better. A videotape is recorded with about 240 lines. By comparison, a videodisc is recorded with 350 lines of resolution. Thus, visuals on a videodisc have a sharper appearance and higher-quality resolution than a videotape.

Videodiscs Offer High-Quality Audio

Videodiscs offer high-quality, stereophonic sound. Additionally, videodiscs can have up to four separate audio tracks—each of which can be independently accessed. Two tracks can be laid down with analog sound and the other two can be recorded with digital audio. A videodisc recorded with digital audio provides the highest-quality sound equal to that of digital CD audiodiscs. Currently, it is more common to have no more than two audio tracks on a videodisc. An excellent example of using the two audio tracks for independent playback is provided on the Vincent van Gogh Revisited Videodisc by The Voyager Company. On audio channel one is a narrator reading from Vincent's letters to his brother, Theo. On the second channel is the voice of Leonard Nimoy describing information about Vincent's life and work. Either audio channel can be selected by simply clicking on a button displayed on the Macintosh computer screen. The Bio Sci II Videodisc by Videodiscovery Inc. makes use of both tracks for bilingual education where one track is in Spanish and the other in English.

In the near future, videodiscs are going to make more use of four audio tracks—one audio track could be in English, the second in Spanish, the third a voice-over narration interpreting the video scene itself, and the fourth another voice-over as told from the actual person being portrayed in the video story.

Videodiscs Are Easy to Use

Using a computer, remote control, barcode reader, or the control panel on the front of the videodisc player, the playback of videodiscs can be easily done. Using a hand-held remote control, you simply press the "play" button and the videodisc starts playing, just like a videotape would in a VCR. For greater interaction, a computer is required. When hooked to a computer, interactive video combines the power and interactivity of a computer with the video and audio qualities of television. Videodisc technology allows students to adjust the pace of learning to better suit their needs and learning styles.

Videodiscs Give the Learner Control

Interactive video makes learning individualized by putting the learner in control. Using a computer, the student can select what frames to view, in what order, and at what speed. The learning is self-directed. Students enjoy having the opportunity to move through a videodisc at their own pace (Corum et al., 1991, p. 25). Because they do have control, faster learners can move more quickly through the information, thus reducing the chance for boredom. Lower-ability students can move at their own pace and repeat any information that they desire. Therefore, they are more motivated to stay on task and learn.

Videodisc players make it easy to repeat video clips, play them in slow motion, or freeze frame them. With the Vincent van Gogh Revisited, the student can jump back and forth on the videodisc to see various video clips of Vincent's life as narrated by Leonard Nimoy, to view motion videos of the actual streets in Paris or the fields in Holland where van Gogh painted, and to admire brilliantly colored stills of his artworks. It is an excellent mixture of stills and full-motion video that can be controlled by the student for self-directed, individualized learning.

Videodiscs Provide Short Access Time to Specific Visuals

It takes less than three seconds for a typical videodisc player to find a specific frame on a videodisc. Frames and motion video clips can be accessed using a remote control, barcode reader, or computer. Unlike a variety of other media devices, including VCRs, the access time of a videodisc player is fast and accurate.

Videodiscs Are Durable

The information on a videodisc is permanent—it cannot be altered, erased, or worn down. Since nothing except a low-powered laser beam touches the surface of the videodisc, it should last indefinitely. It should not wear down or deteriorate with repeated plays, pausing, or freeze framing. The same high-quality video and audio remains unchanged after years of use.

Videodisc Players Can Be Controlled in a Variety of Ways

A videodisc player is like a VCR in that both can be used as multimedia playback systems. Both can play back audio, stills, and motion video. Unlike a VCR, a videodisc can be accessed with a variety of devices, including a remote control, front panel on the videodisc player, barcode reader, or computer. In order for computer control, the videodisc player needs to be interfaced to the computer with a RS-232C interface, which is the standard connection.

Effectiveness of Interactive Video in Instruction

In the last 20 years, there has been considerable research done on the effectiveness of interactive video in instruction. A major report was published in July 1990 by J. D. Fletcher, who summarized a review of 47 studies. Fletcher concluded that interactive video instruction is more effective and less costly than conventional instruction. Following is a summary of Fletcher's conclusions.

Interactive Video Is Used Successfully to Teach

Overall, interactive video was found to improve academic achievement when compared to less interactive, more conventional approaches to instruction (Fletcher, 1990, summary pages 1–2). Another study conducted in 1987–1988 indicated that students who received interactive video in physical science education significantly outperformed students with conventional instruction. The greatest improvement occurred among low-ability students. For this study, a complete two-semester interactive videodisc-based physical science curriculum for ninth- and tenth-graders was developed by the Texas Learning Technology Group (TLTG). The interactive videodisc curriculum consisted of 160 hours of instruction in which students used interactive video for 50 percent of the classroom instruction time. The students receiving interactive video instruction expressed a greater interest in taking additional science courses (Callahan, 1990, p. 24). Interactive video opens doors for learners by providing a new and exciting entry to knowledge.

Even more substantial gains in student achievement were noted by Pioneer—a leading manufacturer of videodisc players. Pioneer stated that average-ability students who learned with interactive video scored 33 percent higher than those receiving conventional instruction.

Another study conducted in Georgia with eighth-graders indicated that interactive video instruction was significantly more effective than conventional methods of instruction. The study also showed that interactive video instruction can be significantly more efficient (White, Mathews, & Holmes, 1989, p. 22).

Teachers in Burkburnett, Texas, came up with the same conclusions. At Burkburnett High School, videodiscs are being used for 70 percent of its physical science class instruction with huge success. The Burkburnett study concluded that students who received videodisc instruction were more likely to enroll in third- and fourth-year science classes, succeed in the physical science courses, have a more positive attitude toward science, and demonstrate a longer retention of science information (Louie et al., 1991, p. 22).

Use of Interactive Video in the Classroom Is Effective for Knowledge and Performance Outcomes

Fletcher (1990) noted that students did equally well on knowledge outcomes as well as performance outcomes. *Knowledge outcomes* include learning about facts, concepts, and other information. *Performance outcomes* include learning about procedures, skills, and other capabilities that students could demonstrate (summary pages 2–3). The

1987–88 study involving the TLTG interactive videodisc physical science curriculum showed that students performed well on both mastery of physical science content as well as process skills (Callahan, 1990, p. 25).

The results of another study published in 1988 indicated that 76 percent of the students polled nationwide had improved content mastery with the use of interactive video for instruction. In addition, 72 percent had a greater use of scientific thinking skills (Optical Data Corporation, 1988, p. 74).

Fletcher (1990) was also able to show a connection between student achievement and the degree of interactivity in interactive video instruction. The more interactive the system was, the more students learned. Students learn better actively, nonlinearly, visually, and cooperatively (Mageau, 1990, p. 23). The greatest achievements were found with the use of level 3 interactive video systems (Fletcher, 1990, summary page 3).

Use of Interactive Video in Instruction Is Less Costly than Conventional Instruction

Students are more engaged in the learning task when using interactive video. Students learned the content in 31 percent less time than with conventional instruction (Fletcher, 1990, summary page 4). Interestingly enough, interactive video has also been shown to increase student attendance, which is a critical factor (Davey, 1990, p. 9). All of these research data demonstrate the capability of videodiscs and new frontiers for learning.

Using Interactive Video in the Classroom

Following is an overview of the various uses of videodiscs in the classroom. For a more detailed account of how to use selected commercial videodiscs, refer to Chapter 2.

Travel to Uncommon Destinations

Videodiscs can take students to places where they have never been before. Using interactive video, students can now travel to destinations that would be impossible for most of us to experience, such as Mars and inside a human being. At the San Jose Museum of Science and Technology (also called the "garage" by the local residents who acknowledge all the computer inventions that took place in garages, such as the invention of the Apple computer), an interactive video setup allows museum visitors to travel over the surface of Mars. Using a joystick, the museum visitor chooses the path of travel, controls the speed of flight, and steers the direction of flight. One can dip down into valleys the size of the Grand Canyon or fly over tall mountain peaks. It is even possible for the user to crash into the side of a mountain if a judgment error is made while steering the flight.

Other destinations of travel via interactive video would be those that are impossible because of our body size, such as entering into a human's body via an arterial vein. Students would be able to observe how blood cells move through an artery and how the heart pumps. Another perspective would be to shrink our view down to the size of an ant to observe the social interactions of carpenter ants moving through the tunnels in their ant colony.

With interactive video, students can also travel and experience other cultures in distant foreign lands. Interactive video stimulates the curiosity of students and motivates exploration.

An Archive

A videodisc is a desirable media for preserving a large archive due to its durable surface, large storage capacity, and ability to maintain high-quality color over the years, which is not a feature found in color slides that deteriorate with use.

Videodiscs are excellent for holding a museum's collection of paintings, such as those by twentieth-century American artists. Students in art history may compare various artists from the same period with the use of an interactive video. An example of using a disc for archival purposes in art is The National Gallery of Art from The Voyager Company. Figure 1–21 displays an artwork selected from The National Gallery of Art videodisc.

With videodiscs, students have easy access to volumes of information. Students can use videodiscs as a research source in the same way that they gather evidence from newspapers, journals, encyclopedias,

FIGURE 1–21   Videodiscs can contain the collection of an art museum. This figure shows one visual image from The National Gallery of Art videodisc by The Voyager Company. Courtesy of The Voyager Company.

and books. Also, many of the film classics are also now available on videodiscs.

Class Lectures

Teachers have ultimate control over the selection, ordering, and pacing of information displayed from a videodisc. Teachers can freeze frame motion video clips at critical points, show entire motion video clips in slow motion, and repeat important visual concepts quickly and easily for clear demonstrations. With barcoding, teachers can simply wave a wand over the barcode to access a specific visual from the videodisc.

With easy-to-use authoring tools such as HyperCard, teachers can create customized software. Figure 1–22 shows a card from HyperCard. Teachers may enter their lesson notes into HyperCard and then synchronize them to the specific audio/visual frames from the videodisc. The visuals from the videodisc can be used to illustrate lecture points and provide demonstrations and simulations of concepts.

Dynamic Textbook

A videodisc can become a dynamic textbook with the use of either commercially or teacher-produced software used in conjunction with a videodisc. The software can be customized by the teacher to ask questions, define terms, point out key ideas, and test students. This is particularly useful for students who need a review or have missed a class.

FIGURE 1–22   HyperCard (by Claris Corporation) is a very popular authoring tool used by teachers on the Macintosh. HyperCard software is © 1987–1993 Claris Corporation. All rights reserved. HyperCard is a registered trademark of Claris Corporation.

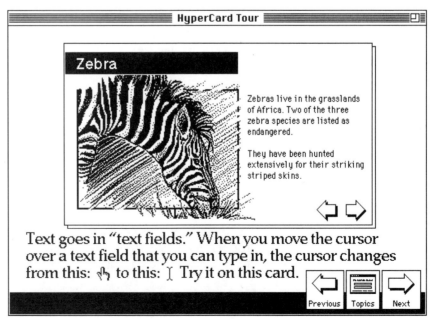

Desktop Publishing

Teachers can create visually exciting class handouts, transparencies, and lab manuals with images taken from videodiscs. Using digitizing software such as ComputerEyes for the Macintosh or IBM, or MacVision for the Macintosh, visuals can be selected from the videodisc, sized, and printed. Using your desktop publishing or word-processing software, headings can be entered and integrated with the visuals to point out key ideas. The finished work can even be printed in color using a color ribbon on your dot-matrix printer. Before you do this, though, make sure that you have permission to reproduce the images from the videodisc by contacting the publisher. Some publishers grant permission to educators and others will state that the visuals are copyrighted and cannot be reproduced in any form or means.

Create Customized Videotapes

To create customized videotapes, transfer motion video clips from the videodisc directly to videotape using software products such as Promotion on the Macintosh. If desired, you can even dub in your own voice as narration in the videotape. Be certain to seek out the appropriate copyright permissions first before doing this, however.

Administer Tests

Teachers can show frames from a videodisc (just as they would show slides) and ask the students to identify the pictures or make comparisons between them. Using a videodisc, teachers can bring up motion video clips that illustrate a scientific phenomenon and ask students to write an essay describing the event.

A computer can also be connected with the videodisc player to perform test management and record keeping. Students could take their tests right at a computer that is hooked to a videodisc player. Their answers would be graded by the software and saved in a file on the computer. Later, the teacher could print out the individual student and class results.

Student Presentations

Students can enliven their own class presentations with the use of videodiscs. They can display images and motion video from videodiscs, just like they would with slides, overheads, and videos.

Creative Writing

Students can create their own stories illustrated with visuals displayed from a videodisc. They can even produce digitized printouts of images from a videodisc to add as figures to their research papers.

Handling a Videodisc

It is wise to handle your videodiscs carefully to prolong their lives as well as the life of your videodisc player. Keep your discs clean by wiping off any smudges with a slightly damp, clean, soft cloth. Even though the smudges will not affect the quality of the information on the disc, over time it will destroy your videodisc player because it takes more laser energy to penetrate the dirt on the disc. Eventually, use of dirty discs can burn out the laser mechanism, which is the most expensive part to replace in the videodisc player. There are even special cloths on sale at stores where videodiscs are sold.

Keep your videodiscs out of direct sunlight and away from high temperatures that may permanently warp the disc. When not in use, store the videodisc in its original sleeve and jacket in an upright vertical position.

The Future

In addition to interactive video, several other technologies are emerging that offer many exciting possibilities for use in education. These include CD-ROM, CD-I, DVI, QuickTime, and the new software and hardware that will be produced at Kaleida Labs. Kaleida Labs is the name given to the newly formed research venture between IBM and Apple. In general, the future of technology is to have greater amounts of multimedia on smaller-sized discs with a diameter of 4.75" or smaller.

CD-ROM

Many schools are already using CD-ROMs (compact disc read-only memory). CD-ROMs are laser-encoded optical storage devices used to store any kind of digital information, including text, graphics, photos, sound, digitized motion video, as well as software programs. Companies such as Discis and The Voyager Company have published a variety of CD-ROMs for use in literature, reading, and music. Figure 1–23 shows a screen displayed from a CD-ROM entitled Exotic Japan by The Voyager Company.

A 4.75" CD-ROM has the storage capacity to contain not only all the information in a textbook but an entire encyclopedia. The small size of a 4.75" CD-ROM is contrasted to a 12" videodisc in Figure 1–24. An entire 20-volume encyclopedia can be carried in your pocket. In fact, Grolier (an encyclopedia company) markets a CD-ROM version of their well-known encyclopedia entitled The Grolier Electronic Encyclopedia. It includes 1,500 full-color illustrations, audio capabilities, 33,000 articles, up to 15 windows of text, full split-screen options, on-line help, pull-down menus, and hundreds of high-resolution color maps. The text, graphics, and maps can be saved to your own computer disk, as well as cut and pasted into any document, such as a word-processing or desktop publishing file.

FIGURE 1-23   A screen displayed on the Macintosh from the CD-ROM entitled Exotic Japan by The Voyager Company. Courtesy of The Voyager Company.

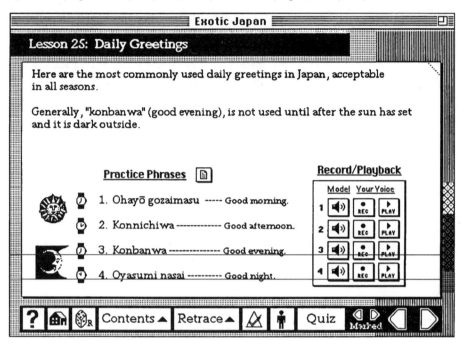

CD-ROMs are becoming so popular that there are even publications devoted exclusively to the CD-ROM industry. For example, *CD-ROM Professional* is a journal focusing on this medium, *CD-ROMS in Print* is a reference book describing over 3,000 titles, and *CD-ROM* is a catalog listing hundreds of titles for every subject area imaginable. Some titles listed in *CD-ROM* include Time Table of History: Business, Politics and Media; United States Supreme Court on Disc; American Heritage Illustrated Encyclopedia; A Visit to Sesame Street—Numbers; How the Camel Got His Hump (Spanish & English versions); Mozart: The "Dissonant" Quartet; North American Indians; Cinderella; Desert Storm; English as a Second Language Series; Mammals: A Multimedia Encyclopedia; Presidents: It All Started with George; and Shakespeare Illustrated—to name just a few!

A Children's CD-ROM Discis publishes a children's CD-ROM entitled Heather Hits Her First Home Run. It is a book on disc that is read using a Macintosh computer. Using a mouse, children can read the story themselves or listen as it is read to them with various musical and sound effects. The gender of the reader's voice can be selected, as well as if it is read in Spanish or English. Teachers can select the rate at which students hear the story read aloud to them. Various rates include phrase by phrase, with up to four seconds between each phrase; sentence by sentence, or page by page. Children can highlight any block of text to hear it pronounced aloud as many times as they wish. Children can also point and click on different objects in the picture, such as hat, bat, and ball to hear its name said out loud. Sound effects, such as the crack of the bat

FIGURE 1–24   A leading manufacturer of CD-ROMs is 3M. 3M masters videodiscs, CD-ROMs, as well as rewritable optical disks. Notice the small size of the 4.75" CD-ROM discs compared to the 12" videodisc. Photo courtesy of 3M Prerecorded Optical Media.

when Heather hits the ball and the applause and cheer of the crowd, further enhance the story. The size of the font appearing on the screen is adjustable so that younger children can read using a larger font size (Discis Knowledge Research, Inc.).

CD-ROM Storage Capacity   CD-ROMs are becoming quite popular because of their huge storage capacity, small portable size, and durability. A CD-ROM is like a computer diskette in that it holds digital information, but a CD-ROM has a much greater storage capacity. The storage capacity of one CD-ROM is about 650 megabytes (MB) which is equal to over 1,500 common floppy disks, 500 high-density 3.5" disks, 270,000 pages of text or data, 6,000 enhanced graphic images, 12,000 scanned images, 72 minutes of high-fidelity music, or any combination of the above. Also, the information on the CD-ROM does not change or deteriorate with repeated use. Each disc is sprayed with a clear protective coating of plastic. When the disc is read in the CD-ROM drive, nothing touches the surface except for the reflection of a low-powered laser beam.

A CD-ROM is a playback medium, meaning that you can read the information on it but you cannot write, edit, or delete files on it. The information on a CD-ROM is originally laser encoded when it is manufactured. Using a computer and CD-ROM drive, you can read the information on a CD-ROM and copy information from it over to your computer. Once the information is in your computer, you can use it, edit it, and save it to a computer disk.

CD-ROM and Digital Information   Information is recorded on a CD-ROM with a laser device that imprints microscopically small pits into the surface. Figure 1–25 displays a magnified view of a CD-ROM disc showing its pits. Like a videodisc, information is read off the CD-ROM with a laser beam that is housed inside the CD-ROM drive. The low-powered laser beam reflects off the shiny disc. But this is where the similarities between a videodisc and CD-ROM end. Information on a videodisc is analog, like a videotape. All the information on a CD-ROM is digital information. Digital information is stored or transmitted as a series of binary digits. Computers, software, and digital CD audiodiscs are digital media. To be able to put motion video on a CD-ROM, the analog video and audio

FIGURE 1–25   A microscopic view of a CD-ROM showing the pits etched into the surface. Photo courtesy of 3M Prerecorded Optical Media.

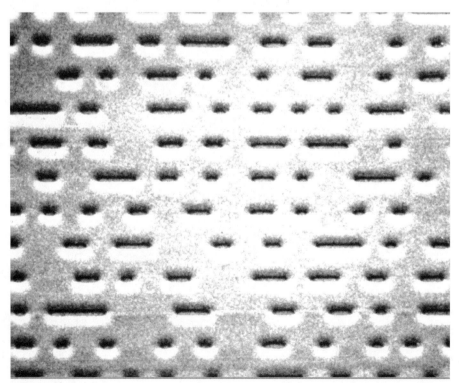

information has to be converted to digital data; that is, it has to be digitized. An analog signal cannot be sent directly to a computer screen without having been converted to digital data. Since the information in a CD-ROM is digital, it can be sent directly to a computer screen. Whatever motion video and audio information is seen or heard from a CD-ROM was first digitized and then recorded onto the disc.

When you first insert a CD-ROM into the CD-ROM drive, a CD-ROM disc icon appears on the computer screen, as in Figure 1–26. If you are using a Macintosh IIsi, you would simply double click on the CD-ROM icon appearing on your computer screen. The CD-ROM icon looks like a miniature disc. This action would display the contents of the disc as a directory in a window on your computer screen. Working with a CD-ROM on a computer screen is done in the same way as you would interact with a 3.5" computer disk. To launch or start up a program from the CD-ROM, you would simply double click on a program icon displayed in the window on your Macintosh screen.

Although a 4.75" CD-ROM looks just like a 4.75" digital CD audiodisc, there are some differences. Like a CD audiodisc, a CD-ROM has the same wonderful capability for CD-quality sound. Both can contain digital audio. But a CD audiodisc does not have the potential to store a software program, whereas a CD-ROM does. The programming code that would be put on a computer disk is the same programming code that would appear on a CD-ROM. Because programs are getting so much larger today, CD-ROMs are an ideal source for holding gigantic

FIGURE 1–26   In this picture taken from the Macintosh desktop, the arrow pointer is pointing to the icon representing a CD-ROM entitled Poetry in Motion by The Voyager Company.

multimedia programs containing sound effects, music, digitized voices, computer animations, digitized motion videos, and graphics. Unfortunately, when motion video is digitized, it takes up a lot of disc storage. To reduce the size of the disc storage taken up by digitized video, newly developed compression and decompression techniques, such as QuickTime and DVI, are used. Although much of the work in compression and decompression of motion video is still emerging, it holds much promise for future use in education. CD-ROMs are becoming the preferred media for educational stacks because a producer can put many QuickTime movies on a CD-ROM, as well as colorful graphics and digital audio—all of which take up a lot of disk storage space.

In addition to being able to use software, graphics, and audio stored on a CD-ROM, the AppleCD 300 drive is also capable of displaying pictures stored on Photo CDs. Photo CD is a new technology developed by Kodak that lets your local, commercial film developer store your photographs in digital format on special compact discs. Then, using the AppleCD 300, photos from the Photo CD can be displayed on your color Macintosh computer screen. The AppleCD 300 is displayed in Figure 1–27.

CD-ROMs require a specialized CD-ROM drive in order to be used. As shown in Figure 1–27, an external CD-ROM drive looks like a box measuring approximately 6" wide × 12" deep × 3" high. The CD-ROM drive is connected to the computer with a cable plugging into the SCSI port at the rear of the computer. The CD-ROM is then inserted into a disc caddy, which is placed in a sliding tray in the front of the CD-ROM drive.

FIGURE 1–27   An external CD-ROM drive, called the AppleCD 300 by Apple Computer, is capable of playing CD-ROMs, digital CD audiodiscs, and the Kodak Photo CDs. Photo courtesy of Apple Computer, Inc., John Greenleigh, photographer.

FIGURE 1-28   The Macintosh IIvx by Apple has a built-in CD-ROM drive. Photo courtesy of Apple Computer, Inc., John Greenleigh, photographer.

CD-ROM drives are made by a variety of manufacturers, including Apple, NEC, Hitachi, Pioneer, and others. A CD-ROM drive can also come built into the computer. The Macintosh Performa 600, the Macintosh Centris 650, and the Macintosh IIvx can be ordered with an internal CD-ROM drive (see Figure 1-28).

A multimedia MS/PC-DOS microcomputer that has a built-in CD-ROM drive is called a *MPC* (multimedia personal computer). Basically, a MPC comes with a built-in CD-ROM drive, audio board, the Microsoft Windows 3.1 graphical environment with multimedia extensions, and a set of amplified speakers or headphones for high-fidelity stereo audio output. IBM produces a MPC named the Ultimedia computer. Tandy Corporation and AST Research Inc. also market their versions of the MPC. Tandy's Sensation! is illustrated in Figure 1-29. The Sensation! is a 486-based MPC. Notice that the slot for inserting the CD-ROM appears in the front of the Sensation!

MPC kits that upgrade an existing MS/PC-DOS computer to a MPC are being marketed by NEC Technologies, Asymetrix Corporation, and MultiMedia Direct. These kits convert your 386SX computer into a full-

FIGURE 1-29   The Tandy Sensation! is a 486-based MPC with an internal CD-ROM drive. Photo courtesy of Tandy Corporation.

featured multimedia system. Typically, a MPC kit includes a CD-ROM drive, sound adapter board for both audio playback and recording, amplified speakers for the CD-ROM drive, multimedia software extensions, some sample CD-ROMs, and multimedia authoring software that allows you to make your own software. Software or CD-ROMs specially marked with the MPC logo will run new MPC. Integrated hardware like the MPC tells you how quickly that multimedia is becoming popular.

CD-I

Compact disc-interactive (CD-I) is a spin-off from CD-ROM. CD-I was first introduced on October 30, 1991, by Philips International. Figure 1-30 illustrates the CD-I 220 System by Philips. CD-I requires a stand-alone CD-I player, which is a cross between a computer, CD-ROM drive, and video game. The CD-I player has an internal microprocessor, 1 MB of RAM, a ROM-based operating system, and audio and video chips. The

FIGURE 1-30   The CD-I 220 System by Philips International with Compton's Interactive Encyclopedia CD-I displayed on the screen.

information from the CD-I plays back through a standard television or video monitor. A variety of entertainment and educational CD-I programs are available that the user interacts with by using a remote control that looks like a joystick. A CD-I program can contain audio, text, digital motion video, and high-quality still images. The display of digital motion video has been an obstacle that Philips addressed by limiting the size of the screen area where a moving picture can be displayed, as well as limiting the number of frames of motion video displayed per second (Oltz, 1991, p. 29).

Presently, CD-I technology is still developing. It is being directed to the home market for entertainment on standard television sets. American Interactive Media (AIM) has developed several CD-I children's products, including A Visit to Sesame Street and the CD-I Cartoon Jukebox (*Multimedia & Videodisc Monitor*, 1991, p. 16). The CD-I Cartoon Jukebox allows children to select a language from English, Spanish, and French; listen to 10 different children's songs; watch cartoon movies; play games; and color the cartoon characters singing the songs. Sonic Images is marketing Children's Musical Theater, a CD-I program that allows children to play back music in a variety of styles (pop, country, or classical) as well as control the instrumental mix, delete certain instruments, and add others to the playback. Another CD-I title by Sonic Images, called Private Lessons, teaches how to play selected musical instruments (*Multimedia & Videodisc Monitor*, 1991, p. 20). Since CD-I is being directed toward the consumer market, it is difficult at this time to say what impact CD-I will have for schools.

DVI

Digital video-interactive (DVI) refers to a file compression standard that allows computers to process and store motion video more efficiently. DVI is owned and marketed by Intel with the support of IBM. DVI allows the playback of motion video on a hard disk or CD-ROM as digital motion video. DVI merges TV and computer technologies, allowing computers to display full-motion video signals. This is usually done with a DVI board on an IBM. A DVI board contains programming code for the decompression and playback of digitized motion video and audio. When played back, the video almost looks as if it is occurring in real time. With further advancements, it will undoubtedly look as if it were playing in real time.

Presently, to author a DVI application, a motion video is sent to Intel where it is compressed as digital data on a mainframe computer. Then, the digital data is transferred to a CD-ROM disc. You can expect 72 minutes of DVI motion video from a CD-ROM.

A DVI movie can be played back in a variable-sized window without any changes in quality. The size of the window can be expanded to be as large as a full screen or decreased to be as small as a 2" × 2" window. Unfortunately, a drawback to DVI is the current expense for purchasing a DVI board for the IBM.

Some educational applications available in DVI format include Burried Mirrors by Films Incorporated Video, which teaches introductory Spanish with motion video clips shot in Mexico City; and Palenque by Bank Street College, which encourages children to explore the Mayan ruins. Another use of DVI is seen in Florida, where roadside tourist-information touch screen systems called "Florida TouchGuides" are located at tourist information centers and rest stops along the Florida turnpike. They provide information on restaurants, hotels, beaches, entertainment facilities, and other attractions. They even allow the user to print out the desired information complete with directions and a map for driving there (*Multimedia & Videodisc Monitor*, 1991, p. 4).

QuickTime

Early 1992, Apple Computer released QuickTime. QuickTime is similar to DVI in that it allows the playback of motion video on a screen, specifically a Macintosh computer. QuickTime is a system software program that can added to your color Macintosh to extend the capabilities of the computer to compress and play back digitized motion video. Compressing a movie reduces the amount of space required to store the movie on disk and display it on the screen. The motion video is compressed using QuickTime and decompressed when it is played back in a small window on the computer screen. On a Macintosh IIsi, QuickTime version 1.5 plays back digitized movies in a small window measuring 240 × 180 pixels at 15 frames per second. Playback on a more powerful Macintosh, such as a Quadra, can reach quarter screen (320 × 240 pixels) at 24 frames per second. By comparison, standard playback of movies on 1/2" VHS videotape is 30 frames per second. QuickTime movies can be played back without the need for any additional hardware cards. QuickTime works with all color-capable (68020 or later) Macintosh computers running system software 6.0.7 (or later) with at least 2 MB of memory. This means that millions of Macintosh owners who are using software applications that support QuickTime can take advantage of its capabilities right away. Also, QuickTime incorporates user-friendly interface features (commands, pull-down menus, metaphors) with which Macintosh users are already familiar—like copy, cut, and paste. QuickTime version 1.5 is being packaged and sold as part of the Macintosh System Software 7.1.

QuickTime standardizes the process for compressing movies so that QuickTime movies can be played back in a variety of different software applications, including HyperCard, MS-Works, Word Perfect, Kids Pix Companion, and PageMaker. In Figure 1–31, a QuickTime movie is being played back in Kid Pix Companion—a highly rated and popular graphics program for children from 3 to 12 years old. The QuickTime movies are created and edited using Kid Pix Companion, which is an add-on product to the Kid Pix drawing and paint program. Using the Wacky TV feature, kids can play QuickTime movies in Kid Pix and add their own special effects by using the Wacky TV controls, such as the Electric mixer and Zoomer effects.

Even though graphic compression techniques are being used, the average storage requirement for a QuickTime movie is still large. One minute of a QuickTime movie is 10 MB, which is equal to what can be saved on about seven 3.5" high-density Macintosh disks.

Many educational products are incorporating QuickTime movies, such as Compton's Multimedia Encyclopedia and Poetry in Motion by The Voyager Company. For example, Poetry in Motion displays Quick-

FIGURE 1–31   QuickTime movies can be incorporated into the Kid Pix graphics program using Kid Pix Companion—an add-on product. Kid Pix Companion by Broderbund Software, Inc. is designed for children from ages 3 to 12.

Time movies of poets reading aloud their own poetry. As illustrated in Figure 1–32, the QuickTime movie of the poet reading his poem parallels the written poem that is presented on the right side of the Macintosh screen.

Kaleida

"Kaleida Labs" is the name given to Apple and IBM's joint venture to develop new multimedia technologies. Kaleida software will form the basic standard for a new era of technological devices that read text and images from special compact discs, communicate with new interactive television programs, and provide a rich variety of electronic information accessible to the average consumer (Weber, 1992, p. D1).

Kaleida wants to develop software that will make it easy to create mullimedia programs that will work on a variety of electronic platforms—computers, consumer electronic services, and interactive television. Interactive television is a specially configured program that lets the viewers play and interact with the game via a communication box hooked up to a standard television. Using interactive television, people would be able to participate in game shows from their homes, order groceries, and look through libraries of information from movies to newspaper articles (Weber, 1992, p. D3).

FIGURE 1–32   Poetry in Motion by The Voyager Company uses QuickTime movies. Courtesy of The Voyager Company.

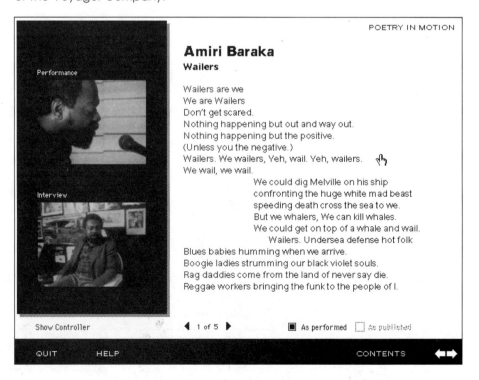

Conclusion

Videodiscs offer new ways for students to learn. Students can use them to see full-motion video demonstrations of such things as scientific phenomena in real time, text, colorful graphics, and the playing of audio on two (or more) separate audio tracks as for bilingual education. When videodiscs are combined with the power of a computer, they provide hypertexting features for obtaining additional information (e.g., definitions and locations on maps), test management capabilities that keep score on a student's progress, and highly interactive qualities that encourage students to become proactive in their own learning by directing the course of action and by making decisions.

Videodiscs truly have the potential to change education. As educators, we need to make changes in the classroom to better prepare students for the twenty-first century. Students in the next century will be faced with greater population numbers; increased global transportation, economy, and communications; advanced technologies; growing environmental problems; and human social issues. Students will need to be able to develop their own critical thinking skills, be sensitive to living in a multicultural world, and understand how to live and work cooperatively with others from diverse backgrounds and cultural attitudes. The use of interactive video in the classroom has the potential to enhance the learning of students by involving them in the exploration and development of critical issues and ideas.

In the next chapter, you will learn how to use commercial videodiscs in the classroom. Chapter 2 describes several lesson plans for using videodiscs in a variety of disciplines.

Suggested Learning Extensions
1. Review an article on the effectiveness of learning with videodisc-based instruction or implementing videodiscs in the classroom.
2. Interview a teacher regarding the features, benefits, advantages, and effectiveness of using interactive video in the classroom. Write a summary of the interview or videotape it.
3. Critique a CD-I system that appears in a retail outlet, such as at a department store or an electronics store.
4. Contact a videodisc company and request their catalog. (Refer to Appendix A for an extensive listing of various companies specializing in videodiscs.) Upon receiving the catalog, select interactive video programs that focus on your particular discipline(s). Then contact the company to preview these products. Give a class presentation of your favorite product.
5. Create a notebook of articles, photographs, and catalogs focusing on videodiscs in your particular discipline, such as videodiscs in art, math, or science.
6. Create an activity sheet that is barcoded to a particular videodisc. Use a software product like Pioneer's Bar'n'coder to do this.
7. Take a field trip to a public institution that uses interactive video, such as a local science and technology museum, a zoo, or an art museum. Write a summary report of your observation.

8. Select a level 1 videodisc. Write a lesson plan that shows how you would use the videodisc for whole-class instruction.

Chapter References and Additional Readings

Alessi, S. M., & Trollip, S. R. (1991). *Computer-based instruction: Methods and development.* Englewood Cliffs, NJ: Prentice Hall.

American Interactive Media (AIM). *A visit to Sesame Street and the CD-I cartoon jukebox.* AIM, Suite 790, 11111 Santa Monica Boulevard, Los Angeles, CA 90025. (213) 473-4136.

AmigaNews. (May/June 1991). Data fact. *AmigaNews.* Scholastic Inc., 730 Broadway, New York, NY 10003.

Apple Computer, Inc. (1992). *Apple CD 300.* 20525 Mariani Avenue, Cupertino, CA 95014. (408) 252-2775 or (408) 996-1010.

Apple Computer, Inc. (1992). *Macintosh IIvx, Performa 600, and Centris 650.* 20525 Mariani Avenue, Cupertino, CA 95014. (408) 252-2775 or (408) 996-1010.

Apple Computer, Inc. (1992). *QuickTime starter kit user's guide.* 20525 Mariani Avenue, Cupertino, CA 95014-6299. (408) 996-1010.

AST Research Inc. (1992). Advantage! (714) 727-4141.

Asymetrix Corporation. (1991). *ToolBook version 1.5.* 110 110th Avenue N.E., Suite 717, Bellevue, WA 98004. (206) 637-1500.

Asymetrix Corporation. (1992). *Level 1 MPC.* 110 110th Avenue, N.E., Suite 717, Bellevue, WA 98004. (206) 637-1500.

Bank Street College. *Palenque.* New York: Bank Street College.

Brittannica Software, Inc. & Compton's Multimedia Publishing Group, Inc. (1992). *Compton's interactive encyclopedia CD-I.* 345 Fourth Street, San Francisco, CA 94107. (415) 595-5555.

Broderbund Software, Inc. (1991). *Kid Pix 1.2 and Kid Pix companion.* 500 Redwood Blvd., PO Box 6121, Novato, CA 94948-6121. (415) 382-4700 or (415) 382-4400.

Bruder, I. (October 1989). Ninth annual survey of the states. *Electronic Learning, 9*(2), 28.

Callahan, P. (January/February 1990). IVD students outperform traditional students with the TLTG physical science course. *Instruction Delivery Systems, 4*(1), 23–25.

CD ROM, Inc. (Fall 1992). 1667 Cole Boulevard, Suite 400, Golden, CO 80401. (303) 231-9373. FAX: (303) 231-9581.

CD-ROM Professional. (1992). Dept. EBS1, 462 Danbury Road, Wilton, CT 06897-2126. (203) 761-1466 or (800) 248-8466. FAX: (203) 761-1444.

Chronicle of Higher Education. (July 25, 1990). Hispanics falling behind in education, report says. *The Chronicle of Higher Education, 36*(45), A2.

Claris Corporation. (1991). *HyperCard 2.1.* 5201 Patrick Henry Drive, Box 58168, Santa Clara, CA 95052-8168. (800) 628-2100.

Corum, C. T., Wotring, E. E., Forrest, E. J., & James, M. L. (Fall 1991). Re: The production & marketing of CD-I & DVI: Lessons from IVD. *IICS Interact, 3*(1), 20-27.

Creative Laser Concepts. (1992). *Barcode maker.* 555 Saturn Blvd., Suite B-281, San Diego, CA 92154. (619) 435-0700.

Cushall, M. B., Harvey, F. A., & Brovey, A. J. (February 1987). *Research on learning from interactive videodiscs: A review of the literature and suggestions for future research activities.* Conference paper presented at the Annual Convention of the Association for Educational Communications & Technology, Atlanta, GA.

Davey, J. (March 1990). Laserdisc shines brighter than the Arizona sun. Interactive Laserdisc. Spring supplement to *T.H.E. Journal, 17*(6), 8–10.

Discis Knowledge Research Inc. *Heather hits her first home run, Cinderella, Moving gives me a stomach ache, The tale of Peter Rabbit, and Ananse the spider.* Discis Knowledge Research Inc., Toronto, Ontario. (800) 567-4321.

Electronic Learning. (March 1991). Optical Data, Panasonic customize videodisc player for Texas. *Electronic Learning, 10*(6), 8.

Electronic Learning. (October 1991). Schools plan to buy technologies, despite economic concerns. *Electronic Learning, 6.*

Emerging Technology Consultants. (April 1992). *The update to the videodisc compendium for education and training, 3*(2).

Emerging Technology Consultants. (1993). *The videodisc compendium for education and training* (5th ed.). St. Paul, MN: Emerging Technology Consultants.

Encyclopedia Britannica. *Compton's multimedia encyclopedia CD-ROM disc.* Encyclopedia Britannica, Britannica Centre, 310 South Michigan Avenue, Chicago, IL 60604. (312) 347-7155.

Farallon Computing, Inc. (1989). *MacRecorder version 2.0.1.* Berkeley, CA. (415) 849-2331.

Fletcher, J. D. (July 1990). *Effectiveness and cost of interactive videodisc instruction in defense training and education.* Alexandria, VA: Institute for Defense Analyses. IDA Paper P-2372.

Grolier Electronic Publishing, Inc. *Grolier electronic encyclopedia 1991 CD-ROM disc.* Grolier Electronic Publishing, Sherman Turnpike, Danbury, CT 06816. (203) 797-3500.

Hitachi America, Ltd. *Hitachi CD-ROM drive.* Hitachi America, Ltd., 2902 Oregon Street, Suite B3, Torrance, CA 90503. (310) 328-9700.

Hoffman Educational Systems. (1991). *Laser learning and reading in the content area.* 1863 Business Center Drive, Duarte, CA 91010. (800) 826-8377, (800) 472-2625, or (818) 359-0977. FAX: (818) 359-0957.

Holzberg, C. S. (February 1991). Interactive aids education. *Electronic Learning Special Edition, 10*(5), 14–16.

Houghton Mifflin. (1992). *American history.* Houghton Mifflin, One Beacon Street, Boston, MA 02108. (617) 725-5000.

IBM Corporation. *LinkWay 2.01*. Marketing Support, IBM Corporation, 3301 Windy Ridge Parkway, Dept. 7EY, Marietta, GA 30067. (800) 627-0920.

Instruction Delivery Systems. (November/December 1990). News briefs. *Instruction Delivery Systems, 4*(6), 30.

Intel Corporation. *DVI*. Intel Corporation, Princeton Operation, CN 5325, Princeton, NJ 08543. (609) 734-2211.

Kranch, D., & Forrest, C. (1990). Videodiscs: An overview. *Tech Trends, 35*(2), 18–20.

Louie, R., Sweatt, S., Gresham, R., & Smith, L. (May/June 1991). Interactive video: Disseminating vital science and math information. *Media & Methods, 27*(5), 22–23.

Mageau, T. (March 1990). Software's new frontier: Laser-disc technology. *Electronic Learning, 9*(6), 22–28.

Market Data Retrieval (MDR). (1991). *Education and technology—A full market report of schools and their use of technology*. 16 Progress Drive, Shelton, CT 06484. (800) 333-8802.

Meckler. (1992). *CD-ROMs in print*. Meckler, 11 Ferry Lane West, Westport, CT 06880-5808.

Miller, R. L. (1987). An overview of the interactive market. In S. Lambert & J. Sallis (Eds.), *CD-I and interactive videodisc technology*. Indianapolis, IN: Howard W. Sams & Co.

Motion Works International, Inc. (1992). *ProMotion*. 1020 Mainland Street, Suite #130, Vancouver, B.C. V6B 2T4. (604) 685-9975. FAX: (604) 685-6105.

MultiMedia Direct. (1992). *Media vision multimedia upgrade kit*. 2105 S. Bascom Avenue, Suite 290, Campbell, CA 95008. (800) 354-1354. FAX: (408) 371-5760.

Multimedia & Videodisc Monitor (January 1991). Breaking new ground in interactive children's programming, 9(1), 16.

Multimedia & Videodisc Monitor (January 1991). Florida touchguide: DVI for tourist info, 9(1), 19–20.

Multimedia & Videodisc Monitor (January, 1991). A look back, 9(1), 28.

Multimedia & Videodisc Monitor (January 1991). New directions in interactive music programming, 9(1), 19–20.

Multimedia & Videodisc Monitor (February 1991). The industry reacts: Notes and analysis, 9(2),5.

National Geographic & LucasArts Entertainment. (1990). *GTV: A geographic perspective on American history* (Videodisc). Washington, DC 20036.

NEC Home Electronics. *NEC CD-ROM drive and multimedia upgrade kit*. NEC Home Electronics, 1255 Michael Drive, Wood Dale, IL 60191. (312) 860-9500, (708) 860-9500, or (508) 264-8000.

nView Corporation. *Viewframe LI+2 LCD*. 860 Omni Blvd., Newport News, VA 23606. (804) 873-1354. FAX: (804) 873-2153.

Oltz, M. (February 1991). Learning digital video interactive hypermedia design through a sample application. *Multimedia & Videodisc Monitor, 9*(2), 26–30.

Optical Data Corporation. (September 1988). Study confirms better learning via videodisc. *T.H.E. Journal, 16*(2), 74.

Optical Data Corporation. (February 11, 1991). *Windows on science.* 30 Technology Drive, Box 4919, Warren, NJ 07060. (908) 668-0022. FAX: (908) 668-1322.

Optical Data Corporation. (1991). *The history of videodiscs.* Module 6.5. Warren, NJ: Optical Data Corporation.

Panasonic Sales Company. (1992). *LX-120 videodisc player.* Division of Matsushita, Electric Corp. of America, Secaucus, NJ. (201) 392-6488.

Philips Consumer Electronics Co. (1991). *CDV-400 multi-format player.* Knoxville, TN. (615) 521-4499.

Philips Consumer Electronics Co. (1993). *CD-I 220 system.* Knoxville, TN. (615) 521-4499.

Phillipo, J. (May 1989). Videodiscs as information archives for the classroom. *Electronic Learning, 8*(7), 42–44.

Pioneer Communications of America. *Laserbarcode tool kit 2.0 and Bar'n'coder 3.0.* 600 East Crescent Avenue, Upper Saddle River, NJ 07458-1827. (201) 327-6400 or (800) LASER-ON. FAX: (201) 327-9379.

Pioneer Communications of America. *LD-V2000, LD-V2200, CLD-V2400, LD-V4200, and LD-V4400 videodisc players.* Corporate Offices, 600 East Crescent Avenue, Upper Saddle River, NJ 07458-1827. (201) 327-6400, or (800) LASER-ON. FAX: (201) 327-9379.

Pioneer Communications of America. *Pioneer laservision videodisc production guide book.* Corporate Offices, 600 East Crescent Avenue, Upper Saddle River, NJ 07458-1827. (310) 522-8600, (201) 327-6400, or (800) LASER-ON. FAX: (201) 327-9379.

Pollack, R. A. (January/February 1990). The state of videodiscs in education and training. *Instruction Delivery Systems, 4* (1), 12–14.

Rogers, M. (June 5, 1989). A new spin on videodiscs. *Newsweek,* 68–69.

Scholastic Software. (1990). *Interactive NOVA: Animal pathfinders.* 730 Broadway, New York, NY 10003. (212) 505-6006.

Silver Burdett & Ginn. (1992). *Science horizons videodiscs.* Product Manager, Science, Silver Burdett & Ginn, 250 James Street, Morristown, NY 07960-1918.

Sonic Images. *Children's musical theater CD-I and private lessons.* Sonic Images, 4590 MacArthur Boulevard, Washington DC 20007. (202) 333-1063.

Sony. (1992). *MDP-1100 and LDP-1450 videodisc players.* Multimedia Systems Division, Montvale, NJ. (201) 930-6034.

Stack, P. (1990). Interactive video—The barriers have fallen. *Tech Trends, 35* (2), 38–40.

Tandy Corporation. (1992). *Sensation!* Ft. Worth, TX. (817) 390-3216. FAX: 878-6508.

Tech Trends (1990). Texas textbook committee approves videodisc-based curriculum, 35(5), 5–6.

Tech Trends (1991). Videodiscs adopted in Virginia Beach, 37(3), 5.

Voyager Company, The. (1987-90). *The National Gallery of Art videodisc companion.* 1351 Pacific Coast Highway, Santa Monica, CA 90401. (310) 451-1383.

Voyager Company, The. (1988-91). *Vincent van Gogh revisited videodisc.* 1351 Pacific Coast Highway, Santa Monica, CA 90401. (310) 451-1383.

Voyager Company, The. (1992). *Exotic Japan.* 1351 Pacific Coast Highway, Santa Monica, CA 90401. (310) 451-1383.

Voyager Company, The. (1992). *Poetry in motion.* 1351 Pacific Coast Highway, Santa Monica, CA 90401. (310) 451-1383.

Voyager Company, The. (1992). *Videodisc toolKit.* 1351 Pacific Coast Highway, Santa Monica, CA 90401. (310) 451-1383.

3M Optical Recording Department. 3M Center, St. Paul, MN 55144-1000. (612) 733-1110.

Van Horn, R. (1991). *Advanced technology in education.* Pacific Grove, CA: Brooks/Cole.

Videodiscovery, Inc. (1990). *The Bio Sci II videodisc.* Videodiscovery, Inc., 1700 Westlake Ave. N., Suite 600, Seattle, WA 98109-3012. (206) 285-5400 or (800) 548-3472.

Weber, J. (September 27, 1992). In search of computing's holy grail. *Los Angeles Times,* Section D, D1-3.

White, B. M., Mathews, K. M., & Holmes, C. T. (December 1989). The cost-effectiveness of an interactive video system for science instruction. *Educational Technology,* 19–23.

2
Educational Applications of Interactive Video Programs

Chapter Objectives

After completing this chapter, you will be able to:

❑ *Understand the format and major capabilities of a sample of leading interactive video programs that can be used in the classroom.*

❑ *Use the lessons outlined in this chapter and modify them for your own classroom needs and the way you work with interactive video.*

❑ *Extend the lessons presented in this chapter and create new interactive videodisc-based lessons.*

❑ *Develop critical thinking in students through studying concepts across disciplines and working within cooperative learning teams.*

❑ *Utilize multiple approaches to learning, including lectures, demonstrations, community research strategies, multimedia shows, video simulation games, and simulated lab experiments.*

❑ *Structure lessons that integrate both cognitive and affective domains into learning and assessment.*

Introduction

The purpose of this chapter is to familiarize you with some of the leading commercial interactive video programs and how you can adapt them or ones similar to them for use in your classroom. Interactive videodiscs have tremendous potential for illustrating a lecture; recreating a lab experiment, a field study, or a museum trip; and allowing your students to create their own multimedia reports and videos. The material in this chapter can be used for selecting video programs as well as developing your own videodisc-based lessons. (Refer to Chapters 4 and 5 on how to author your own interactive video programs.) The lessons for videodiscs in this chapter were set up with a Macintosh computer, but software is also available for the IBM. When making presentations to a whole class, an LCD projection panel will need to be used so that every student can observe what is happening on the computer screen.

Multicultural Classrooms

Classrooms have become increasingly multicultural with students who are recent immigrants or who represent a mix of different cultural backgrounds and traditions within this country. It is important that teachers are knowledgeable about the process of culture in order to promote students' self-esteem and understand how values, attitudes, and beliefs are transmitted and become internalized. The lessons included in this chapter stress the importance of students learning about their own cultures as well as the cultures of other people.

Cooperative Learning Teams

An excellent way to encourage students to get to know each other and their cultures is to provide opportunities for them to work cooperatively. Lessons should provide opportunities for cooperative learning teams, whole-class activities, pairs of students working on projects together, as well as individuals working independently with the videodisc programs. When students interact together as a team with the videodisc and software, the potential exists for increasing their academic achievement and for improving their communication skills. For example, the concept of *peer experts* can work well in cooperative learning teams, where particular students may have more in-depth experience in an area such as computers or other skill areas. These peer experts can be leaders in certain activities or help out in tutoring individual team mates. Teachers can motivate students to reflect on what skills they need to practice in order to work together as a team. Problems can be identified and the team can brainstorm solutions. Cooperative learning teams achieve greater results if the team has specific objectives and each team member has a particular role and responsibility, as in the following suggested list:

- *Team leader:* Facilitates and organizes group meetings and final presentations.
- *Recorder:* Keeps track of meetings and takes minutes; keeps computer records of compiled research and reports.
- *Data collectors:* Uses such resources as the library, videodisc, film, interviews, and newspapers to obtain data and write up reports.
- *Librarian/Media specialist:* Keeps track of collected data, books, picture files, newspapers, and so on in an organized format.

These roles in the team are suggestions only; the team might include additional roles as a need becomes apparent. Roles could be rotated, shared, or two positions could be held at one time. For example, every team member could be working on data collecting. Lessons should include the spontaneity of discovering, sharing, and searching for new material within interactive video programs, as well as using outside resources, so that working in teams can be an exciting and rewarding way to learn.

Selection of the Videodisc-Based Programs

The major criteria for selecting the particular interactive video programs for this chapter included the following:

- Programs should use level 3 discs with software and a computer to drive the videodisc player. Many of the programs can also access images on the disc with both a remote control and barcode reader.
- Programs should represent a variety of subjects taught in schools, such as art, science, social studies, and English. In addition, it is important that there is flexibility within the program for teaching more than one subject and that an cross-discipline approach was possible.
- Programs should be forerunners in the field of education and in use by teachers in the classroom.

The selected videodiscs represent a sampling of quality videodisc programs.

Components of the Lesson Plans

The lessons in this chapter can be modified to fit your own curricular needs, your teaching style, and your students' abilities, or be used as models for lessons you design. For example, the worksheets could be rewritten for a lower level of comprehension with limited vocabulary for students who have special needs. Time schedules, time allotted for the lessons, and the emphasis to be placed on the lessons within any given curriculum would have to be determined by the teacher. Different classes will work at different rates, depending on grade level, ability level, and the particular curriculum emphasis. Since many classrooms have equipment only for small groups of three or four students at a time to work with the computer and videodisc, the lessons allow you to create other related activities where students can rotate using the technical equipment and at other times work at their desks or do research in the library.

Description of Videodisc-Based Programs

Each videodisc-based lesson is introduced with a brief description of the disc and software content. There are also figures illustrating graphics and main menus. Significant features and highlights of the disc and software program are discussed. The *description* section provides enough information to familiarize you with the general structure of the program and how the branching capabilities access the content.

Lesson Plan Title

The title of the lesson indicates the major focus and purpose of the learning experiences.

Materials and Vocabulary

The *materials* section of the lessons lists the source for the discs and software program, the number of discs, and if there are user's manuals, teacher's guides, lesson plans, or other supplementary materials. Refer to Appendix A for lists of companies to obtain educational videodiscs and software. The *vocabulary* section is not exhaustive but it highlights major terms and concepts important to the lesson.

Suggested Grade Levels

General *grade levels* are designated for each lesson. Certain lessons can be used with grades 4 through 6, and these are referred to as an *elementary*-grade level. Middle school, grades 7 and 8, and high school, grades 9 through 12, are referred to as *secondary*-grade levels. Teachers can modify any lesson by incorporating elementary- or secondary-level learning experiences appropriate for their particular classroom.

Purpose and Objectives of the Lesson

The *purpose* section of the lesson introduces the major idea and global perspective of the lesson. Specific student objectives are listed, including a hierarchy of thinking and research skills, ranging from recall and descriptive abilities through higher-level analytical, interpretive, and evaluative skills. Most importantly, both cognitive and affective types of learning are stressed with subjective experiences, feelings, and critical thinking working together.

Procedures

The *procedures* section of the lesson plan details the steps to be taken by both the teacher and the students. Alternative approaches are also suggested. Questions that can be duplicated and used as worksheets are included to provide guidelines for focusing students' research as well as for assessing what learning takes place. The questions help motivate the students to interact with and utilize the software.

Assessment and Extension of Lesson

The *assessment* section of the lesson plan provides suggestions for multiple evaluation approaches and parallels the student objectives. Both cognitive and affective areas of evaluation are included. The content on a videodisc is often so large that there is a tendency to focus on the encyclopedic qualities of the database and limit learning to collecting, sorting, describing, and recalling data. Therefore, it is important that the objectives, learning experiences, and assessment extend to higher-level critical and imaginative thinking skills. The *extension* section suggests other related learning experiences that include multidisciplinary approaches and encourage further in-depth and creative thinking.

The National Gallery of Art Videodisc

Description

The National Gallery of Art videodisc contains a motion sequence describing the history of the National Gallery on Side I lasting 22 minutes, 17 seconds. Side II contains 1,645 artworks plus a brief film covering an overview tour of the National Gallery lasting 27 minutes, 22 seconds, which begins with the first card on Side II. The HyperCard software used to drive the videodisc was The National Gallery of Art: A Videodisc Companion (The Voyager Company, 1987, 1991) and used with a Macintosh. The Videodisc Companion, which provides clear instructions for setting up the video with the Macintosh, consists of two main parts:

- The *Gallery Index* contains the Main Index, which includes the Videodisc Player Setting; a Help Button, which when highlighted, allows the pointer to be placed over a button or text and information is displayed about them; a Utilities Index that can sort the catalog in different ways; and a Home icon. In addition, there is an index of categories to access, which includes the Artist, Style/Period, Date, Nationality, and Subject of the artwork. A museum icon, when clicked, allows you to go to the Gallery Catalog.

- The *Gallery Catalog* displays information on the Macintosh screen for each work of art it brings up on the video screen.

The Gallery Index

Each of the indexes has complete instructions that are brought up on the first card of the index.

Main Index   This index includes all of the indexes in the Videodisc Companion as well as the Gallery icon to access the first card of the Gallery Catalog. See Figure 2–1 for the Main Index of the National Gallery of Art. This facilitates going back and forth between the Gallery Index and the Gallery Catalog. The artworks are arranged chronologically by date of completion. You can arrange the complete collection by another category, such as by artist, style, or nationality, by using the Utilities Index. This sort feature can be used only if the Videodisc Companion is installed on a hard disk providing for at least 800K memory. There is also a Home icon in the Main Index that closes the Videodisc Companion and takes you back to the HyperCard Home stack. When first becoming familiar with this software, remember to click the Help button (question mark) and leave it on to provide you with information on all the button functions and text as you use them.

Artist Index   The Artist Index is arranged alphabetically in a loose-leaf booklet format with tabs. Clicking on a letter of the alphabet brings up a list of artists whose last name begins with that letter. Clicking on an artist's name allows you to look at the earliest work in the Gallery by that artist. To search for additional works by the artist, continue to click on the artist's name in the Gallery Catalog Card.

FIGURE 2-1   Main Index of the National Gallery of Art: A Videodisc Companion. Courtesy of The Voyager Company.

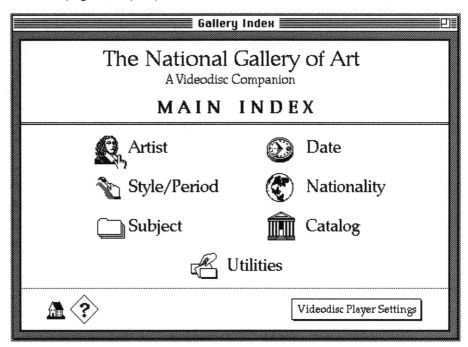

Style/Period Index   Clicking on Style/Period provides you with a card listing of styles and periods. Clicking on a specific style provides a concise definition and description of the Style/Period with examples of three artists and a representative work by each artist to click on and view. Clicking on the Catalog button at the bottom of the screen will take you to the first work in the catalog from this period or style.

Date Index   This index is arranged chronologically by century and you are taken to the first work of art in the collection created in that century. If you wish to find a particular date, you can go to the Gallery and use the Find button near the bottom of the screen to search for the specific year.

Nationality Index   Using the Nationality Index allows you to access works by country. When in a particular Gallery Catalog card, you can also click on the nationality if you wish to go to another work by an artist from that country.

Subject Index   This index is organized by specific categories. For example, if you clicked on Activities, a list of activities would appear. Clicking on one activity, such as Sailing, would take you to the first artwork in the Catalog collection that had to do with sailing. Click on the Subject menu at the bottom of the screen and click on Sailing again to bring up another work of art related to this activity. Clicking again each time on Sailing, Ship, or Boat in the Subject menu as it comes up would allow you to view the other artworks having to do with that specific subject. An educational feature of the Subject Index is that teachers or students can add their own search words using the Find button tool since the Subject Index is not exhaustive.

The Gallery Catalog

Icon Buttons   Figure 2–2 illustrates a sample Catalog Card. Clicking on the icon button in the upper right of this card allows you to type in your own notes of the artwork on a Notes screen by clicking on the note paper icon. There is a dotted corner in the upper right-hand part of the screen, and if clicked it folds down to mark a catalog card for future reference. You can also view a close-up of an artwork by clicking on a magnifying glass icon or bringing up a film by clicking on a movie projection icon when they are displayed on a particular catalog card.

Find Button   The Find button allows you to type in a descriptor for a work of art you are searching for. The Subject button provides a list of key-words to use with the Find button to search for related works. Other text from the title, medium, artist's name, and nationality may also be used with the Find button. The Find button is an excellent feature of Videodisc Companion. It allows you to make your search as wide or as narrow as you want. For example, you can view all the twentieth-century sculptures in the collection or only those that are abstract and made of marble. To access each painting, click the Find button and then click OK in the dialog box (see Figure 2–3).

FIGURE 2–2   Sample Catalog Card of The National Gallery of Art: A Videodisc Companion. Courtesy of The Voyager Company.

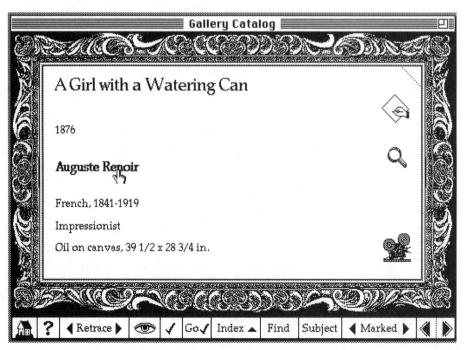

FIGURE 2-3 Find tool: Dialog box in the National Gallery of Art: A Videodisc Companion. Courtesy of The Voyager Company.

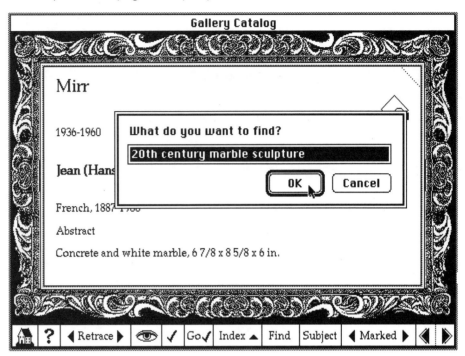

Slide Show Buttons   The check button records the frame number, title, and artist on a list for later reference and creates a slide show of your own design. The information can be brought up and controlled by clicking on the Go Marked button on the bottom of each catalog card.

Navigating Through the Collection   The Browse button (an eye icon) takes you at random to another work of art . The Retrace button allows you to go back to the last card you have seen or go ahead. The Arrow buttons, standard on HyperCard stacks, allow you to go backward or forward in the cards. In addition, a Help button, a HyperCard Home button, and an Main Index button are included.

Lesson Plan: The National Gallery of Art Videodisc

Title

Critiquing Social-Cultural Values Depicted in Paintings: Attitudes Toward Women

Materials

National Gallery of Art Videodisc (1983, Videodisc Publishing Inc., 381 Park Ave. South, Suite 1601, New York, NY 10016)

A Videodisc Companion—User's Guide and one compressed floppy diskette (1987,1991, The Voyager Company, 1351 Pacific Coast Hwy., Santa Monica, CA 90401).

Vocabulary

Style, historical periods, cultural assumptions, values, attitudes, beliefs, symbolic meaning, analysis, interpretation, social-cultural roles, qualitative properties, composition, expressive properties

Grade Level

Secondary

Purposes

Cross-curricular objectives are promoted in this lesson through a focus on history, art, aesthetics, anthropology, and sociology. A critical issues approach is used to examine works of art as a reflection of a people's culture and creative expression. Students are involved in researching paintings using methods in art history, criticism, and aesthetics to examine cultural assumptions. Transitions in art styles, social attitudes, and the students' own taken-for-granted knowledge are contrasted through critical dialog and cooperative learning approaches. This lesson is most appropriate for high school students; however, teachers could adapt the National Gallery of Art Videodisc and Videodisc Companion software for elementary-age students. For example, students could be encouraged to play detectives; using the Subject Index button or Subject pull-up menu, they could search for paintings with dogs. They could then create a slide show comparing the different ways dogs have been illustrated, what activities they are depicted in, their placement in the paintings, and what kind of feeling or meaning a particular painting has for them because a dog is in it. Other topics of interest to children can be selected, as well as major themes related to specific curriculum objectives.

Lesson Objectives

Students will be able to:

- Identify paintings by style and periods in history.

- Identify specific roles of women depicted in paintings by examining the visual elements and symbols used by the artist.
- Interpret and contrast the artists' depiction of women in the past with contemporary art and the roles of women today.
- Interpret how cultural themes and values have changed over time.
- Create their own slide show from a particular time period gathered from cooperative research learning experiences.
- Contrast their own taken-for-granted cultural values with those depicted in the works of art.

Procedures

1. Use the brief Tour of the National Gallery of Art to introduce the whole class to an overview of the Gallery collection. The Tour is on side II, Chapter 17, of the videodisc. It lasts 27 minutes, 22 seconds and can be accessed by using a remote control. The Tour segment can also be used by the teacher to highlight the vocabulary and some of the main concepts that will be dealt with in this lesson. For example, the Renaissance period is discussed with representative works of art and major artists. Symbolic meaning, style, and social-political issues, as well as compositional techniques used by artists, are identified in selected periods of history. The remote control can be used to stop the video and examine a work more closely and to motivate the students to question and analyze the concepts presented. The eighteenth-century decorative style of Fraggonard can be compared to David's political portrayal of Napoleon. Constable's technique of leading the viewer into his pastoral landscapes can also be observed and contrasted with a Corot landscape. The video can be reversed and later works of art can be analyzed in relation to twentieth-century values in painting. Specific artists works can also be accessed in the Tour film by typing in the artist's name or work of art with the Find Tool and then clicking on the film projector icon in the catalog card. For example, discussion of Fraggonard's painting in the Tour film can be accessed this way through the Videodisc Companion software (The Voyager Company, 1987, 1991).

2. Demonstrate the Gallery Catalog and the Gallery Index with particular emphasis on the Subject Index and how different artwork with related themes can be identified and saved for retrieval. Describe the purpose of the lesson. Define and describe *culture* as the shared values, attitudes, and beliefs of a group of people (see Boyer, 1987; McFee & Degge, 1992). Discussions should include what values and beliefs the students have, how they might be different in other cultures, and how values, attitudes, and beliefs are reflected in works of art.

3. Divide the class into small cooperative learning teams of four to five students and assign them a particular time period. A team will include a team leader, recorder, class reporter, and data collectors. (Refer to the beginning of this chapter and brief descriptions of each of these responsibilities.) Each team is to identify and analyze the cultural roles and values toward women as depicted in paintings for their particular time period. For example, a team could concentrate on analyzing a sample (three paintings) from only nineteenth-century French paintings of fe-

males or sixteenth-century Italian paintings by using the Find button, bring up the Find dialog box and then type in the nationality, the word *female,* and then the particular century. Refer back to Figure 2–3 as an example of a dialog box.

4. Provide a duplicated worksheet for each team to help them analyze cultural assumptions in relation to the historical period, style, composition, context, symbols, expression, and function of the particular paintings.

Worksheet for the National Gallery Videodisc

*   Title: _____

*   Artist: _____

*   Date: _____

*   Style: _____

*   Theme: What is the painting about? Is there a particular event or activity taking place? What shared values, attitudes, and beliefs are illustrated? For example, what rituals, heroes, or traditions do people hold in common? Are certain symbols, clothing, objects, or food highly valued? Can you also tell something about the artist's values by the style and what is being expressed?

    _____

    _____

    _____

*   Qualitative Properties: Identify the nature of the shapes, texture, colors, sizes, lines, values, and use of space. Describe how they appear to you. Is the use of color or space particular to a specific ethnic or racial group?

    _____

    _____

    _____

*   Compositional Properties: To what extent is each part of the painting necessary—for example, the shapes, colors, lines, and use of space? How is a sense of unity maintained? What colors, shapes, and textures are repeated, touching, or overlapped? What parts are more dominant? How does the viewer lead into the work and what kind of path does the eye follow? How does this indicate the values and attitudes of the period?

    _____

    _____

    _____

- Context: Where is the setting? What does it tell you about the people or the artist of that period? In what relationship are people shown to their environment? How is the natural or built environment shown? What values are emphasized because of the setting?

  _____

  _____

  _____

- Symbols: How are objects, animals, and religious symbols depicted? Of what value or significance do they have in the painting for illustrating shared beliefs and attitudes?

  _____

  _____

  _____

- Expressive Properties: What particular mood or sense of feeling do you get from the painting? Is there a quiet feeling about the work of art or is it dynamic or explosive in feeling? What statement do you think the artist is trying to make? How does that relate to the cultural values or attitudes of the people portrayed or the times they lived in?

  _____

  _____

  _____

- Cultural Significance: What meaning did this painting have for the people of this culture? Are certain taken-for-granted values depicted that are the same today or are they different? Are these values the same for every cultural group? What kinds of roles are depicted for women in the paintings? Are they in leadership positions or are they shown in supportive roles to men? What relationship is there between the age, race, and religious or ethnic background of women and their cultural roles? In what ways have roles for women changed through time and in what ways have they stayed the same? Are women portrayed as artists or are any of the works painted by women? What cultural assumptions are related to these findings?

  _____

  _____

  _____

5. Each team will select representative works that clearly demonstrate the findings of its group. The team will use the Check button to record the works and create a slide show, presenting their research orally to the entire class.

6. Have the class identify and critically discuss (in both written and oral form) the similarities and differences between the various styles and cultural beliefs in the works of art presented by the teams. Were the

teams able to analyze the cultural meaning in the paintings? How accurate were they in their interpretations and conclusions?

Assessment

1. Identify the level of understanding from the written research gathered by each team. Were the students able to identify, analyze, and interpret the cultural assumptions from their particular time frame in the National Gallery of Art Videodisc?

2. What was the level of participation, motivation, and enthusiasm of each team for their cooperative learning experience? Were the slide presentations to the entire class effective in terms of timing, interest level, and clarity of ideas?

3. Was the class, through critical dialog, able to recognize different styles and discuss relationships across the presentations?

4. Written tests can be used to evaluate vocabulary and major concepts identified in this lesson.

Extensions

1. Students could develop research and slide shows of other cultural issues related to art, such as comparing differences in the way artists depict men, elderly, disabled, children, or particular ethnic or racial groups. Cultural issues could also center on large themes and changing attitudes toward such areas as industrialism, technology, war, homelessness, and concern for the environment.

2. Extensions of this lesson could be made into the area of students creating their own artwork. Current social issues reflective of a student's cultural value system could be the central focus for a painting. A cooperative art project (painting, sculpture, or video) with students working in groups could also be developed around the history and pride of particular cultural groups.

Vincent van Gogh Videodisc

Description

The Vincent van Gogh Videodisc (Side I) contains full-motion video, a collection of stills of van Gogh's major works from his early Dutch Period all the way through to his final days at Auvers, maps, related photographs, artworks by artists who influenced him, and two audio tracks—one a commentary by Leonard Nimoy and the other a narrator reading Vincent's letters to his brother Theo. Side II, Vincent: The Play, on the original 1982 videodisc, is a one-man play in two acts, starring Leonard Nimoy. This play was produced and videotaped at the Guthrie Theater in Minneapolis.

Indexes

The van Gogh Videodisc Companion by The Voyager Company (1988, 1991) includes extensive indexes of video, stills, and text. The HyperCard software makes it possible to access time periods, artworks by theme, video clips on selected topics, an illustrated time line, as well as indexes with descriptions and illustrations of techniques, influences, and keywords (see Figure 2–4). You can easily go back and forth between full-motion clips, slides, maps, and different audio tracks, all through the use of the various indexes.

FIGURE 2–4   Main Menu for Indexes in the van Gogh Videodisc Companion. Courtesy of The Voyager Company.

Catalog

The Catalog section of the Videodisc Companion has a separate card of information for each of Vincent's works of art in the videodisc. The works are arranged in chronological order. The information text contains the title, date, period, theme, medium, name of museum that has the work, museum identification number, reference in Vincent's letters, and more keywords (see Figure 2–5).

The graphic icons in Figure 2–6, a catalog card on the Potato Eaters, include a magnifying glass for studying details in the work of art, two cameras to view a photograph related to the subject matter, a motion projector to view a motion clip about the work, and a voice balloon to view a motion clip with excerpts from Vincent's letters. There is also a checkmark icon "✓" in the upper left section of the screen to create a still frame or motion sequence of your own. In addition, there is a memo, control panel, and find/search function. In the Find section, there are three pull-up menus: Period, Theme, and Date. You may use these or type in the name of a particular work of art.

There is also a Notes feature that allows you to write your own notes, combining text and image access. Notes can be accessed from anywhere in the Videodisc Companion by clicking on Notes.

FIGURE 2–5   A Catalog Card from the van Gogh Videodisc Companion. Courtesy of The Voyager Company.

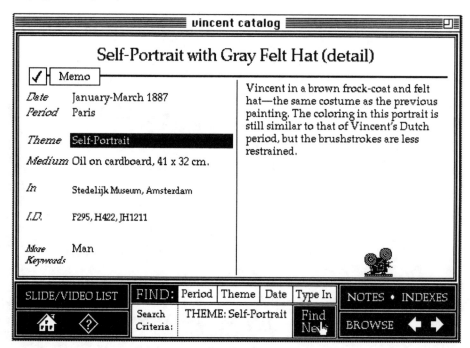

FIGURE 2–6   The Potato Eaters Catalog Card in the van Gogh Videodisc Companion. Courtesy of The Voyager Company.

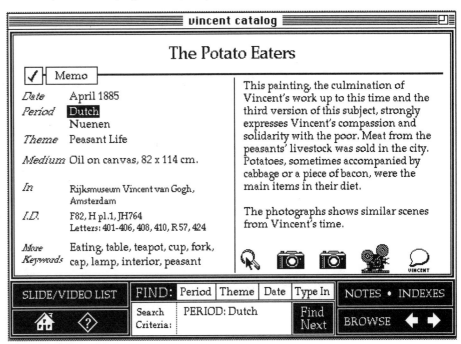

Lesson Plan: Vincent van Gogh Videodisc

Title

Vincent's Expressive Use of Color

Materials

Vincent van Gogh Videodisc: A Portrait in Two Parts (1982, Philips International and North American Philips Corporation, Wilmington, Delaware)

Vincent van Gogh Revisited: A Videodisc Companion—1 floppy diskette, and User's Guide (1988,1991, The Voyager Company, 1351 Pacific Coast Hwy., Santa Monica, CA 90401)

Vocabulary

Art criticism, hue, value, primary, secondary, tertiary, complementary, local color, expressive qualities, composition, cultural influences

Grade Level

Levels of learning for elementary or secondary

Purposes

In this lesson, language arts, history, and visual art disciplines are integrated. The major purpose of this lesson is to develop both the art of writing (literature) with learning in the social sciences and visual arts. Students can observe the relationship between Vincent's writings to his brother Theo and the actual paintings Vincent was talking about. This lesson focuses on one major aspect of van Gogh's artwork—his expressive abilities with his use of color. Other themes could be developed around his portraits of people, his self-portraits, observations and feelings toward nature, and specific transitions in his paintings.

Different Learning Levels   This type of lesson develops perceptual, inquiry, critical thinking, and expressive skills at different levels of ability. Students in grades 4 through 6 could work with questions that involve describing, identifying, and recalling material and their feelings about artworks in the videodisc. In grades 7 through 9, students could focus more on concepts such as providing examples of how complementary color approaches were used by Vincent and for what purposes. They could also analyze and contrast works of art and ideas in the letters, and express their personal perspectives. In grades 9 and up, students can work toward more evaluative questions, critical thinking, and create a particular style for expressing their feelings. Teachers can decide what learning levels or combination of levels are best suited for the students with whom they are working. A good foundation for teaching this lesson would be to have students become familiar with "talking about" reproductions of works of art by a variety of artists in different periods of history and in different cultures. Trips to museums and/or galleries would provide firsthand encounters with actual works of art.

Lesson Objectives

Students will be able to:

- Identify primary, secondary, and intermediate colors and how they are used in Vincent's paintings.

- Understand the difference between *hue* and *value* and how color is used to strengthen the compositional qualities of a work of art as well as its expressive qualities.

- Compare Vincent's writing about color in his letters to Theo and the actual way he used color in his paintings.

- Identify how Vincent's cultural values, attitudes, and beliefs affected the way he painted.

- Analyze other artists' works shown in the program and how they influenced Vincent and his use of color.

- Compare the meaning and use of color in their own environment and culture with the way Vincent used color. Contrast the meaning and use of particular colors across different cultural groups.

- Critique the expressive qualities in Vincent's writing and demonstrate a relationship to the expressive style in his painting. Expressive qualities include moods and feelings communicated through the works of art.

- Focus on a particular painting by Vincent and write on how the colors affect their own feelings and emotions when looking at that work of art.

Procedures

1.   Demonstrate how the Indexes and Catalog work to access material. To do this, first launch the Voyager Videodisc Companion software by clicking twice on the Vincent Index stack.

Once at the opening title screen, Vincent van Gogh Revisited: A Videodisc Companion, click anywhere on the screen to bring up the Main Menu for Indexes. Click next on Periods from selection of Indexes and you will be on the Index to Periods screen (see Figure 2–7). In the Index to Periods, click once on Auvers (or any of the other periods in Vincent's life) to illustrate how to move around in the Index section.

To go to the Catalog section, click once on Catalog, which is in the bottom right-hand corner of your screen. This section allows you to access all of the artworks on the videodisc with information cards for each work. Once in the Catalog section, you can then click on Type In in the Find section and a dialog card will appear for you to type in.

Next, type in a theme, title, or word that you might want to find in Vincent's artworks. For example, type in *sunflowers* and click OK. This will bring up one of Vincent's painting of sunflowers (in chronological order) on the video screen and an Informational catalog card for that painting on the computer screen (see Figure 2–8). By clicking on Find Next at the bottom of the screen, you can view all of Vincent's paintings on the videodisc containing sunflowers or text with references to sunflowers.

Students can be prepared for this lesson by viewing the summary in Chapter 16 on side I of the videodisc and by using the remote control.

FIGURE 2-7   Index to Periods in the van Gogh Videodisc Companion. Courtesy of The Voyager Company.

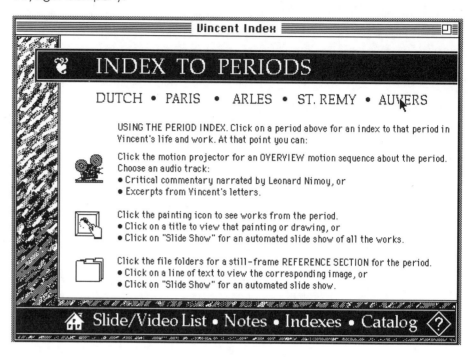

FIGURE 2-8   Catalog Card for a Sunflowers Painting in the van Gogh Videodisc Companion. Courtesy of The Voyager Company.

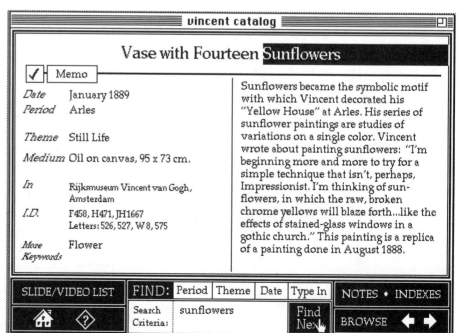

The summary categorizes Vincent's work into five major themes, such as portraits, still lifes, landscapes, urban settings, and self-portraits. Use the remote control and press on Chapter, 16, and then Search. Select a theme, such as *self-portraits*. Use the Still/Step button to click through the chapter and study the works by Vincent. Provide a list of questions for the students to watch for in the summary related to the self-portraits. Include a list of new vocabulary words they will be using and that can be discussed following the viewing of the videodisc. For example, discussion could follow on how Vincent's approaches to self-portraits changed through his use of color, brush strokes, as well as changes in his feeling and expression. What are the primary, secondary, and tertiary colors and how did Vincent use them in his self-portraits? How did he use complementary colors? What feelings do you have by looking at Vincent's self-portraits?

2.   Optional: You may also wish to show The Play or parts of it from Side II, if you have the original disc (1982, Philips International and North American Philips Corporation) to emphasize the drama and feeling of Vincent's letters to his brother Theo.

3.   Explain the purpose of the lesson to the class and divide the class into cooperative teams of four or five members. Each team will be assigned to one of the five time periods in Vincent's life (Dutch, Paris, Arles, St. Remy, and Auvers). If there are more than 25 students, time periods can be duplicated. The major task of each team will be to create a text and visual presentation of Vincent's culture, expressive style, and use of color for their specific period. Materials about Vincent can also be researched from books, articles, and reproductions. There is to be a team leader, recorder, class reporter, and data collectors. In addition, each team member must be assigned a specific task that will contribute to the final presentation and must be held responsible for a specific segment of information. The following questions in the worksheet can be divided among the team members. For example, one member might be responsible for identifying and collecting additional references related to major influences on Vincent's work, such as other artists or particular interests in his life during the period.

Following is a list of questions that can be copied and given to each team. Writing out responses for each question will help students keep a record of their progress and keep them focused on their research topic. The team should follow Steps 4 through 11 as they attempt to answer the questions on the checklist.

Checklist for Vincent van Gogh Videodisc

*   Identify the period your team will be studying.

_____

_____

_____

- What artists influenced Vincent during this period and how did they influence his use of color?

  _____

  _____

  _____

- What subjects or themes were most important to Vincent during this period and how did this affect his selection and approach to color?

  _____

  _____

  _____

- How are Vincent's colors described through text on the computer software or commentary on the videodisc?

  _____

  _____

  _____

- How is light shown in the paintings and how is this related to color? Do certain colors seem to come forward while other colors seem to go back into the painting? Describe how this appears to you.

  _____

  _____

  _____

- What does Vincent say he is trying to do in his paintings? In what way do you feel the same or different about these paintings he describes?

  _____

  _____

  _____

- What does Vincent say about other artists and their work?

  _____

  _____

  _____

- How did the culture and people around where Vincent lived during this period influence what and how he painted?

  _____

  _____

  _____

- How are Vincent's feelings and cultural values expressed in his use of colors and in the words he writes about his paintings?

  _____

  _____

  _____

- Provide examples of how colors are used in your culture and the meaning they have for expressing status, rituals, feelings, celebrations, or specific ceremonies. Contrast the meaning and use of colors in other cultures and provide examples.

_____

_____

_____

- Write your response to one of Vincent's paintings, emphasizing your feelings and emotions. Exchange and discuss these writings with members of your team to better understand how others write and feel about the paintings. Do some of you have similar or different feelings about these paintings? Listen to what others have to say and learn to understand where they are coming from. Some of you may choose to write about the same painting.

_____

_____

_____

4. The first step for the team is to become familiar with the particular time period. Go to the Periods Index, click on the assigned period, such as Paris, and click on the motion projector for an overview motion sequence (see Figure 2-9). Take notes on any material referring to Vincent's use of color and artists that influenced him. Stop the video by clicking once on Done. Use the list of questions and discuss the use of

FIGURE 2-9   Paris Period Card in the van Gogh Videodisc Companion. Courtesy of The Voyager Company.

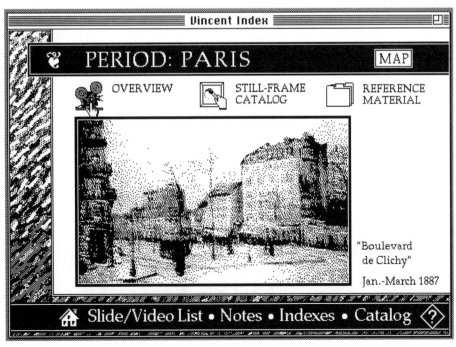

color in some of the paintings. Be sure to listen to both the commentary by Leonard Nimoy and excerpts from Vincent's letters. Go through the entire full-motion video by clicking on Play.

5.   Click once on the Still-Frame Catalog (along the top of the screen) for a list of works from the period. Notice that there is a scroll menu to view the complete works included for this period.

View a sample of work from the period, such as two portraits, two still lifes, and two landscapes. Do this simply by clicking once on the title of the artwork you wish to view. Keep notes on all the references on color as well as your responses to the paintings you observe. Note the differences between the early works and the last works Vincent painted for this period.

Click once on the map at the top of the screen to identify where Vincent was living during this period. Clicking on a name on the map will take you to the catalog section to a representative work of art done in that geographic area. To return to the Period section, pull up the Index Menu from the bottom of the screen and click on your particular period.

Back in the Period section, click on the Reference Material for text and still photographs related to Vincent's art. View these slides by clicking on the desired paragraphs describing a specific artist or artwork. The reference section focuses on the culture and influences of the period.

6.   Return to the Main Index Menu and click on Topics. From the Topics Index, click on Color and Technique. This will take you to video clips related to Vincent's use of color throughout the various periods of his life. Select a video clip by clicking once on it. Adjust the video with the Video Controller near the bottom of the screen. A bullet (•) before each clip indicates that there is a audio sequence drawn from Vincent's letters. Explore this section and select material that can be used in your final presentation.

7.   You should also feel free to explore the other indexes, such as the Influences Index and Keywords Index, to add other pertinent material to your research.

8.   Finally, go to the Catalog section. Pull up the Period Menu in the Find section and release the mouse button on your particular period. To view all the artworks in your period, continue through by clicking on Find Next. Study the text for each painting, paying particular attention to what is stated about color. Refer to your list of questions. Are you able to answer all of them as well as add additional questions and material?

9.   Click on the Notes at the bottom of the screen and bring up the Notes screen. This feature acts as a word processor to help you to organize and put together your ideas for your multimedia presentation. The Notes screen is in the edit mode, so you can type, cut, paste, and print your material with the usual Macintosh commands. Type in your introduction for the class presentation, at least three major points about your findings, and a conclusion. Clearly describe your ideas and the research you have gathered.

10. Organize the slide/video portion of your presentation by using the Slide/Video List feature. Clicking on the checkmark "✓" in the upper left of the screen puts the frame numbers and description of still frames or

motion sequences you are viewing onto a list for later reference. Clicking on the Slide/Video List button at the bottom of a card takes you to the Slide/Video List. This will display a list of slides and motion sequences you have marked. To view any of the images on this list, simply click on one of the lines. You can use the scroll on the right side to move the list up or down. By clicking on the commands at the bottom of the screen, you are able to design and edit your own show.

11. Critical discussion and exchanges of ideas should be encouraged during the class presentations by the teams.

Assessment

1. Collect the responses from the questions and research of each team. Determine the level of the responses:
   - Level One: Description, identification, and recall type of answers
   - Level Two: Understanding concepts, contrasting ideas, and analysis of concepts and expression of feelings
   - Level Three: Evaluation, critical thinking, creative expression, creating further questioning, interpreting meanings related to the assignment, and developing own expressive style to communicate findings and new concepts

Each level should deal with both cognitive and feeling-expressive types of responses. Teachers will determine which levels are most appropriate for students to concentrate on and guide them toward that goal.

2. Determine the level of participation, motivation, and enthusiasm of each team for its cooperative learning experience. Students can be given opportunities to reflect on their work and the quality of their interactions though group discussions, checklists, and written assignments.

3. Were students able to feel comfortable about critiquing both Vincent's writing and his works of art? Were they able to observe a relationship between the two forms of expression? Were they able to incorporate new vocabulary and concepts into their responses?

4. During the team presentations, was the class able to observe similarities and differences between the five periods of Vincent's life? Using the checklist, was there a high level of participation and exchange of ideas between the presenters and the class?

5. Have the students exchange their writing assignment with someone else in the class. Have them read the other student's work, select particular strengths in the writing, and briefly describe how they support their critiques with constructive criticism and guidelines.

Extensions

1. Students could work on their own artwork using one of the themes from the Videodisc Companion. They could write a short essay about the work, colors, subject, composition, cultural influences, and expressive qualities.

2. Students could examine published writings by other artists such as Pablo Picasso, Georgia O'Keeffe, or Freida Kahlo and write about

the different cultures, artwork, and writings of these artists. They could compare their own culture and values to other artists living in different cultures around the world.

3. Students could create a short one-act play about a particular artist's life and writings they have studied. Observing and analyzing the play on Side II (1982, Philips International and North American Philips Corporation) of the videodisc for a model, they could also design simple backdrops, props, costumes, and lighting.

Interactive NOVA: Animal Pathfinders Videodisc

Description

Interactive NOVA: Animal Pathfinders is the first in a series of multimedia videodiscs focusing on natural science. It includes video footage and slides of animals and habitats, plus a one-hour film "The Mystery of Animal Pathfinders" that deals with migration patterns. The full package contains 2 videodiscs, a handbook, reference chart and navigator guide, 10 software discs, and a teacher's guide with lesson plans, strategies, and black line masters. Going to the Main Menu of Animal Pathfinders allows you to move among the four major categories of Pathfinders: Overviews, Database, Activities, and Resources (see Figure 2–10). Following are brief descriptions of the four areas:

Overviews

Clicking directly on the square icon in the Main Menu will take you to Overviews. Included in this area is a video description of how to use the icons to move through the program. There is a video introducing the topic of migration and video explorations containing short films that introduce six categories of animals, six types of habitats, and three basic categories of animal behaviors. The one-hour NOVA film: "The Mystery of Animal Pathfinders" is in this section and on Sides C and D of the laserdisc. You can view the entire film or select a particular segment

FIGURE 2-10   Main Menu in Interactive NOVA: Animal Pathfinders (published by Scholastic Software).

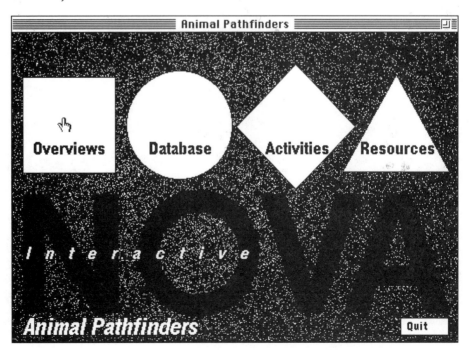

from Overviews. The software is designed for easy navigation from one area to another. In the lower left-hand section of the screen is a miniature of the Main Menu. Click on NOVA and go back to the Main Menu.

Database

Click on the circle icon to go to Database. This area contains more than 600 database cards that describes animals, habitats, and behaviors, with short related video or slide sequences (see Figure 2–11). In addition, there is a Theme Tours section that explores six biological themes, including such areas as Why Animals Migrate, Protective Coloration, and Metamorphosis. Click on NOVA to return to the Main Menu.

Activities

Click on the diamond icon to go to Activities. This section includes three interactive educational activities: Butterfly Field Study, Bee Dances, and Turtle Mystery. Butterfly Field Study allows you to work with a research team in both the field and the lab to discover the mystery of the migration patterns of monarch butterflies. Bee Dances allows you to explore how scout bees dance to communicate the location of nectar sources to worker bees. Once you learn the intricacies of the bee dance, then you have the opportunity to "be the bee," view samples of

FIGURE 2-11   A Database Card in Interactive NOVA: Animal Pathfinders (published by Scholastic Software).

bee dances, and attempt to determine the location of the nectar-bearing flowers (see Figure 2–12).

Turtle Mystery is a multimedia adventure game where you become an investigative journalist to discover why there are fewer loggerhead turtles in Florida. It simulates places and activities so that you ride in a taxi, fly in a plane, figure out clues and use them, and do such things as drive a boat using radar. The emphasis in these activities is on active learning with simulations, feedback, and a variety of options that you control. When finished with exploring Turtle Mystery, click NOVA on the bottom of the screen and return to the Main Menu.

Resources

Click on the triangle icon and go to Resources. This section has six different resources for using and getting the most out of Interactive NOVA. These resources include Help, Navigator, ReportMaker, VideoEditor, References, and Videodisc Controller. These sections not only make it easier to move through the program, as well as provide further information, but they also enable you to create your own multimedia reports, videos, slide shows, and games. In addition, clicking on the Navigator button in the lower right-hand corner of most screens takes you to the Navigator screen and a diagram of the entire program, and from

FIGURE 2–12   Sample screen from You be the Bee in Interactive NOVA: Animal Pathfinders (published by Scholastic Software).

there you can jump directly to any part of the program (see Figure 2–13). The NOVA box is located in the lower left-hand corner of most screens and allows you to return to the Main Menu from wherever you are in the program, or clicking on one of the four shapes takes you directly to one of the four major areas. Clicking on the Help button (a question mark) in the lower right-hand corner of most screens will take you to a card that explains what each button does.

FIGURE 2-13   Navigator Card in Interactive NOVA: Animal Pathfinders (published by Scholastic Software).

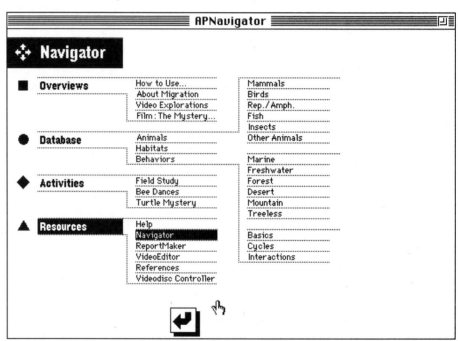

Lesson Plan: Interactive NOVA: Animal Pathfinders Videodisc

Title

Cultural Attitudes Affecting the Preservation of Animals and Their Habitat

Materials

Read Me First Handbook, Teacher's Guide, Icon Reference Chart and Navigator Guide, 2 12" videodiscs, and 10 3.5" diskettes (1990, WGBH Educational Foundation, Peace River Films, Inc., and Apple Computers, Inc. with Scholastic Software Publishers, 730 Broadway, New York, NY 10003)

Vocabulary

Extinction, habitat, endangered species, predators, ecosystems, cultural attitudes, taken-for-granted assumptions

Grade Level

Secondary

Purposes

Teacher's Guide   This lesson is an extension to several of the lessons in the Teacher's Guide that are in the packet for Interactive NOVA: Animal Pathfinders. The Teacher's Guide contains 12 lessons, and each lesson includes the following sections: Objectives, Background, Teaching Strategies, Questions for Discussion or Writing Assignments, Suggested Activities, Recommended Readings, and Student Worksheet. Teaching methods and strategies suggest various techniques for using the material with the whole class, small groups, pairs of students, and individuals.

Three Levels of Cognitive Skills   Thinking skills are geared for grades 5 and up using three levels: (1) recall recommended for grades 5 through 10, (2) analysis appropriate for grades 7 through 10, and (3) evaluation for grades 9 and up. However, flexibility is provided to the teacher by listing questions in each lesson that represent all three levels. Cooperative learning skills are also stressed in group activities that incorporate interaction, positive interdependence, individual accountability, and group social skills.

Multidiscipline Approaches   The Suggested Activities in the Teacher's Guide encourages multidiscipline approaches to the natural science lessons with related experiences in such areas as art (drawing), geography (map studies), and journalism (newspaper writing and reporting.) This lesson utilizes Lesson 6 (Human Threats to Animals) and Lesson 10 (Turtle Mystery) as a foundation for involving students in identifying their own cultural attitudes toward environmental issues and contrasting attitudes of other cultures. In addition, students are to come up with possible solutions for helping preserve animal life. The affective areas of subjective observation and feelings are significant in this lesson as well as the three cognitive levels of recall, analysis, and evaluation.

Lesson Objectives

Students will be able to:

*   Identify major issues concerned with the endangerment of animals.
*   Relate personal experiences and their feelings about the preservation of animals and their habitat.
*   Critically examine the cultural origins and assumptions embedded in society's attitudes and their own cultural attitudes and values toward preserving animal life.
*   Compare their own cultural attitudes toward animals with other cultures and how these cultures are different and/or similar in terms of caring for and protecting animals.
*   Use Pathfinder's ReportMaker and VideoEditor to create a video/slide presentation of their findings and possible solutions related to Cultural Attitudes and the Human Threat to Animals.

Procedures

1.   Use Lessons 6 and 10 to develop an understanding of what human threats there are to animals. Brainstorm as a class to create a list of threats to animals caused by human activities.

2.   Divide students into cooperative learning groups of four. Follow Lesson 6 and 10 and distribute student worksheets. Some groups could work on Lesson 6 while other groups are doing Lesson 10, the Turtle Mystery Activity. All groups should have turns working with the videodisc and computer with both lessons.

3.   Have each group use the questions for discussion and writing and include all three levels. Each student in a group should have one of the following responsibilities:
    *   Scribe: Records group's answers
    *   Reporter: Reports findings to whole class
    *   Facilitator: Keeps track of turn taking and makes sure everyone is doing their share; leads discussions
    *   Librarian/Media: Keeps group's papers, drawings, photos, magazine, newspaper clippings, and books in order

4.   Have groups work through the Suggested Activities in Lesson 6 and 10. For example, in Lesson 6, have them contact one of the listed conservation organizations in their local area and invite a representative to talk to the class. In the Suggested Activities for Lesson 10, they could start keeping a scrapbook from newspaper and magazine clippings concerning human threats to animals.

5.   Define and discuss the concept of *culture* with the whole class using the following strategies:

- Focus on the definition of *culture* as the shared values, attitudes, and beliefs of a particular group of people. Cultural groups may be differentiated by their geography, region, race, occupation, or historical traditions and beliefs. Identify each of these areas in relation to a particular group.

- Have the class brainstorm to create a list of different types of cultures, such as the Japanese, Amish, Pennsylvania Dutch, Appalachian Coal Miners, and Australian Aborigines. Discuss how we differentiate between these groups through their dress, designed living spaces, language, dialect, religion, values, beliefs, or folk arts.

- Invite a speaker or speakers representing different cultural groups to show films or slides that reinforce the concept of culture and differences in values and traditions among various groups. Emphasize attitudes toward animals and what part they play in particular cultures.

6.   Have groups develop a list and critique how particular threats to animals are related to their own cultural values, attitudes, and beliefs. For example, ideas about progress and efficiency, which are taken for granted, influence people's behavior about disposable plastic packaging that litters and is harmful to animal habitats. Have attitudes and beliefs about animals and the environment changed through time? Provide examples through history books and old newspapers. How do the students' own attitudes and values compare with attitudes they have been examining?

7.   Have the groups select a culture different from their own and contrast how that particular culture protects their animal life and environment. Identify similarities and differences between the values, attitudes, and beliefs of the two cultures. Refer to library resources, social studies texts, and additional references at the back of this chapter related to culture.

8.   Using Pathfinders, have each group present their findings and possible solutions to preserving animals and their habitat to the whole class by using both ReportMaker and VideoEditor. Presentations should include audio, visual, and text material. Students can describe how their own cultural attitudes have been modified or changed because of their research projects.

Assessment

1. Assess the level of understanding from the written research gathered by each group. Were they able to research and answer questions for recall, analysis, and critical thinking? Were they able to balance cognitive responses with more subjective, feeling responses?

2. Were the students comfortable using the laserdisc and computer to explore and research the topic? Did they get involved and use the interactive capabilities of Pathfinders extensively?

3. Did the students comprehend the concept of *culture* and how it relates to people's behavior and feelings toward animals and the environment?

4. Was the class, through critical dialog, able to compare and discuss the different cultural assumptions presented by the group research?

5. Were the students able to decode their own cultural values and beliefs and how that influenced their actions toward animals and the environment?

6. Were the groups able to come up with realistic and workable solutions to the problems involving animal preservation?

Extensions

1. Have students join a local chapter of a conservation group or a student chapter of their choice—such as the National Wildlife Federation, the National Audubon Society, the Nature Conservancy, or the Sierra Club—and contribute some group time toward a endangered animal project. It will be important for each group to set up goals, objectives, specific steps, and a time line to finish a particular project. Some of the areas they could get involved in might be designing posters to educate about endangered animals, helping to clean habitat areas, or helping to plant trees. The group should keep a log/diary of their involvement with the organization and participant observations throughout the project.

2. Have students project their ideas into the future and create an imaginary world where people and animals could live within a balanced relationship of each other. What would their culture be like? What would they look like? How would they dress? What kind of transportation and living habitat would they have? This is an excellent project for motivating fantasy and creative imagination. The project could take the form of both writing and visual illustration.

The Bio Sci II Videodisc

Description

The Bio Sci II Videodisc contains one side of a disc with over 7,000 still images, 400 diagrams, and 25 minutes of motion pictures and 3-D computer graphics. The videodisc is divided into 22 chapters that include everything from frog development, using the microscope, blood circulation, plant structures, dissections, and evolution diagrams. Videodiscovery, Inc. (1983, 1990) produced both the videodisc and the Bio Sci II Stack software to interact with the video. There is a content directory indexed by concept/classification, common name, scientific name, and frame number. The complete main index is also barcoded to interface with the Pioneer Laser Barcode Reader. The Slide Show and The Notebook allow teachers or students to produce their own slide/video shows and a video overlay capability allows text to be typed over the video images.

The Main Menu

Click twice on the Bio Sci II Index to go to the Main Menu. The Main Menu is arranged as a flow diagram of the structure of the Bio Sci II Stacks (see Figure 2–14). It maps the connections of all the features of the program and provides access to every section of the stacks. The Main Menu is made primarily of buttons, with the Index and Lesson Menu included in this card. Placing your pointer over text or buttons provides information about these functions in an information box.

FIGURE 2-14   Main Menu in Bio Sci II Videodisc. Used by permission of Videodiscovery, Inc., Seattle, WA., publishers of interactive video for science education.

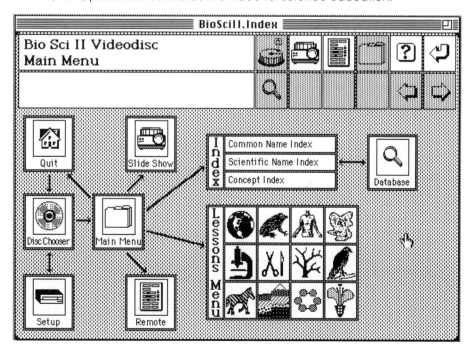

The Video Identifier

Click on the magnifying glass icon to go to the Video Identifier. The Video Identifier cards are the main core of the database. Each image and motion clip has a card in the Identifier. The triangle buttons allow you to go forward or backward through respective directories one entry at a time or one frame number at a time. This feature is helpful for browsing through several indexes Bio Sci simultaneously and for checking others with the same common name or finding related organisms.

Clicking on the icon showing hands searching through a card file allows you to make global searches across the entire database. By entering a word to search (e.g., *desert biome*) on this card, every card in the database that contains that word will be added to the end of the slide show list.

Lessons

There are 12 HyperCard Lesson themes with illustrated cards containing active buttons and descriptive text related to the video. These can be accessed from the Main Menu through icon buttons. The 12 topics are:

1. Biomes: Allows you to view scenery, plants, and animals within different biomes (a major community of living organisms)
2. Frog Development: Contains 10 different stages
3. Anatomy/Histology: Shows the human torso or human head graphic
4. Cell Biology: Computer graphic animation, diagrams, and movies present the cell organelles in detail
5. Microscopy: Teaches how to use the microscope, lighting, stains, magnification, and types of electron micrographs
6. Dissection: Eight dissections using mouse instead of scalpel
7. Family Tree: Diagrams the organization of all living organisms through the five-kingdom phyllogenetic tree
8. Bird Adaptations: Variations in birds relating to survival of the species
9. Animal Behavior: Demonstrates such areas as communication, feeding, locomotion, defensive, and social behavior
10. Geology: Includes major earth processes as well as other topics such as tilted strata
11. Biochemistry: Carbohydrates, fats, proteins, and nucleotides are introduced on various levels and the basic synthesis of each group is included
12. Angiosperm Life Cycle: Goes through every stage from sporophyte generation to growth of the seedling

Biome Data Cards

In the Main Menu, click on the World Globe icon to go to the world map of biomes. There are different biomes or biological communities of the earth presented on the map of the world (see Figure 2–15).

The Biome Data Card can be accessed by clicking on icon buttons on the World Map, the Washington State Transect, or the Temperature/

FIGURE 2-15   World Map of Biomes in Bio Sci II Videodisc. Used by permission of Videodiscovery, Inc., Seattle, WA., publishers of interactive video for science education.

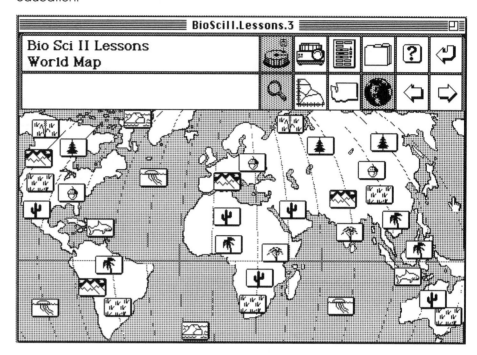

FIGURE 2-16   Alpine Biome Data Card in Bio Sci II Videodisc. Used by permission of Videodiscovery, Inc., Seattle, WA., publishers of interactive video for science education.

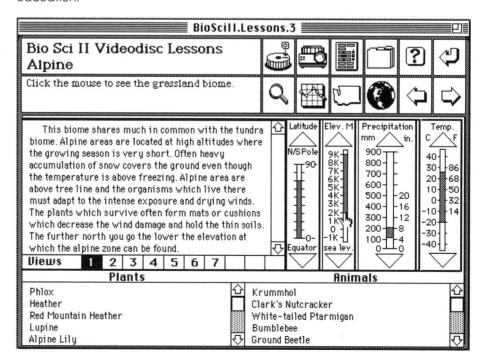

Rainfall graph boxes in the upper right-hand of the computer screen. They can also be accessed by clicking on the slide bars such as rainfall, temperature, elevation, and latitude (see Figure 2–16). Clicking on these slide bars links the biomes to each other according to their rank order—those either high or lower in rainfall, temperature, elevation, or latitude. A selection of general views of a typical terrain can be accessed on the video monitor for each biome, as well as specific plants and animals. Clicking on a Graph icon takes you to a graph of that biome's temperature and rainfall by month in a typical year.

Lesson Plan: The Bio Sci II Videodisc

Title

Human Adaptation to Biomes Around the World

Materials

Bio Sci II Software-Bio Sci II Stacks, Bio Sci II Videodisc, & Manual (1983, 1990) (Videodiscovery, Inc., 1515 Dexter Avenue North, Suite 400, Seattle, WA 98109-3017)

Image Directory—barcodes with Wm. C. Brown Publishers, Dubuque, Iowa 52001)

Vocabulary

Biome, transect, latitude, elevation, precipitation, temperature, climatogram, adaptation, culture, ecology

Grade Level

Elementary through secondary

Purposes

Bio Sci II was created for students in grades 4 through 12. The manual that comes with Bio Sci II Stack provides a section on sample activities and suggestions for possible lessons. This lesson has students studying different biomes from around the world and could be presented at either the elementary or secondary grades. Descriptive and recall skills could be emphasized more at the elementary grades, whereas analysis and critical thinking skills would be more of a focus at the secondary grades. However, teachers should feel free to determine the focus and learning experiences for their particular class. This lesson at one level encourages students to research both individually and in groups to understand the physical conditions of each biome and the plants and animals that inhabit it. At a higher level of thinking, the lesson involves students going beyond merely data collecting and analysis by problem solving and creating new scenarios based on the data.

Lesson Objectives

Students will be able to:

* Identify and describe the physical conditions of a particular biome as well as the plants and the animals that inhabit it.
* Analyze and contrast physical conditions between biomes, comparing both similarities and differences.
* Determine why and how certain plants and animals have adapted to their biome.
* Design a simple shelter for people that would allow them to live in a specific biome all year round.

- Examine how people in the same type of biome (e.g., desert or rain forest) but in different parts of the world adapt to their environment (through their shelter, clothing, foods).
- Determine the culture of people in different biomes and examine the relationship between their cultural attitudes, values, and beliefs and the biome they live in.
- Identify the relationship between the students' own values, attitudes, and beliefs, and the biome they live in.

Procedures

1.   Demonstrate the use of the computer with the Bio Sci II videodisc to the class with the purpose of the lesson and assessments. Illustrate what a biome is by using the Biome Data Cards and emphasizing the text, general views, organism lists, four physical data gauges, world map, temperature and rainfall graph, and transect. Have a class discussion about what biome they live in and what adaptations they have had to make.

2.   Divide the class into cooperative learning teams of four or five members. Each team should select a particular biome from the world map. Each team member should have a responsibility, such as facilitator, recorder, librarian/visual media, reporter, or researcher. Members can take turns being leaders in these areas.

3.   Have each team explore and search through the program for images and pieces of information related to their biome. Refer to the Bio Sci II Stacks Manual for activities using the biome data cards.

4.   The teams will be involved in writing, sketching, and gathering library research in addition to searching through Bio Sci II.

5.   Following is a checklist that can be duplicated and given to each team to help guide the members' research and gather their data.

Team Checklist for Bio Sci II

- What is the general description of your biome? Include latitude, elevation, precipitation, temperature, and a climatogram for a typical year.

  _____

  _____

  _____

- How can you describe the illustrations of the biome from Bio Sci II in your own words? What do these views tell you about the biome?

  _____

  _____

  _____

- What plants live in the biome and what characteristics do they have for coping in the biome?

  _____

  _____

  _____

- What animals live in the biome and how have they adapted and learned to cope? Where do they live and do they have a kind of shelter to live in?

  _____

  _____

  _____

- Where geographically is your biome located and where are other locations of the same biome on the world map? Name the specific countries, or states if in the United States, that are contained within these biomes. Are there similarities or differences between them?

  _____

  _____

  _____

- Are the animal and plant life in the same biome the same no matter what part of the world they are located in? Describe similarities or differences.

  _____

  _____

  _____

- What people live in your biome and in biomes like it in other parts of the world? Describe their different cultures, such as their language, dress, shelter, foods, music, art, rituals, beliefs.

  _____

  _____

  _____

6. Have each team design a shelter of its own that would help the students adapt to their biome and complement the environment. For example, they would use materials dominant in their area. Discuss and provide examples of architects who have consciously designed with the environment in mind, such as Frank Lloyd Wright in the desert at Taliesen West in Arizona. Have teams explore and research samples of different forms of architecture in their biome. Their final design can take the form of a drawing of floor plans, elevations, or a three-dimensional model of the exterior design.

7. Have teams critically analyze the relationship between a particular group of people and the biome they live in as well as their relationship to their plant and animal life.

Assessment

1. Each team will present its biome and highlights of their research findings to the class through text, motion clips, and slides from Bio Sci II. The focus will be on defining clear relationships between human adaptation, culture, and characteristics of a biome. Presentations demonstrating skills in description, organization, analysis, interpretation, problem solving, and evaluation will be emphasized.

2. Each team will present its shelter design in a visual format with a written description of the materials and functions, adaptability to the biome, considerations for preserving the plant and animal life, and comfort and aesthetic factors for the inhabitants.

3. Students will write short essays to demonstrate their understanding of the relationship of their own culture (values, attitudes, and beliefs) to the particular biome they live in. They will include individual or family experiences to illustrate their own feelings, their abilities to adapt, and their own value system.

Extensions

1. Have students create a play about a particular group of people who have traveled to a biome different from one they were familiar with and how they were able or not able to cope. An example would be the pioneer people who traveled across the western plains and mountains in North America. The animal and plant life of the biome should be incorporated into the plot of the play.

2. Have students write short adventure stories demonstrating coping in different biomes and a different culture, with an emphasis on a caring and adaptable leading hero or heroine. An example would be the leading character of the film "Dancing with Wolves," who cared for the animals and became involved with the people of a different culture (the Sioux Indians). The character not only was able to cope within the biome but adapted to and joined the Indian culture and its belief system.

3. Students could study how people have changed over time because of having to adapt to their biome. They could examine history books, old newspapers, biographies, and documentary films.

GTV: A Geographic Perspective on American History Videodisc

Description

GTV is a geographic perspective on American history that is designed for social studies classes in grades 5 through 12. The package contains two double-sided videodiscs, seven diskettes, maps, and a teacher's guide. It features 34 videos, or two hours worth of surveys, that cover American history from pre-Columbian times, the Colonial period, the Civil War, the Industrial Revolution, and other major events up to the present day.

The first videodisc emphasizes how the geography of the land influenced American history and it brings you all the way to the Revolution. The second disc focuses on the Colonists' expansion to the West and events that led up to the Civil War. The third disc moves from the expansion of the railroads through the Industrial Revolution, World War I, and to the United States as a new world power. Finally, the fourth disc brings this country through the twentieth-century by way of inventions in transportation and communication, as well as conflicts and hope for the future. GTV software clearly divides the program into the following four sections: Introduction, Directory, Activities, and Showtime. All can be accessed from the main menu, which is illustrated in Figure 2–17.

FIGURE 2–17   Main Menu in GTV: A Geographic Perspective on American History. National Geographic Society/LucasArts Entertainment Company.

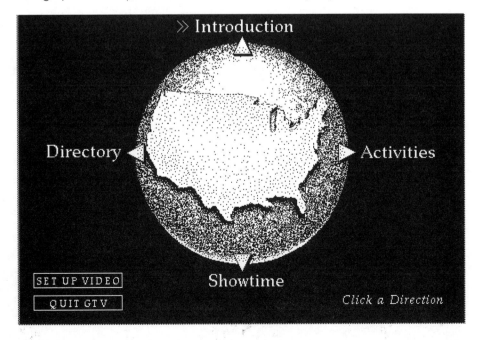

Introduction

This section describes the shows and how to use the software. Going through both the Introduction in the software and the Teacher's Guide provides help in navigating the program as well as an understanding of the content and how it is organized.

Directory

The Directory contains four different directories that let you access shows by date, theme, keywords or pictures.

- Date Directory: There are more than 60 shows that are listed in chronological order and represent two hours of video.
- Theme Directory: This directory clusters related shows into themes. By clicking one of the themes, a description appears. Then click Related Shows and there is a list of all the video shows related to that theme.
- Keyword Directory: This is an index or list of words that will bring up all the videos related to that word or term. Names of ethnic groups, states, cities, famous people, or concepts (such as Manifest Destiny) are examples included in the Keyword Directory. This directory not only makes researching easier but gives you ideas for different ways to search for a topic (see Figure 2–18).

FIGURE 2-18   Keyword Directory in GTV: A Geographic Perspective on American History. National Geographic Society/LucasArts Entertainment Company.

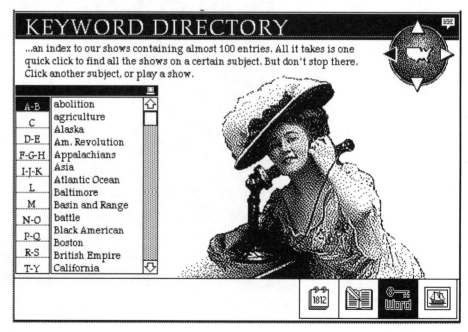

- Picture Directory: This is another way to access the video shows. Picture illustrations are used on drawings of file cards and then you click on those with which you wish to work.

Activities

This section includes maps and graphs. There are animated maps that show population, transportation, and communication growth throughout the history of the United States and a map that illustrates the extent of forest depletion in this country (see Figure 2–19). You can also access music in the Activities section. The music activity provides data on all the music used in GTV. It includes the sound, score, lyrics, and background information, which can be accessed first by clicking on the name of a particular video show and then the name of the music used in that video.

Showtime

This is a tool to create and present your own shows using visuals, sound, and text from GTV. You can pull up shows and write your own captions and text, and delete as well as add and rearrange material. Students can write stories or poetry to accompany their newly created visual show.

FIGURE 2–19   Forest Depletion Map in GTV: A Geographic Perspective on American History. National Geographic Society/LucasArts Entertainment Company.

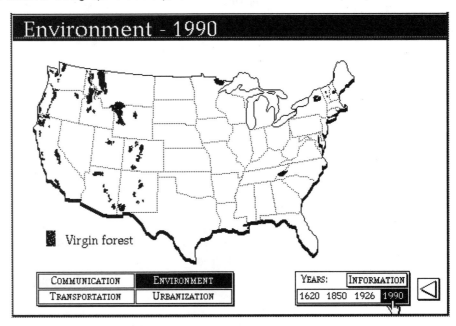

Lesson Plan: GTV: A Geographic Perspective on American History Videodisc

Title

Exploring One Major Theme in GTV: Communication

Materials

GTV: A Geographic Perspective on American History Videodisc, seven floppy diskettes with compressed files, and Teacher's Guide (1990, National Geographic and LucasArts Entertainment, Washington, D.C. 20036)

Vocabulary

Communication, primary sources, secondary sources, technology, historical methodology, influences, historical periods, values, attitudes

Grade Level

Secondary

Purposes

The major purpose of this lesson will be for students to develop methods to research particular periods in history focusing on a theme or concept. They will use a variety of sources from GTV and expand on these to use library sources and, if possible, other community resources, such as interviews, film archives, and newspaper morgues. A major concept developed throughout this lesson on communication is that factors such as geography, expansion to the West, conflicts and wars, population growth, inventions, and the development of new technologies all contributed to changing the way we communicate and in turn changed our values and perceptions of ourselves and others.

Lesson Objectives

Students will be able to:

* Develop research methods using a theme approach to identify and analyze a particular time period in history.
* Understand the difference between primary and secondary resources in researching history.
* Identify specific influences that contributed to changes in communication.
* Understand how relationships between the land of a country, politics and government, natural resources, and technology and the media worked together to form and reinforce the values and attitudes of a people.
* Identify, interpret, and evaluate a major belief (such as Manifest Destiny) and its origin within a particular cultural group, time period in American history, and influences of geographic factors.

- Create a multimedia presentation using GTV Showtime to demonstrate critical thinking and research conclusions.

Procedures

1. The teacher will demonstrate the basic operation of GTV to the whole class by using menus and the navigation system. There are nine themes in the Theme Directory; this lesson will focus on the Communication theme. The class will be divided into four or five teams with each team being responsible for researching the communication systems in a time period—such as a particular century, a war period, or a decade. This selection will depend on the teacher, the curriculum, the ability of students, and the focus. There needs to be a large enough difference in the time periods studied by the teams to provide an overview history of communication. GTV separates the program into four time periods according to the disc side, as follows:

   - Side 1: 1492–1781
   - Side 2: 1781–1865
   - Side 3: 1865–1920
   - Side 4: 1920–1990

2. Each team will explore GTV and how it operates. Each team will be responsible for a specified period of time with a focus on communication, including the influences, changes, and affects on people and society. Each member of the team is to have a team responsibility, such as chairperson, recorder, or class reporter. In addition, each member will also have a specific research responsibility. Following is a sample worksheet that could be developed for the teams.

Worksheet for GTV

- Theme: Communication
- Time Period: _____
- Describe briefly the culture of this period. Include such areas as urban and rural living styles, the land, form of government, trades and major occupations, transportation, and the arts (painting, music, architecture, etc.). (Each team member could be responsible for a particular area.)

  _____

  _____

  _____

- What kinds of communication systems were used? Describe.

  _____

  _____

  _____

- What factors created problems for communication? Describe.

  _____

  _____

  _____

- What groups had trouble communicating with one another? Describe the reasons for these conflicts. Were these problems resolved? Why or why not?

  _____

  _____

  _____

- What innovative ideas, industry, or inventions affected the way people communicated during this time period?

  _____

  _____

  _____

- How did systems of communication affect people's values and their perceptions of each other?

  _____

  _____

  _____

3. The various teams will take turns using the GTV videodisc program and computer station, since it is assumed that most classrooms will not have one station for each team. Teams not working at the station can begin to research background material for their particular time period by using library resources, videos, art books, newspapers, and magazines. Teams may even want to interview community people to gather more data; resource people could be brought into the classroom. After a team at a station has become familiar with the operation of GTV, it would start its research by clicking on the Directory of the Main Menu and then on the Theme Directory. Nine themes will come up on the screen, and clicking on the Communication theme will start the team's research on GTV.

4. A dialog box will appear and will ask how communication has changed (see Figure 2–20). The team member will click on Related Shows on the bottom of the box to bring up a scroll menu on the screen listing those shows related in some way to communication. The team will select shows that provide information about its time period. For example, in the show "The Rise of Cities" (1680–1770), students can observe how waterways were significant for trade and transportation and how this affected communication with other groups of people.

5. As the shows are studied, the Keyword Directory can be used interchangeably to access related data. If the show "The Rise of Cities" is being studied, then the Keyword Directory can be used to search for such words as *colonial, England, people, and transportation.* The focus

FIGURE 2–20   Dialog Box for Communication Theme in GTV: A Geographic Perspective on American History. National Geographic Society/LucasArts Entertainment Company.

of the research will be on what factors influenced change in communication and how systems of communication affected people's attitudes and perceptions.

6.   A final presentation for the class will be prepared by each team. The Showtime tool, which includes Showmaker and Showplace, can be used to create a multimedia show from the GTV videodisc program. In addition, material researched in the library or videos of interviews of resource people can also be incorporated into the presentations. Members of the team are to write a report on what their particular responsibility was and what their major contribution was to the final report.

7.   Presentations by all of the teams will allow the students to observe how communication has changed or how some areas have stayed the same. These class presentations can motivate more in-depth dialog and debates about social issues related to communication. Other lessons can be developed to use the other themes in the GTV program in a similar way.

Assessment

1. Make an assessment on the involvement of a team in using different types of research. Were they able to obtain primary as well as secondary resources? For example, did they use film, slides, newspapers, autobiographies, biographies, interviews, video, and history books to obtain their research data?

2. Determine the level of enthusiasm and involvement of each team for the team learning experience. Read the individual team member's reports—how well did each student assume responsibility for the project and what was a major area of contribution?

3. Evaluate the levels of understanding observed from the written and visual research gathered by the teams. Were levels of recall, description, analysis, interpretation, and evaluation developed in the reports? Were students able to do critical and creative thinking? Were the teams able to identify the most significant data about communication for their research?

4. Did presentations take into account timing and organization? Did they motivate the interest and critical thinking of the students? Were students able to recognize significant transitions and trends that affected the history of communication in the United States?

Extensions

1. Students could focus on the arts—such as visual arts, music, dance or drama—of a particular period and analyze how the arts are influenced by different modes of communication. They might also investigate how the arts have helped to influence perceptions and abilities to communicate.

2. Students could compare the communication of the United States with another very different culture and study the ways they are different and similar. They could examine how cultural attitudes and beliefs affect the way a culture develops modes of communicating.

3. Students could project into the future how new communication systems might be developed in outer space as well as here on earth.

Conclusion

This chapter reviewed a sample of leading educational interactive video programs and how they could be adapted for use in the classroom. Major features and capabilities of the programs were described along with illustrations. Lessons with objectives and step-by-step procedures were described for each interactive video program. Areas such as cooperative learning, understanding the concept of culture, and both affective and cognitive learning were emphasized. These sample lessons with specific formats and subheadings can be used as a framework for developing your own lessons with interactive video.

The sample programs were flexible and many of them allow teachers and students to create their own multimedia shows. The interactive computer software was designed to help users move easily through the programs by being able to branch through levels of their choice. One could access either still frames or motion clips and move back and forth between them.

Many of the interactive video programs included helpful guidelines or provided strategies for teachers to work within the classroom. There were also programs that incorporated lesson plans with computer graphics and games as part of the software program. This review of the interactive video programs for education provides an understanding of the type of programs available to teachers and the wide range of possibilities for using them in the classroom. Next, Chapter 3 concentrates on teacher evaluation of interactive videodiscs and software and identifies specific criteria for use in selecting quality programs for education.

Suggested Learning Extensions
1. Select one of the lessons in this chapter using a specific interactive video program. Modify the lesson to incorporate two or three learning objectives that you would teach in the classroom. Include both cognitive and affective domains.
2. Select one of the extension ideas for a lesson. Create a new lesson plan from your selection by using the format in the chapter lessons.
3. Create a new lesson for one interactive video program. Include cooperative learning teams and multidisciplinary approaches.
4. Observe a teacher using interactive video in the classroom and write up a two- to three-page summary or videotape the experience with permission.
5. Teach a videodisc-based lesson from this chapter and provide a written, photographed, or videotaped summary.

Chapter References and Additional Readings

Boyer, B. A. (1987). Cultural literacy in art: Developing conscious aesthetic choices in art education. In D. Blandy, & K. Congdon, (Eds.), *Art in a democracy* (pp. 91–106). New York: Teachers College Press.

Boyer, B. A. (April 1989). DBAE and CLAE: Relevance for minority and multicultural students. *Journal of Social Theory in Art Education, 9,* 58–63.

Boyer, B. A., & Semrau, P. (1990). Gender and ethnic imagery in interactive video: A lesson for secondary art students. In P. Taylor (Ed.), *Art with a capital A.*(p. 63). California Art Education Association.

Eggen, P., & Kauchak, D. (1988). *Strategies for teachers: Teaching content and thinking skills* (2nd ed.). Englewood Cliffs, NJ: Prentice Hall.

Hurwitz, A., & Madeja. S. (1976). *The joyous vision.* New York: Van Nostrand Reinhold.

McFee, J. K., & Degge, R. M. (1992). *Art, culture, and environment.* Dubuque, IA: Kendall/Hunt.

National Geographic Society. (1990). *GTV: A geographic perspective on American history* (Videodisc). Washington, DC.

Philips International and North American Philips Corporation. (1982). *Vincent van Gogh: A portrait in two parts* (Videodisc). Wilmington, DE.

Scholastic Software. (1990). *Interactive NOVA: Animal pathfinders* (Videodisc, software, & teacher's guide). 730 Broadway, New York, NY 10003.

Semrau, P., & Boyer, B. A. (Fall 1991). Examining educational software from both an aesthetic and cultural perspective. *Journal of Hypermedia and Multimedia Studies, 2*(1), 25–29.

Semrau, P., & Boyer, B. A. (December/January 1991–92). Using Interactive video to examine cultural issues in art. *The Computing Teacher, 19*(4), 24–26.

Taba, H. (1967). *Teacher's handbook for elementary social studies.* Reading, MA: Addison-Wesley.

Videodisc Publishing, Inc. (1983). *The National Gallery of Art* (Videodisc). 381 Park Ave. South, Suite 1601, New York, NY 10016.

Videodiscovery Inc. (1983, 1990). *Bio Sci II videodisc & Bio Sci II stacks.* 1515 Dexter Ave. N., Suite 400, Seattle, WA 90109; and Image Directory for Bio Sci II Videodisc published for Wm. C. Brown Publishers, Dubuque, IA 52001.

Voyager Company, The. (1987, 1991). *The National Gallery of Art: A videodisc companion.* 1351 Pacific Coast Hwy., Santa Monica, CA 90401.

Voyager Company, The. (1988, 1991). *van Gogh revisited: A videodisc companion.* 1351 Pacific Coast Hwy., Santa Monica, CA 90401.

3

Teacher Selection
of Interactive
Video Programs

Chapter Objectives

After completing this chapter, you will be able to:

☐ *Identify and use specific criteria to select interactive video programs for your classroom.*

☐ *Understand how good instructional design of the computer and video screens plays a major role in the learning process of students.*

☐ *Identify the important factors of human interface design that facilitate learning.*

☐ *Develop and use checklists and guidelines in the selection process.*

☐ *Apply different strategies and resources for the selection and evaluation of interactive videodisc programs.*

Introduction

This chapter is concerned with teacher selection of interactive video programs for the classroom. Selecting criteria from the checklists and material in this chapter will help you develop your own evaluation instruments. Evaluating interactive video programs on a continuing basis will help you gain a better understanding of what is involved in a well-designed program. Some quality design factors include providing alternative ways to navigate through the program, simple easy-to-read screens, the choice of selecting quality film and visuals rather than screens merely replicating textbook formats, and the option for learners to receive feedback and develop their own visual and text solutions to problems. Some aspects of poorly designed interactive video programs include the students feeling lost or frustrated, feeling confused by the screen directions and text information, not being able to access data, and having limited interactivity with the program.

When teachers select interactive video programs for their classroom, they need to consider the following factors:

- How does the interactive video program fit into my curriculum?
- Are the objectives for this program compatible with my learning objectives?
- Can I use this program with large groups as well as small groups?
- Does this program already replicate what I have?
- Is this the best use of the media?
- Does this program provide the maximum effectiveness for my type of students?

Although this chapter does not involve cost factors of interactive video programs, teachers will need to account for economic considerations in the selection process. In addition, technical factors—such as unnecessary delays in operating the program, slow loading of graphics, and program "crashing"—are all important aspects of interactive video programs that teachers need to be aware of and avoid.

Selection and evaluation of interactive video programs begins with knowing what to look for and how to look for it. The first step is to establish evaluative criteria and then develop a comprehensive order of procedures for examining programs that might include support people to assist you in reviewing programs. Understanding what is involved in the evaluation process will increase your confidence about selecting the best possible interactive video programs for your school district and students.

Identifying the following major areas will help in the development of criteria for evaluating interactive video programs in the classroom. Checklists are included under each of these major areas throughout the chapter. You can include all or part of these checklists in making up your own evaluation instruments.

- Content and the Learner: What is to be learned and who will be using the program?
- Instructional Design: How will the content be presented?
- Interface Design: How will the learner use the software and navigate through the program?
- Evaluation Process: What procedures and support resources can be used for improving selection?

Content and the Learner

Analyzing the content of interactive video programs in relation to your curriculum and your learners needs is a major step in establishing criteria for evaluation. A beautiful-looking multimedia package can be useless if its content is either incorrect or inappropriate for the classroom and type of students that will be using it. In Figure 3–1, teachers and students are going through lessons developed for the Laser Learning videodisc by Hoffman Educational Systems.

Program Guide

The documentation that comes with interactive video programs concerning both the content and operation of the program needs to be examined for its accuracy and ease of use. A guide is usually provided for the user that includes such features as a table of contents, tabbed pages, and an index. These should be organized so you can begin to access important information about the program and feel comfortable using it. The following general areas need to be considered when examining the program's guide:

- Is there detailed information about required hardware?
- Is there a description about the intended audience?
- Is there a listing of instructional or learner objectives?
- Are there suggestions for classroom use and recommended student learning activities?

FIGURE 3–1   Teacher Doloris Flint (left) demonstrates the Laser Learning videodisc lesson with Duarte, California, students Chad Parodi, Katie Montgomery, Jennifer Ballantyne, Casey Parodi, and teacher Suzanne Owens. The program, produced by Duarte firm Hoffman Educational Systems, has won national recognition. Courtesy of Hoffman.

- Has the program been field tested—that is, used in real classrooms with real students?
- Are telephone numbers and addresses provided for component replacements or other consumer assistance?

Some interactive video programs include separate documentation, one of these being a User's Manual that explains the operation of the program. If the program was designed to be used in a classroom, then there would also be an Instructor's Manual. With an interactive video program that is more open ended and includes simulation programs, there might be a Student's Manual that has instructions and guided activities for the students. The following provides a checklist of what to look for in these various manuals.

User's Manual

For better organization and ease of understanding, the following components should be included in the User's Manual:

- Title Page
- Table of Contents
- Installation and Operational Procedures
- Introduction (including an Overview, Purpose, Particular Requirements such as a textbook), and System Requirements
- Basic Steps for Using the Program
- Instructions for Specific Tasks or Processes
- Reference Section
- Glossary
- Index

Instructor's Manual

Any interactive video program that will be used in the classroom should benefit from additional information for the instructor; however, these are not commonly included with most programs. The following are some of the areas that would be helpful in an Instructor's Manual.

- Curriculum Integration: This describes how students can best be introduced and prepared for the program. Suggested content topics are illustrated for use in curriculum. Educational experiences are provided that can be incorporated into the classroom following the use of the program.
- Educational Background: This includes educational goals and objectives, and provides the type of courses or programs of study that work well with the program.
- Implementing the Program: This describes the kind of classroom required for using the program. Guidelines are included for using the program with individuals, small groups, or the whole class.
- Lesson Plans: Related lessons are provided that include student objectives, procedures, and evaluation of learning.

- Exercises: Included are sample exercises that will help guide the instructor and ensure that the program will be used effectively.
- Ancillary Materials: There are referrals to other materials that an instructor could use. For example, additional types of software or multimedia resources might be listed.

Student's Manual

A self-contained guided experience for students could be useful. Such a manual would be used without the support of an instructor and would include the following:

- Summary of Academic Concepts and Principles: This provides the conceptual link between the academic content and the computer-based instructional (CBI) activities.
- Step-by-Step Explanation of What the Student Does and Sees: This tutorial guides the student through an activity.
- Practice Problem or Activity: This poses higher-order thinking questions that require students to relate problems to academic content.
- Solution Set: This demonstrates how to use the program to arrive at a specific solution. It stresses correct conceptualization of the problem as well as the proper strategy for using the software.

The content presented in the interactive video program must be closely examined. Information needs to be up to date and accurate in regard to the topic that is presented. Opposing points of view within the academic community should be included and fairly represented within the program or in the supporting documentation. Most importantly, the information must be presented without particular prejudices or biases.

The appropriateness of the interactive video program to fit into your classroom instruction is a major criterion. You will be the best judge of the selection of the material for your students and the objectives you have for their learning activities. Your understanding of the physical and intellectual maturity of the students will need to be considered when you are weighing criteria for selection. The concepts and vocabulary used in presenting the content should be relevant to the students' developmental abilities and experiences, and be able to capture their interests and imaginations. In addition, the courseware needs to relate to your particular curriculum and instructional methods.

Management Component

Teacher control of the content presentation can be an important factor when selecting programs. Records and helpful information about student progress can be maintained through certain programs, but you need to determine what kind of control over the information you will require. For example, will the program allow for specific student responses and a compilation of their work so that you have data to study and can better develop your instructional priorities? How much control will you have over the content presentation? Will you be able to set up a mastery level of questions or problems within the program that would determine higher or lower levels of difficulty or challenges for students?

All of these questions need to be taken into consideration when selecting programs that you will be adapting for classroom use.

Learner Characteristics

Characteristics of learners interact with the instruction of interactive video programs and influence the outcomes and effectiveness of learning. These characteristics include prerequisite knowledge, information processing capacity, metacognitive skills, motivation, prior experiences and knowledge, and learner expectations. Following is a sampling of program criteria related to learner characteristics that need to be considered when selecting interactive video programs:

- The program provides the learner with questions and the opportunity to respond throughout the program rather than just viewing and listening activities. This increases the students' ability to remember what they have learned (their information processing capacity).

- The program allows for testing and gathering information on students' prior knowledge regarding the subject. The teacher can observe how students make inferences about new material based on their past experiences, feelings, and knowledge base.

- The program analyzes students' progress and guides and coaches students through appropriate paths of differing complexities.

- The program controls how much practice students will need to be knowledgeable in an area (metacognitive skills) and provides guidance in those areas. If students are not able to evaluate how much practice they need, then such controls must be an essential criterion for selection. Knowing how much control of instruction to assign students should be based on knowledge of learner characteristics.

- The program provides clear operating directions and allows students the opportunity to be involved and "doing" something. Student expectations are based on their interaction and previous experiences with television, computers, or computer games. They will expect to be active and will not want to read screens with lengthy text explanations or descriptions.

- The program uses color, sound, animation, and screen displays selectively for appropriate learning outcomes that are appealing to and motivate students. Techniques of sound and dazzling screen displays can be overdone or even become abrasive to the learner.

It is important to recognize that interactive video programs need to be evaluated not only in terms of the quality of the content but with an understanding of how the characteristics of the learners will influence learning outcomes. In addition to general learner characteristics, learning styles—which are the individual ways that students process information—need to be taken into account when selecting interactive video programs.

Learning Styles

Knowledge about student learning styles is significant to include when evaluating interactive video programs (see Geisert & Dunn, 1992). Learning styles include the characteristic ways that individuals process and retain information in long-term memory.

Interactive video programs can be selected by teachers to enhance their students' different learning styles. Some students tend to process information in a step-by-step, sequential, analytical, and detailed mode. Other students learn through holistic processing—examining the big picture first and then attending to details. Teachers can select multimedia technology that offers different options for the way their students process information and further develop their critical thinking skills. For example, programs that allow for open-ended exploration and multiple ways for solving problems can promote higher-level thinking processes for more advanced, motivated students. Whereas greater guidance, direction, feedback, and reinforcement need to be built into programs at beginning levels for students who have difficulty mastering material or may be less experienced.

The newer technology does not have to be regarded in the same way as traditional classroom strategies that utilize linear media approaches, such as replicating linear video, page turning textbooks, or slide shows. Teachers have the unique opportunity to provide alternative ways of learning and to stimulate intuitive thinking and discovery learning in their students. Students can now be encouraged to learn the way they naturally learn outside of the classroom environment, through networking, exploration, and simulated environments, in addition to the more traditional linear classroom approaches. Teachers can challenge students to increase their skills in critical thinking and creative expression through the use of newer technologies.

Effective Cueing Strategies

Chapman and Olson (1992) noted that an essential factor for enhancing high degrees of learner interactivity in well-designed computer-based instruction (CBI) was the incorporation of effective cueing strategies. Cueing strategies can direct learner attention, structure content, and help organize conceptual segments within CBI lessons. Although limited research has been done in this area, guidelines can be identified for using effective cueing strategies that promote interactive learning and higher achievement of students. Following are particular strategies used in well-designed interactive video programs with CBI:

- Students are required to act on or cognitively process information that they receive in the interactive video program.
- The processing of information is enhanced by the use of visual cues. The cues are selected carefully, and critical visual thinking precedes the use of the cueing devices.
- Visual techniques for cueing attention can be obtained through the use of color, texture, movement, rotation, and explosion/implosion techniques. Text can be highlighted by placement in boxes, underlining, or using bold type, different text fonts, or italics. However, visual and color cueing must be used judiciously so as not to overpower the content or make it confusing.
- The interactive video program uses simple, uncrowded visual presentations.
- Questions and feedback are used that encourage students to come up with answers by actively reconstructing their prior learning with new information.

- The interactive video program incorporates mnemonic aids such as note taking and outlining, which require students to become more active in the learning process.

Knowledge of these criteria for selecting educational interactive video programs will ensure greater quality learning experiences for students and an higher level of interactivity. The lack of effective cueing strategies can be a major factor in limiting the usefulness of interactive video programs for the classroom.

Philosophical and Cultural Factors

Helsel (1987) noted that interactive videodisc programs reflect the value system of the larger society in which they are developed. Helsel further suggested that interactive video programs on a more local level may transmit the cultural values of the design team, as well as values from what might be called a video *subculture* nourished by conferences and professional publications. There is no question that interactive video programs do have the potential to create a particular view of reality in the minds of viewers that is very powerful. Therefore, it is important that teachers be aware of how the interactive video programs are structured, how students are expected to process information, and what are the expected outcomes. Interactive video programs may be based on the following:

- Linear-goal expectation models using individual experts and linear-directed activities with specified outcomes
- Conceptual models using multiple perspectives with more individual learner flexibility and options
- Critical values models promoting the development of critical consciousness in learners with the opportunity to develop their own questioning strategies

There could be variations on these models as well as possible combinations within one interactive video program. For example, if the interactive video program was based on the linear-goal-directed model, then students might be led through the program in a more sequential way and with more direction for a prescribed outcome. However, if a critical values model was used, the program might present a societal problem and expect the student to develop critical thinking skills by arriving at possible solutions. Interactive NOVA: Animal Pathfinders (Scholastic Software, 1990) promotes critical thinking and develops social consciousness about how we treat animals. Teachers who are aware of what philosophical foundation an interactive video program has will be able to select programs more in line with the learning objectives that they are implementing in the classroom.

Instructional Design

Instructional design is a major factor in interactive video programs, for it is concerned with how the instruction or content is presented as well as the type of instructional context it will be presented in. The appearance of the text, visuals, and sound, and how they are organized, all affect how the students will learn. The instructional design, if well done, will reinforce what the interactive video program is trying to accomplish and make the purpose clear to the students.

Introduction to Instructional Design

When students first open an interactive videodisc program, they need to learn its purpose, how to use it, and the rules that have been established for running it. The following short list used for HyperCard stack design (Apple Computer, Inc., 1989) can be helpful when getting started with instructional design criteria in evaluation:

- The program should be simple to use and the purpose should be clear.
- The student should be involved with doing something immediately, such as clicking a button or typing a name.
- Introductory material should be presented in small segments so students do not have to take in too much material at once.
- Specific help or directions should always be available.

Computer-Based Instruction

According to Alessi and Trollip (1991) interactive video is an extension of computer-based instruction (CBI) that provides the instructional designer capabilities that just would not be available by using the computer alone. The major concept is that interactive video as CBI is enhanced by the high quality of visuals and sound.

The connection of video to the computer, as well as compact disc-interactive (CDI) and digital video-interactive (DVI), has made CBI an educational interactive medium that is rich in visual and aural content. The videodisc allows for fast and constant interaction and is able to jump to any segment of a program in a few seconds or less. The fast access time provides interactive instruction that is responsive to the user and is more realistic and enjoyable.

A videodisc has the capacity to store a large number of still images, but this could be a problem if you were trying to find a particular photograph out of, say, 54,000. A printed catalog with a barcode scanner would help, but it would still take a while to go through the catalog—a linear medium. Instead, the videodisc has the capacity for computer control with branching and random access capabilities that make finding your photograph practically a cinch.

Types of Instructional Methodologies

There are various types of instructional methodologies that can be used in interactive video programs. Some of these, such as simulations and instructional databases, use the full capabilities of interactive video programs much better than tutorials or drill approaches. However, there is a place in the classroom for different ways of learning using interactive video and knowing these differences is a major component in evaluation. The following material will discuss interactive video programs such as tutorials, drill, simulations, games, databases, help systems, and generic videodiscs.

Tutorials   Interactive video programs have not been commonly used for tutorials in education. Tutorials have often been combined with other methodologies, as in The Puzzle of the Tacoma Narrows Bridge Collapse (Fuller, Zollman, & Campbell, 1982). Students first work in a simulation, observing various effects of wind on a model bridge. Then a tutorial methodology is used to teach concepts in mathematics to analyze how wave motion can actually cause a large bridge to collapse. A tutorial not only provides information that the student is to learn but allows the student to examine the material and review it. Students can then be quizzed on the material, obtain feedback on the results, and even refer to dictionaries and other references for help.

Drill and Practice   The use of drills as an instructional methodology is not often found in interactive video programs. Drills are much more common in standard CBI programs where a student needs to practice a concept or skill over and over again using verbal material and receiving continual feedback and guidance. Instructional designers could include drill and practice formats in sections of interactive video programs to reinforce the content or skills to be learned, particularly if visuals were a major component of the information to be learned.

Simulations   Interactive video programs have the greatest capacity to create simulations with the use of a wide range of visuals, animations, and sound. The interactive video program can place students in a specific setting with a realistic environment that presents problems or challenges, and all complete with visual and audio simulations. The user is then able to "walk through" the simulation, being presented with a variety of options, and fully able to participate in making decisions and taking action. Bio Sci II (Videodiscovery, Inc., 1983, 1990) includes simulations such as laboratory experiments. Figure 3–2 illustrates one of the computer screens for working on a frog dissection in Bio Sci II.

Interactive video programs are particularly powerful in the area of simulations. The user has access to interacting with a whole range of media such as film, computer graphics, sound, text, and still designs. Combining these capabilities within a large screen creates simulations that are more lifelike and effective. New environments can be created for students to explore based on accurate models and directly related to experiences significant to the students' lives. Simulations can take students back into time or forward in time to imaginary places. Simulations can also take the place of activities that could be time consuming, dangerous, costly, or too difficult to accomplish in the classroom. The military uses flight simulations in training pilots to fly expensive aircraft.

It is important that simulations be an important area to focus on for evaluation. Such things as whether the learner becomes an active participant in the learning simulations and whether the program is intrinsically reinforcing to the learner are areas to be evaluated. In simulations, there should be opportunities for nondirective techniques, such as discovery or exploration of knowledge. The simulation should provide continual feedback to learners regarding their achievement level

FIGURE 3–2   Frog dissection simulation in Bio Sci II Videodisc. Used by permission of Videodiscovery, Inc., Seattle, WA., publishers of interactive video for science education.

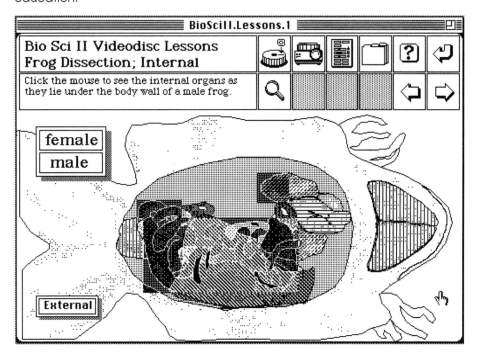

throughout the program. In addition, the simulation should be appealing with a high level of interest for learners.

Educational Games   Educational games can be incorporated into interactive video programs and are another type of instructional methodology. Alessi and Trollip (1991) found it surprising that there were so few games among level 3 videodisc programs. It may be that during this period of time interactive video programs have been used primarily for adult instruction and instructional games are more associated with children. Games can be used with the addition of simulations like those used in Interactive NOVA: Animal Pathfinders (Scholastic Software, 1990). A mystery game is part of Animal Pathfinders and within the game are such simulations as riding in a cab, driving a boat, and being able to move around an office and click on objects that become animated and provide clues. Figure 3–3 illustrates an office interior in the Animal Pathfinders game.

Games are particularly effective for developing critical thinking and problem solving. The best of them pose problems that provide multiple options and responses and allow students to create their own problems. They involve high levels of interactivity and critical thinking, and students find them to be fun. Educational games can be a challenging and excellent way to learn. Examining the interactivity of educational games, their levels of difficulty, feedback, and relationship to students' interests are all factors to evaluate when selecting interactive video programs.

FIGURE 3-3   Office simulation in Interactive NOVA: Animal Pathfinders (published by Scholastic Software).

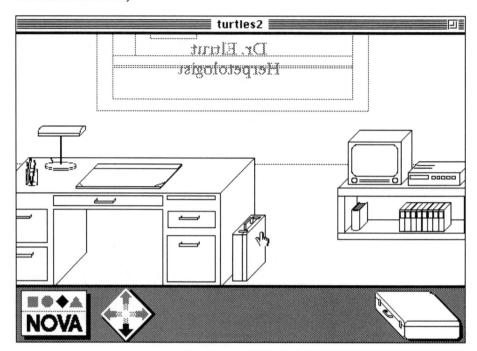

Databases   Videodiscs are particularly appropriate in the area of storing, cataloging, and accessing large amounts of visual information. Students can explore and retrieve thousands of still images, such as those in the van Gogh and the National Gallery of Art Videodiscs (see Chapter 2). The videodisc connected to the computer via a software interface allows users to research and analyze large quantities of visual data related to such disciplines as the visual arts and sciences. It allows students to sort, categorize, contrast, and evaluate large archives that would just not be possible in slide form. First of all, the complete archive would not be available to students; second, an immense amount of time would be required to access the right visuals.

Help Systems   An interactive video program could be used as a help system at a work station to provide demonstrations with narrations on how to run equipment or computer programs. This would be useful for operations that have lengthy manuals that users might have trouble translating. The interactive video program would be available for help as the user begins to master the required skills and could be passed on to others working through the beginning stages.

Generic Videodiscs   There are many instructional videodiscs on the market without any educational software to go with them. If software has been developed to go with the videodisc, it frequently does not incorporate lessons into the program. More often than not, there is a show-and-tell format or a data retrieval system with little concern for lessons that focus on higher-level critical thinking, and assessment of student responses. (Refer to Chapter 2 for lessons developed for generic videodiscs.)

When establishing criteria for evaluating interactive videodiscs, it is important to identify what type of instructional methods are being used, such as tutorial, simulation, or games. The quality of the method and how it is designed should then be determined, as well as whether the method is appropriate for the lesson objectives and the ability level of the students.

Presentation of the Subject Matter

The appropriateness of the context of the subject matter to what is to be learned is an important factor in evaluation. The subject matter in interactive video programs can be presented as a slide show, an animated movie, a game, or a software application. A *metaphor* is often used to help grasp ideas between real-world environments or objects and environments or objects in the program that share similar characteristics. For example, picture book metaphors with tabs that can be clicked to turn the pages can be used for searching for material that is in alphabetical or chronological order. An example of a book-type metaphor is the Artist Index presented in the National Gallery of Art (The Voyager Company, 1987, 1991) (see Figure 3–4). An office metaphor can be used that has file cabinets that can be opened and searched or desktops that have calculators or calenders that can be used. Format presentation is important for how easily students will be able to access material and how motivated they will be about learning.

FIGURE 3–4   Book metaphor used in National Gallery of Art: A Videodisc Companion. Courtesy of The Voyager Company.

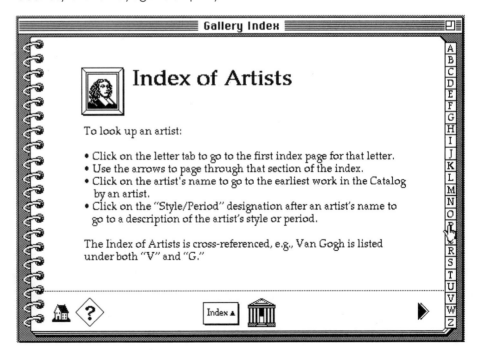

Presentation of the Visual Images

Being able to evaluate the organization and appearance of the visual imagery of interactive video programs is central to the selection of outstanding instructional multimedia. If you are using two screens, you need to take into consideration both the visuals on the video monitor and the graphics and visuals on the computer screen. The quality of the stills and animation on the monitor is not something that can be easily ignored. The monitor is large and allows for clear color stills and sharp professional animations. It is disconcerting to see fuzzy, poor-quality stills, amateur filming, or even bits of film from other sources that have not duplicated well. Companies that produce interactive video programs cannot afford to cut corners in the area of graphics or animations. Teachers need to be aware of the importance of good-quality visuals when selecting programs and expect the best for their classrooms.

Screen Design and Layout

The layout of the computer and monitor screens are an integral part of what users are going to pay attention to and what they will learn. Weak screen designs have the potential to block rather than reinforce learning. The following are some criteria that you can use to evaluate the effectiveness of the screen design and layout.

Screen Organization   Text and visuals should be presented in a visually organized format. The user should be able to locate essential information easily and to focus on primary areas. Information should be easily identifiable and comprehensible. The van Gogh Videodisc Companion (The Voyager Company, 1988, 1991) is an interactive software program that contains good screen organization. What design principles can you identify in Figure 3–5 from the van Gogh program?

Screen Clutter   Learners cannot understand material if the screen is cluttered or crowded. The computer screen is not meant to deliver large amounts of text information. It should contain only what is pertinent to motivate interest and promote learning.

Design Principles   Graphics, color, and sound enliven the instruction, add a dimension of realism, and provide cues to the learner. However, indiscriminate use of these capabilities can confuse the user and should be used only to reinforce the program content. Basic design principles can be used to evaluate screen layout and should include the following:

- Unity: The concept of unity can be created by repeating concepts such as similar shapes, color, lines, or textures, and focusing on just a few of these. Having elements touch, or overlap, or clustering similar elements together also helps give a sense of unity to a design.
- Balance: Various types of balance can be used in a visual layout. One of these is *symmetrical* balance, where elements on the left are mirrored on the right, with both sides identical. This is a very formal type of balance. Another type of balance is *asymmetrical*, where elements are not identical on each side of the design but there is a

FIGURE 3-5　　A screen design in van Gogh Videodisc Companion. Courtesy of The Voyager Company.

visual weighing of the elements. There might be a small area of red color and a texture on one side and a large amount of red and texture on the other side, but, because they are repeated on each side in a balanced way, they present a visual equilibrium. *Radial* balance is a third type of balance where the elements radiate from the center and create a dynamic formal arrangement.

- Dominance: One element of the design is selected to stand out and be different from the rest. It brings attention to that area of the screen by being larger, smaller, or different in color, texture, or shape.

- Repetition: Repetition can also create interest and movement to the overall animation or graphics of the screens. Interactive NOVA: Animal Pathfinders (Scholastic Software, 1990) incorporates good design principles throughout the program (see the Overviews Menu in Figure 3-6).

Layout and design of the visuals both on the computer screen and monitor should be consistent. If there is a sense of consistency to the design graphics, students will be given a feeling of stability and have a sense of confidence in navigating through the program. For example, Figure 3-6 of Animal Pathfinders demonstrates a bold and simple design. The geometric shapes and the text use strong contrasts of dark over light and light over dark. In Figure 3-6, the square for overviews is displayed in the upper left-hand corner, telling users where they are in the program. The Main Menu is reproduced in the lower left-hand corner, allowing the

FIGURE 3-6   An example of consistent style and layout in the Overviews Menu from Interactive Nova: Animal Pathfinders (published by Scholastic Software).

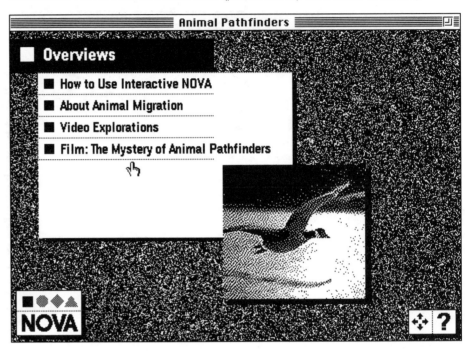

user to exit to another area if he or she wishes. In addition, the square is repeated and enlarged with a bird photograph in it, reminding the user that he or she is in the Overviews Menu. Animal Pathfinders demonstrates how you can take a simple but aesthetic design and use it to reinforce the learning content as well as help the user navigate through the program. Following are some criteria to look for when assessing visual layout and design in interactive video programs:

- Designs are simple and easy to understand.
- Color and visual quality are excellent.
- It is easy to identify priority items through size, different texture, shape, color, or contrast.
- The layout of elements in the design imply obvious relationships between the items.
- The screen design visually leads the user to the right areas.
- Visuals do not offend users, such as being nationalist, racist, or sexist.
- The potential usable life of the program, such as clothing and hairstyles that can be dated, are a consideration when selecting an interactive video program.
- Visual and audio effects support the metaphor or navigation method you have chosen.
- Special effects are effectively employed.
- Transitions between video sequences are not distracting.

- Edits are not noticeable.
- Motion sequences are of high technical quality.
- Narration is clear, well-paced, and easy to listen to.

The instructional designs of interactive video programs have to take into account which information should be presented by the computer and which by the videodisc player. This decision can be complex because it depends on what the visual presentation is: text, graphic, live action, still, or a combination of these. These are all areas that you need to be aware of because of the affect it will have on your use of the interactive video program and the affect on the learning process. Factors such as whether the visual information is to be modified frequently, how much user control over the stimulus is desirable, and what kind of color effects or realism are required are all important areas to be considered. Certain information that is continually changing, such as addresses and phone numbers, would be better presented by the computer. If both visual information on the computer screen and video monitor is to be changed and there is a need to have lifelike motion, perhaps interactive video—such as digital video-interactive (DVI)—would be an option.

Choices and considerations for selection of interactive video programs for the classroom should be based on what is known concerning both the motivation and development of learning, as well as such things as the logistics and costs. Alessi and Trollip (1991) noted that some kind of audio combinations—such as narration with pictorial information—increase learning, whereas narration with displayed text tends to impede learning and should be avoided. Stills may be appropriate for presenting content and take up less space on the videodisc. However, drawings and diagrams may simplify a concept and emphasize major features. When reviewing an interactive video program, it is important to consider whether such approaches as text or animation, or a combination of both, are the most appropriate way to present the concept to your students.

Interface Design

Evaluating the interface components of an interactive video program is an especially important procedure for teachers. Human interface is the communication system between the computer and the user. It is the way the user receives information from the computer and is able to input information back to the computer.

Interactivity

The first thought to consider when selecting an interactive video program is the fact that it involves interactive learning. The design of an interactive video program is approached differently than the design of a noninteractive medium, such as videotape. The contents on a videotape are arranged with the intent that the user is going to view it in a linear progression from start to finish. An interactive video program is organized to allow for various branching opportunities and involved decision making. *Branching* refers to how a software program changes its current path of instruction to another learning path based on the user's input. The interactive video program may offer various choices for the user to select from, depending on the user's previous responses and ability level. In fact, two users working with the same interactive video program might each take a different journey through it.

A key feature of an interactive video program is its interactive, branching capability, if coupled with highly interactive learning. Interactive video programs should not only provide opportunities for selecting options and branching but allow learners to create their own material, demonstrating imagination as well as critical thinking and problem-solving skills. If the interactive video program does not attempt to provide directions for students, be concerned with levels of student achievement, or account for different individual learning styles, then whatever interactivity exists is of limited worth in an educational setting. Passive video viewing, lecture formats, the use of multiple choice, and student-chosen paths without direction or feedback tend to be the poorest use of interactive video programs (Yoshii, Milne, & Bork, 1991).

Global and Local User Control

Global user controls include the ability to review, return to a menu or directions, and exit from a program. An interactive video program may also include global user control of the video information, providing such options as being able to pause and play or the ability to search or browse the video material in fast or slow motion. These capabilities allow the user to have control over the material that is similar to the control they have when reading a book. However, they can configure or even change material, combining visual and text presentations, for example, in ways that would not be possible with a book.

Global user controls are available anywhere in a program, whereas *local user controls* are available only at appropriate designated times. Asking for answers or hints to problems are types of local control. There are advantages of having global control over local control in that global control is always available and the screen does not have to be cluttered with options. For example, options can be combined into a single menu, thus avoiding clutter.

Appropriate Learner Control and Pacing

People using computers and interactive video programs want to feel like they are in control. It is usually desirable to allow the learner to control the pace for going through the program. Feedback from the program to the user is another essential part of users feeling in control. When the mouse is clicked, a menu selected, or a move to another part of the program is made, there needs to be a response from the computer and the videodisc monitor. People like to hear some sort of sound, see an animation, have something highlighted, and have an indication of where they are in the program. Good interactive video programs clearly indicate that the user's request is being carried out. Programs also provide easily marked buttons or controls that help the user perform necessary tasks. People like to begin immediately exploring and going through an interactive video program by themselves without doing a great deal of reading in a manual first. So, an interactive video program that allows your students to get involved quickly and provides clear directions and feedback will be highly motivating.

Designers of interactive video programs refer to three kinds of learner controls and they should be easily available in any of the programs you are reviewing.

- Pacing Control: This is the ability to control the pace of the materials that are being viewed. This feature allows students to set the speed of the lesson at a pace that matches their own particular learning style.
- Sequence Control: This is the ability to choose the sequence or order that the presented material will be viewed. However, all or parts of the sequence may be controlled by the program, depending on the learning objectives and ability of the students.
- Content Control: This feature allows students to select which module or section of the program they will study. As mentioned earlier, options provided to the learners should be on a continuum according to their ability level, motivation, and learning style.

Symbol Systems

An easily recognizable visual symbol system can help students operate interactive video programs. For example, interactive video programs may use actual compass points and symbols of the world for the user to click on to navigate through the program. They can see an icon on the screen and point to it rather than rely strictly on the keyboard to perform a command. If the symbol is well designed, students will not be required to memorize it but merely recognize what desired task it activates. GTV (National Geographic and LucasArt Entertainment, 1990), an interactive video program, uses symbols to help make navigation through the program easier (see Figure 3–7). Icons of maps or arrows can guide students through programs, and highlighting directional icons can tell them where they are in the program.

Consistent Applications

Students should not be surprised or confused by different approaches to applications. There should be a particular way for users to implement activities. Familiarity and consistency are necessary components for a strong working interface that can be relied on. It is important that navigation procedures be consistent and predictable; They need to provide a conceptual sense of stability. There should be a clear indication of where you are in the program and how to get to other areas. Both students and teachers need to feel comfortable using an interactive video program and working with applications that they can count on. Following are basic criteria for interface design guidelines:

- The visuals and operation of the program are consistent throughout.
- Applications for controlling the program (e.g., menus, button icons) clearly communicate their functionality.
- Users always know what their options are, how to communicate with the program, and when the program has accepted the user's input.

FIGURE 3-7   Clearly defined symbols in GTV: A Geographic Perspective on American History. National Geographic Society/LucasArts Entertainment Company.

ACTIVITIES

The more time you spend with some folks, the more you learn. That's (mostly) true with GTV, too. So reveal new aspects of GTV's basic personality—with these activities.

 MAPS lets you see all the maps in GTV, tosses in even more—and provides some new angles.

 GRAPHS brings a heightened visual dimension to GTV's Population Clocks.

 MUSIC opens up a data base that gives the inside info on every scrap of music from the GTV Features. Meet the composers. Read the lyrics. Learn where all the words and music are coming from.

Evaluation Process

Procedures for evaluating the interactive video program are as important as being able to identify criteria for evaluation. First, you will want to look at all the documentation that comes with the interactive video program, such as the manuals and the teacher's and user's guides. Second, you should be able to sit down with the program and run through it. You will want to do several reviews to become familiar with major concepts of the content, how it will fit into your curriculum, how it operates, and how you and your students will navigate through it.

Examining Manuals and Other Documentation

When beginning your review of the interactive video program and examining the documentation that comes with the program, you need to keep in mind how the program will fit your particular curriculum and your individual classroom. Any documents that come with the interactive video program should clearly define the content, objectives, and how the program is to be used. The hardware needed and instructions for its use should be made explicit. In addition, it is important that there are examples of on-screen visual displays and clear descriptions of the functions, such as menus, prompts, and buttons for navigating. It is also helpful if the manual provides a bibliography or reference list of related information, a comprehensive index, and possible sources to contact if there are questions regarding the interactive video program.

In addition, there should be manuals directed specifically to education and how the program may be used in the classroom. Suggested learning activities and lesson plans should be educationally sound, with instructional objectives written in terms of the learner. Lesson plans should include both scope and sequence of content with levels of difficulty appropriate to the identified learners.

Running Through the Program the First Time

When going through the program the first time, you will need to follow instructions carefully, review student activities, and estimate timing and the sequences of events that students will be going through. Ask yourself if the program matches the vocabulary and learning styles of your students. You should note whether the program is challenging and interesting. Would you want to use it again and share it with others, and would your students learn any new concepts or ways of thinking? The first run-through should accomplish the following:

- Identify any major problems in running the program and how much time it takes to work through it.
- Assess the quality of instructions and ease of navigating and branching.
- Note relevance for your curriculum, style of teaching, and age and characteristics of your students.
- Observe quality of animations, graphics, and general aesthetics of program and how well they relate to the instructional content.

Running Through the Program Again

In evaluating an interactive video program, it is necessary to go through the program enough times so you are familiar with it and can make sound judgments about its educational worth. Running through a program only once before making a decision will provide you with a limited understanding of what the program can do. The approach to take for the second or third run-through should be to examine the program through the novice's perspective. Ignore instructions and press wrong keys. Go through the program a second time by giving a variety of correct and incorrect responses, providing a check for branching and randomization. Take every opportunity to make mistakes and observe how the program handles this. Feedback should be provided to the user that an input error has been made and a reminder about what input or range of input is being requested. Perhaps clever graphics will appear for incorrect responses. You should also document your observations and assessments of the program as you go through it. Writing a short summary of the content, strengths, weaknesses, and possible extensions for future uses of the program is an excellent idea.

Using Checklists

You may want to use some form of checklist to document your evaluations. The 1986 edition of the *Standards for Evaluation of Instructional Materials with Respect to Social Content* by the California State Department of Education, for example, is used to guard against selecting technology resources containing demeaning labels or role stereotyping of the following groups:

- Male/female roles
- Ethnic and cultural groups
- Older persons and the aging process
- Disabled persons

Guidelines for Computer Software in California Schools

The 1991 Guidelines for Computer Software in California Schools, although focusing primarily on software, do provide excellent criteria for helping to evaluate interactive video programs. The Guidelines were field-tested by educators and software publishers who were invited to provide suggestions. There are five specific sections for evaluation: Instructional design, content, curricular match, interest, and technical quality, and each section lists criteria according to (1) essential, (2) desirable, and (3) exemplary. Following are highlights from the Exemplary rating for each section, starting with the instructional design category.

Instructional Design The Guidelines emphasized three areas under instructional design:

- Program Design: Problem solving, higher-order thinking, creativity, high degree of interaction, and deeper and broader understanding of concepts are emphasized. It was noted that when software is used with other technologies, there must be a significant increase in learning experience over that with use of one medium alone.
- Learner Interface: Users find the operating program intuitive and transparent. Opportunities are provided to go back to review, and open-ended natural language responses are given.
- Teacher Support: Suggestions and materials for pre- and postcomputer activities, models of instructional applications in different settings, results of classroom field-tests, and training and publisher-provided support are included.

Content Learning is promoted across disciplines. Some textual and/or audio is presented in one or more non-English languages. *Note*: It is considered essential for content to be without cultural, gender, or racial bias.

Curricular Match Instructional themes in the California curriculum frameworks are integrated and correlations to widely used textbooks are included.

Interest Students are eager to use the program repeatedly and share it with friends. They are motivated to develop problem-solving skills, are intellectually challenged, and are encouraged to be creative.

Technical Quality Publisher/distributor support is provided. Teacher help is readily available in the form of a free information hotline or 800 number for service.

A School Field-Tested Checklist

Char and Tally (1986) of the Center for Children and Technology at the Bank Street College of Education identified seven major areas for improving videodisc designs and the use of videodisc technology in the schools. Understanding what they found to be successful through field testing in actual classroom situations reinforces a set of criteria for teachers selecting their own interactive video programs.

Archival Discs with Visuals   The programs are only as good as the visuals you have to work with. Two important factors noted in their findings and worth mentioning here are the marketing of archival discs, which is a step in the right direction. But without including adequate indexing, software support, and curriculum frameworks, they tend to be unwieldy and educationally inadequate. The second factor they discussed is that while developing the majority of archival discs in the sciences, there needs to be increased development in language arts, art, social studies, and history if videodisc designers are going to expand their base among teachers.

User Control Over Video Options   This is an area that Char and Tally found to be significant for a successful rating in the classroom. The more the user controls could be maximized and with clarity and ease for the students, the higher the teachers rated it.

Importance of Audio and Text   The role of language in elucidating pictures needs to be recognized. Appropriate use of narration and text and taking into consideration the age level of the students were major criteria for the success of an interactive video program.

Indexes and Databases   Archival discs were unwieldy for teachers and students alike. The way visuals were sequenced or clustered often made using the data difficult. It appeared that raw archives, no matter how significant, did not constitute valuable educational materials for the classroom. How you are able to access the visual data, as well as the indexing, and use of a search system are all major components when rating an educational program.

Simulations, Games, and Problem-Solving Activities   There was no question that the use of game scenarios and problem contexts through the use of level 3 systems highly motivated students, focused their thinking, and encouraged problem solving. It was noted that interactive video programs should not only include more games, simulations, and problem-solving contexts, but should also allow teachers to create their own simulations and game scenarios.

Classroom Management Problems Introduced by Scarce Videodisc Resources   It was found that the most successful videodisc activities were games and simulations that were best used by small groups of children at a time. Therefore, teachers had to orchestrate disc-related and nondisc activities in order to engage all the students. It was suggested that designers and publishers include print materials of ideas for related, hands-on learning activities for students, as well as small-group activities that could be carried out without requiring continual teacher intervention. (Refer to Chapter 2 for learning activities written for selected interactive video programs.)

The Role of Teachers in the Videodisc Arena   These field tests found that teachers could contribute valuable insights rather than being simply passive consumers of existing videodiscs—which is the major premise of this chapter on teacher evaluation. The problem is that designers and publishers of interactive video programs have to be willing to listen to teachers as well as work with them. The field test findings concluded with the strong recommendation that videodisc designers must actively involve teachers in the design process.

Published checklists are invaluable in helping you establish criteria for the selection of high-quality interactive video programs. You may also want to make a compilation of these checklists as well as create your own lists unique to your students and setting. Certainly, you will want to include the title of the program, publisher, date, subject content, program objectives, and age of students it would be appropriate for. The prerequisite knowledge required by the students to use the program effectively is information that both you and your colleagues will find important when selecting interactive video programs. It is worthwhile to know if the program has been field-tested in a real classroom setting. Perhaps you or a colleague could test it first with a class before purchasing it. Most all of this type of assessment material can be incorporated in a checklist, but you should realize that using a checklist alone will not be sufficient documentation. You might want to include summaries of your impressions of the program or students' responses. In addition, you might include abstracts of program reviews that appear in computing magazines or educational journals.

Student Reviews

Although teacher evaluations of interactive video programs are essential, student evaluations are also an important component in the selection process. If possible, students need to be involved in reviewing programs and testing them out before programs are purchased. Students can indicate how easy it is to understand instructions, how help menus are provided, or how easy it is to exit the program. It is important also for students to document how they respond to both the visuals and audio components of the interactive video programs. They should be able to indicate what specific areas and techniques motivate them in the program and their particular level of interest.

Developing an Evaluation Framework

Following is a sample evaluation framework taken from major headings in this chapter. Using the headings is only one approach for the development of your own evaluation format. You can also select criteria from the checklists in this chapter or you might want to combine evaluation formats using a variety of resources suggested in the chapter. Reviewing the chapter and major criteria lists for evaluation, as well as using the headings as your guide, will help you design an evaluation checklist that fits your particular teaching style and curriculum.

	Above Average	Average	Below Average
CONTENT AND THE LEARNER			
Program Guide	___	___	___
User's Manual	___	___	___
Instructor's Manual	___	___	___
Student's Manual	___	___	___
Includes Management Controls	___	___	___
Consistent with Learner Characteristics	___	___	___
Provides for Individual Learning Styles	___	___	___
Effective Cueing Strategies	___	___	___
Structured Around a Particular			
Philosophical Model			
Linear-Goal Directed	___	___	___
Conceptual, Open Ended	___	___	___
Critical Consciousness	___	___	___
Other	___	___	___
INSTRUCTIONAL DESIGN			
Types of Instructional Methodologies			
Tutorials	___	___	___
Drill and Practice	___	___	___
Simulations	___	___	___
Educational Games	___	___	___
Databases	___	___	___
Help Systems	___	___	___
Generic Videodiscs	___	___	___
Presentation of Subject Matter	___	___	___
Presentation of Visual Images	___	___	___
Screen Design and Layout	___	___	___
Overall Screen Organization	___	___	___
Screens Not Cluttered or Crowded	___	___	___
Design Principles	___	___	___
Unity	___	___	___
Balance	___	___	___
Dominance	___	___	___
Repetition	___	___	___
INTERFACE DESIGN			
Interactivity with Direction and Feedback	___	___	___
Global Control	___	___	___
Local Control	___	___	___
Learner Control and Pacing	___	___	___
Use of Symbols for Navigating	___	___	___
Consistent Applications	___	___	___

Content and the Learner

This evaluation framework can be used as a beginning to develop your own evaluation instrument. The lists within the chapter can help you develop more in-depth criteria lists for evaluation. Go back to each major area and select criteria and checklists that fit your particular educational concerns and objectives. For example, under Effective Cueing Strategies on page 109, there is an extensive list of criteria related to cueing strategies used in well-designed interactive video programs. All or some of these criteria can be included in an evaluation instrument that you develop. Over time, you may modify and update instruments and formats to become more compatible with current educational objectives your are trying to accomplish.

Conclusion

Selecting the appropriate interactive video program for your students is an important process and one that must take into account (1) the content and learner, (2) the instructional design, (3) the interface capabilities, and (4) the review guidelines and procedures. Students enjoy using interactive video with its flexibility, real-life simulations, and having the opportunity to be active rather than passive learners. It will be the teacher's responsibility to select the highest-quality programs that are educationally sound. Interactive video programs have the capability to bring another dimension to classroom teaching that contributes to instructional effectiveness. They provide students with opportunities to explore and manipulate limited artificial realities. A constant issue in the learning process is how to relate abstract, formal knowledge to particular real-world situations. Students have difficulty linking their abstract understanding to actual applications. Being able to alter and manipulate microworlds in interactive video programs allows students to use both formal cognitive information and applied knowledge in the sciences, arts, and humanities. It will be significant for teachers to differentiate between quality programs that incorporate high-quality instructional technology with the latest innovative learning theories.

Technology in the future promises to synthesize telecommunications, computers, and interactive video to allow individuals to "walk through" museums such as the Louvre in Paris and examine the artwork in any order, at different angles, for any length of time, with or without a narrator, and with hypermedia links to related resources both historical and cultural. It would not take the place of a real trip to the Louvre, but it definitely would be better than viewing a set of slides or even a videotape. Teachers will play a major role in advancing the capabilities of these newer technologies by continuing to use and evaluate their significance for the classroom.

A Shift in Evaluation Criteria for the Future

Education continually goes through changes and new multimedia technology will continue to have profound effects on classroom teaching and student learning. Collins (1991) described some informed speculations about the impact of new technologies on the schools. Following are some of these predicted shifts in education that will affect how teachers evaluate interactive video programs for their students.

- Shift from Whole-Class to Small-Group Instruction   Teachers will evaluate interactive video programs on how well the programs can be used with small groups and what kind of support materials can be used with other groups of students who are not working with the program.

- Shift from Lecture and Recitation to Coaching   Much of the learning is taking place between the student and computer; therefore, the teacher becomes a guide, coach, and facilitator who ensures that beneficial learning takes place. In this shifting role for the teacher, it is even more significant that the teacher's evaluation skills of the interactive video programs be highly developed.

- Shift from Working with High Achievers to Working with Students Who Need More Help   This particular shift may encourage teachers to demand more quality interactive video programs that use tutorials or have greater instructional design potential.

- Shift Toward More Engaged Students   This movement toward more involved students may encourage teachers to be more selective regarding creative and problem-solving types of interactive video programs.

- Shift from Assessment Based on Test Performance to Assessment Based on Products, Progress, and Effort   Qualitative types of assessment will need to be built into the programs and designed for evaluating students as they progress through interactive video programs.

- Shift from Competitive to Cooperative Social Learning Structure   Evaluation of interactive video programs will need to include criteria that promotes cooperative learning objectives as well as individual learning objectives.

- Shift from All Students Learning the Same Things to Different Students Learning Different Things   Interactive video programs will need to address teacher as well as student management of learning assessment to allow for individualized learning styles and outcomes.

- Shift from Primacy of Verbal Thinking to the Integration of Visual and Verbal Thinking   The education of teachers will need to include assessment skills for both visual and verbal learning instruction. This is a major change that needs to be implemented throughout the educational system. Such areas as the arts and humanities will need to be given higher priority in the restructuring of teacher training and student learning objectives.

Interactive video programs will continue to have tremendous impact on education for the future. The teacher's role in assessment should be of vital importance to the design and development of interactive video programs. Teachers need to be encouraged to become full participants in this very important process and fully aware of the potential of newer technologies for the classroom. Students must have the opportunity to be involved in critical thinking, questioning, and creative problem solving, rather than merely comparing data, selecting categories, and organizing data. Teachers who are knowledgeable about and involved in assessing the strengths and weakness of interactive video programs today will be an important part of the development of well-designed, educational technology programs for the future.

Suggested Learning Extensions

1. Design your own evaluation instrument using checklists and material from this chapter. Be sure to include material from each of the major areas, such as Content and the Learner, Instructional Design, and Interface Design.

2. Create a list of procedures and support people you would include to evaluate and select interactive video programs for a school district.

3. Evaluate a particular interactive video program for the classroom using an evaluation instrument or checklist from a published journal, text, or document.

4. Interview students regarding their attitudes and knowledge related to a specific educational interactive video program they have used in their classroom. Format your report in relation to the headings used in this chapter.

5. Find and read several reviews of a particular interactive video program published in journals. Using the same interactive video program, write your own review.

6. Construct two or three student activities for a particular videodisc that describe how you would evaluate the students' work with that videodisc.

Chapter References and Additional Readings

Alessi, S. M., & Trollip, S. R. (1991). *Computer-based instruction: Methods and development.* Englewood Cliffs, NJ: Prentice Hall.

Apple Computer, Inc. (1987). *Human interface guidelines: The Apple desktop interface.* Reading, MA: Addison-Wesley.

Apple Computer, Inc. (1989). *HyperCard: Stack design guidelines.* Reading, MA: Addison-Wesley.

Burns, M. S., Goin, L., & Donlon, J. T. (1992). A computer in my room. In J. J. Hirschbuhl & L. F. Wilkinson (Eds.), *Computers in education* (pp. 78–83). Guilford, CT: Dushkin Publishing Group.

California Instructional Video Clearinghouse & California Computer Software Clearinghouse. (1991). *1991 guidelines for computer software in California schools.* Administered by the Stanislaus County Office of Education, Martin G. Petersen, County Superintendent of Schools.

California State Department of Education. (1986). *Standards for evaluation of instructional materials with respect to social content.* Education Codes 60040-60044.

Chapman, W. D., & Olson, J. S. (1992). *Comparative effects of visual augmentation on CBI achievement.* Presentation at NECC Conference, Dallas, TX.

Char, C., & Tally, W. (October 1986). *Getting the picture: Four classroom case studies of videodisc use in schools.* Technical Report No. 41. New York: Bank Street College of Education, Center for Children and Technology.

Collins, A. (September 1991). The role of computer technology in restructuring schools. *Phi Delta Kappan, 73*(1), 28–36.

Dede, C. J. (1990). Empowering environments, hypermedia and microworlds. In J. J. Hirschbuhl & R. M. Konet (Eds.), *Computers in education* (pp. 194–199). Guilford, CT: Dushkin Publishing Group.

Floyd, S. (1992). Hurricanes, computers, and classrooms. In J. J. Hirschbuhl & L. F. Wilkinson (Eds.), *Computers in education* (pp. 109–111). Guilford, CT: Dushkin Publishing Group.

Fuller, R. G., Zollman, D. A., & Campbell, T. C. (1982). *The puzzle of the Tacoma Narrows Bridge collapse* (Videodisc). New York: John Wiley and Sons.

Gayeski, D. M. (Autumn 1988). Breaking all the rules in IVD design. *Journal of Interactive Instruction Development, 1*(2), 3–5.

Geisert, G., & Dunn, R. (1992). Effective use of computers: Assignments based on individual learning style. In J. J. Hirschbuhl & L. F. Wilkinson (Eds.), *Computers in education* (pp. 70–75). Guilford, CT: Dushkin Publishing Group.

Helsel, S. K. (March–April 1987). The curricular domain of educational interactive videodisc. *Optical Information Systems,* 107–112.

Henderson R. B., & Sales, G. C. (July 1988). A guide for the review of interactive videodisc instruction. *Performance & Instruction,* 17–20.

Hoffman Educational Systems. (1991). *Laser learning.* 1863 Business Center Drive, Duarte, CA 91010.

Lathrop, A. (1992). Evaluating computer software programs. In E. Murdock & P. Desberg (Eds.), *Computers in the curriculum: Exercises for integrating technology into instruction* (pp. 367–377). Long Beach, CA: The California State University Foundation.

Martin, B. (1990). *Computers in education.* In J. J. Hirschbuhl & R. M. Konet (Eds.), Computers in education (pp. 119–123). Guilford, CT: Dushkin Publishing Group.

Megarry, J. (1992). Hypertext and compact discs: The challenge of multi-media learning. In J. J. Hirschbuhl & L. F. Wilkinson (Eds.), *Computers in education* (pp. 192–197). Guilford, CT: The Dushkin Publishing Group.

Milheim, W. D. (September/October 1988). Learner control options as an effective strategy. *Instruction Delivery Systems, 2*(5), 4–6.

National Geographic and LucasArt Entertainment. (1990). *GTV: A geographic perspective on American history* (Videodisc and software). Washington, DC 20036.

Price, R. V. (1991). *Computer-aided instruction: A guide for authors.* Pacific Grove, CA: Brooks/Cole.

Scholastic Software. (1990). *Interactive NOVA: Animal pathfinders* (Videodisc and software). 730 Broadway, New York, NY 100103.

Schwarz, I., & Lewis, M. (1992). Basic concept microcomputer courseware: A critical evaluation system for educators. In J. J. Hirschbuhl & L. F. Wilkinson (Eds.), *Computers in education* (pp. 88–94). Guilford, CT: Dushkin Publishing Group.

Semrau, P. & Boyer, B. A. (Fall 1991). Examining educational software from both an aesthetic and cultural perspective. *Journal of Hypermedia and Multimedia Studies, 2*(1), 25–29.

Semrau, P., & Lu, M. (Spring 1992). Design issues and trends in creating hypermedia. *Journal of Hypermedia and Multimedia Studies, 2*(3), 8–17.

Steinberg, E. R. (Winter 1990). The centrality of learner characteristics in computer-assisted instruction. *Journal of Computing in Higher Education, 1*(2), 49–58.

Voyager Company, The. (1987, 1991). *The National Gallery of Art: A videodisc companion.* 1351 Pacific Coast Hwy, Santa Monica, CA 90401.

Voyager Company, The. (1988, 1991). *Van Gogh revisited: A videodisc companion.* 1351 Pacific Coast Hwy, Santa Monica, CA 90401.

Videodisc Publishing, Inc. (1983). *The National Gallery of Art* (Videodisc). 381 Park Ave. South, Suite 1601, New York, NY 10016.

Videodiscovery, Inc. (1983, 1990). *Bio Sci II videodisc & Bio Sci II stacks.* 1515 Dexter Ave. N., Suite 400, Seattle, WA 90109.

White, C. S., & Hubbard, G. (1992). Tips for evaluation, documentation, and preview of software. In J. J. Hirschbuhl & L. F. Wilkinson (Eds.), *Computers in education* (pp. 84–87). Guilford, CT: Dushkin Publishing Group.

Yoshii, R., Milne, R., & Bork, A. (November 1991). *Highly interactive programs with video for learning languages.* In Proceedings of the 33rd Annual International Conference of the Association for the Development of Computer-Based Instructional Systems, St. Louis, MO.

4

Authoring Tools for Macintosh and Apple Computers

Chapter Objectives

After completing this chapter, you will be able to:

❑ *Describe what an authoring tool is.*

❑ *Identify criteria for selecting the best authoring tool.*

❑ *Explain the term* repurposing.

❑ *Name popular authoring tools for Macintosh and Apple computers.*

❑ *Use an authoring tool, such as HyperCard 2.1 and The Voyager Videodisc ToolKit 2.2 to create an interactive video program.*

❑ *Differentiate between the two layers of a card, such as Background and Card.*

❑ *Copy and paste video buttons from Videodisc ToolKit 2.2 to your HyperCard stack to control a videodisc player.*

Introduction

In this chapter, you will learn what an authoring tool is and how it is different from a programming language. Appendix C provides an extensive listing of various authoring tools. Later in the chapter, you will gain some hands-on experience using an authoring tool on the Macintosh. If you are an MS/PC-DOS user, you will want to read this chapter until reaching the section entitled A Comparison of Authoring Tools for the Macintosh and Apple Computers, which provides a general overview of authoring tools. From there, skip over to Chapter 5, which covers authoring tools specific to the MS/PC-DOS machine.

There are many ways to create an interactive video program. An interactive video program has software to control the playback of the videodisc in the videodisc player. This is level 3 interactivity (Chapter 1 explains the different levels and interactivity associated with each). Using software, the user selects specific video segments to play back. Traditionally, the software interfaces to videodiscs were written with programming languages, such as BASIC, COBOL, and Pascal. Today, programmers use modern languages like C++. To be really proficient in a programming language takes years of experience. Although many teachers would like to create their own customized software, most are not experienced programmers because they have not had the time nor perhaps the interest in learning a programming language to the extent that a computer programmer would. Fortunately for us educators, some high-level, user-friendly authoring tools are available for nonprogrammers. (*High level* means that the software is user-friendly and easy to use, as compared to learning how to program.) Using an authoring tool, such as LinkWay or ToolBook on the IBM PS/2 or HyperCard on the Macintosh, a teacher can now focus her or his energies on developing the content and objectives of the interactive video lesson rather than learning how to program. Thus, teachers can spend more time on developing instructional programs that meet the needs of their students.

Teachers can also teach their students how to use an authoring tool. Authoring tools such as HyperCard and LinkWay are easy enough that children as young as fourth-graders have been using them. In fact, some wonderful applications have been created by elementary children. One teacher, Diane Munson at Garfield Elementary School in Alhambra, California, had her children research Creepy Critters. She assigned each student a Creepy Critter to investigate in the library. Each of the alphabet letters stood for a critter, as in *I* for *Iguana*, *L* for *Leatherback Turtle*, and *P* for *Pipe Snake*. In the library, they wrote up a description of the critter and drew a picture of it on a 5" x 7" index card. When they returned to the classroom, the children took turns at the computer typing in their descriptions and drawing their critters with HyperCard.

In the end, this group of elementary school children created an entire stack on Creepy Critters, as illustrated in Figures 4–1 and 4–2. After the HyperCard stack was finished, they spent hours going through the stack and reading the descriptions and looking at each other's drawings. They marvelled at the artistic quality of certain drawings. This was a successful project because the teacher allowed the children to create their own project. As an extension to this project, the students could synchronize their cards to frames from a videodisc on lizards, frogs, and snakes, such as the Encyclopedia of Animals Volume 6—Reptiles and Amphibians. Then, when a particular critter card is up on the computer screen, a video clip showing that critter in full motion in its natural environment would be displayed on the video monitor.

FIGURE 4-1 A card from Creepy Critters—a HyperCard stack created by an elementary class using the HyperCard authoring tool on the Macintosh. This stack was made in Diane Munson's class at Garfield Elementary School in Alhambra, CA.

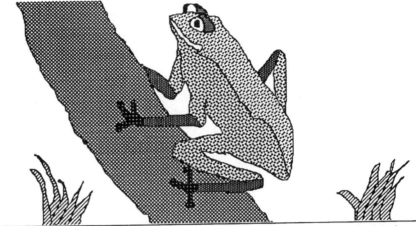

R   is for Red-eyed Tree Frog. This frog might be the most interesting of all rain forest frogs but soon they may become extinct. People are destroying the forests they live in. Poor things.

Betty Tong, age 12 and Shirley Liu, age 11 Garfield Elementary School, Alhambra, Ca

FIGURE 4-2 Another card from Creepy Critters.

O   is for Ornate Box Turtle. Box turtles have a hinged bottom shell which they can completely shut to protect their bodies. They are the prettiest of all the turtles.

Sylvia Martinez, age 12   Garfield Elementary School   Alhambra, California

Authoring Tools

An authoring tool is a specialized, easy-to-use software product that allows nonprogrammers, such as educators and children, to create customized software applications. One type of software application is to control a videodisc player. Authoring tools are multimedia presentation tools that let you assemble and present various kinds of visual, textual, and audio information in an easy and flexible way. Teachers, as well as students, can use an authoring tool, such as LinkWay, ToolBook, or HyperCard, to develop exciting multimedia presentations, combining text, pictures, sound effects, animations, digitized music, digitized voice, synthesized music, and full-motion video. With an authoring tool, software applications can be developed mostly with simple mouse clicks, by selecting commands from pull-down menus, and choosing drawing tools from a palette of tools. Selections are also made by clicking on the appropriate dialog boxes that provide several choices from which the user may select. Additionally, most authoring tools offer on-line tutorials on how to start using the authoring tool. Many users are able to start developing their own software application within a few hours of instruction.

For more sophisticated operations, authoring tools offer a built-in authoring language called a *scripting language*. The scripting language in HyperCard is called HyperTalk. HyperTalk is a specialized, English like programming code for writing scripts to enact certain actions. Scripts are performed when an action spot on the screen (called a *button*) is clicked on. When the user uses the mouse pointer to click on a button, a certain action is performed. For instance, a button could be scripted to display the next page when clicked on. Commonly, a button that displays the next card of information is referred to as a *next card* button and the one that goes backwards is a *previous card* button. In Figure 4–3, the previous and next card buttons are shown in the lower left corner. When the arrow pointer clicks one of these buttons, such as the right arrow, the next card is displayed.

The ease with which a user can write a code using the scripting language is an important consideration in selecting an authoring tool. Is it easy enough for you to use?

Advantages to Using an Authoring Tool

Why not just use the software that you purchased with the videodisc? Why would you want to create your own software interface? Many teachers are interested in creating their own customized software to meet the individual needs of their students. They feel that some of the commercial software does not address the needs of their students— some of whom are bilingual, advanced learners, and visual learners. Thus, they resort to using an authoring tool to create their own customized software application for an existing videodisc. When a teacher develops the software interface to accompany an existing videodisc, she or he is *repurposing* the videodisc. *Repurposing* means writing a specialized software application for an existing videodisc to accomplish a task other than the one for which it was originally designed. In other

FIGURE 4-3   In this picture, taken from The Voyager Videodisc ToolKit, the arrows in the bottom left-hand corner are buttons for navigating through this stack. Courtesy of The Voyager Company.

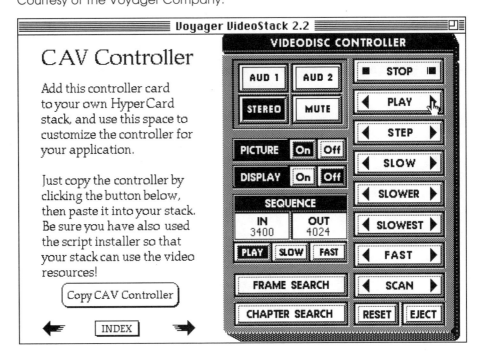

words, if you buy a science videodisc, you could repurpose it to be used for a social studies lesson or repurpose it using Spanish text.

By repurposing videodiscs, teachers can create a multitude of software applications to fit their curriculum for a whole year. Students could use their software to review for quizzes, to catch up on material missed during their absence, to enhance their knowledge by looking at other examples, and for remediation. Also, think of all the money you will save by developing your own software.

Teachers can also author their own software to meet the needs of bilingual learners. Besides presenting the text on the screens in Spanish, with voice digitizing software, concepts could be presented in the teacher's own voice in Spanish. To hear an explanation of an important concept, the students would simply click on a button and hear their favorite teacher speaking to them in Spanish!

The customized software could include quizzes to evaluate how well the students are comprehending the material. The software could also grade the students, which the teacher could then record into her or his gradebook.

Most teachers and students who learn an authoring tool such as HyperCard on the Macintosh continue to use it for many years after learning it. Whereas many teachers and students who learn a programming language for educational applications do not continue to program throughout the years. Use of an authoring tool is more of a life-long commitment to software development.

Disadvantages to Using an Authoring Tool

A big advantage to learning an authoring tool is the minimal time it requires to learn it. Within a few hours of instruction, many teachers are able to start creating their own software application. Yet, the skill needed to produce a very sophisticated operation does require time and an in-depth knowledge of scripting. So, the amount of time invested in becoming proficient at scripting may be equivalent to learning how to program in BASIC, COBOL, Pascal, or C++. On the other hand, for complex programs, it would be better to program in C++ because the programs will run faster. If speed is a significant factor, then you may want to consider learning how to program in a programming language because sophisticated programs generally run slower when they are developed with an authoring tool.

A Comparison of Authoring Tools for the Macintosh and Apple Computers

At this point, if you are an MS/PC-DOS user, you might want to skip over to Chapter 5. The following material compares the features of several authoring tools for the Macintosh and Apple IIGS computers. Following that, you will gain some hands-on experience using HyperCard 2.1 with The Voyager Videodisc ToolKit on the Macintosh. For the Macintosh, three popular authoring tools include HyperCard 2.1, Authorware Professional, and MediaText. HyperCard is described at length since it is the most popular tool for the Macintosh. In addition, several tools used on the Apple IIGS are also discussed, including HyperStudio, HyperCard for the IIGS, and Tutor-Tech. These tools are briefly described. For more information regarding these authoring tools, please contact the companies listed in Appendix C.

Following this description of authoring tools is a hands-on exercise using HyperCard 2.1 and The Voyager Videodisc ToolKit 2.2. In this hands-on exercise, you will be making a HyperCard stack with buttons to control a videodisc player.

HyperCard 2.1

HyperCard, published by Claris Corporation, is the most widely used authoring tool for the Macintosh. HyperCard requires system software 6.0.5 or higher and at least 1 MB of RAM. Typically, a finished HyperCard stack can easily fit on one 3.5" diskette. Stacks created by a teacher or student can be freely distributed throughout the class without any special licensing arrangements. Yet, if you plan on commercially distributing your stack, this does require a special license from Claris.

HyperCard is so easy to use that not only have teachers created their own software applications with HyperCard but so have their students—as young as fourth-graders. Software applications can be created in HyperCard using a variety of pull-down menus that are full of commands. The user makes selections from *pull-down menus* by simply clicking on the desired menu with the mouse. Selections can also be made from *dialog boxes* that present various choices on the screen. Dialog boxes let the user make selections regarding the characteristics or appearance of an object such as buttons. Dialog boxes let the user change the type of font, font style, and font size for the textual characters appearing on a button. Using a dialog box, the user may set the button to such characteristics as boldface lettering, Helvetica labeling, and shadowing. For example, in Figure 4–4, characteristics for a button called Initialize Player are being set by selecting them from a dialog box.

In HyperCard, the basic unit in which information is entered is called a *card*. A card is the equivalent of a screen. A grouping of cards is called a *stack*. A stack is considered to be a finished software piece.

To create an application, a HyperCard author typically would create a number of cards and link them together. Three objects can be put on a card—buttons, text fields, and graphics. When a button is clicked on, a specified action is performed, such as linking one card to the next, displaying a definition for a term, playing a digitized voice, animating a graphic, or presenting a full-motion video clip from a videodisc. Buttons are rectangular in shape and can be visible or transparent. Although a user may not actually be able to see a transparent button, it is still there and will perform its specified action when clicked on. Transparent buttons are useful for laying them on top of pictures. For example, a picture of a robin could have transparent buttons placed over its various body parts. When the user clicks on the beak, a textual description of the bird's diet would appear, along with the playing of a digitized recording of its singing.

FIGURE 4–4   In HyperCard, dialog boxes are used to select choices, such as setting the characteristics of a button, as in this picture. HyperCard software is © 1987–1993 Claris Corporation. All rights reserved. HyperCard is a registered trademark of Claris Corporation.

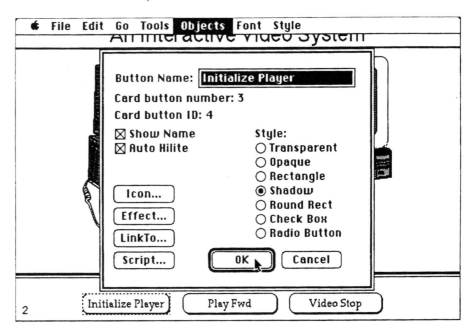

A *text field* is a rectangular shape where text is entered and displayed. It is used for titles, definitions, textual descriptions, headings, menus, and other kinds of textual information. In Figure 4–5, a text field is being created on a card in HyperCard.

Sophisticated graphics can be drawn directly on the card using drawing tools from a Tools palette and commands selected from various pull-down menus. Figure 4–6 shows a graphic created using the Tools palette shown on the left side of the card and the Patterns palette on the right side.

Graphics can also be copied and pasted to your stack. HyperCard comes with a broad collection of public domain art which can be easily copied to your cards where they can be edited to your liking. Figure 4–7 shows the directory of public domain art called Art Bits. Any graphic from the Art Bits collection can be freely copied and pasted to your own stack. For example, in Figure 4–6, the picture of the Macintosh IIci computer was copied to the card from Art Bits. The videodisc player and monitor were drawn freehand using the tools from the Tools palette.

HyperCard includes an on-line interactive tutorial called HyperCard Tour, which is excellent at demonstrating the various HyperCard features. It shows many well-designed graphics and is very instructive. This Tour introduces the basic HyperCard concepts and shows you what you can do with HyperCard. Using the Tour, most users will be creating stacks in less than a few hours. The HyperCard Help stack is an on-line help system that answers questions as you use HyperCard. HyperCard also comes with five user manuals aimed at various levels of users.

In HyperCard, every card consists of two layers—a foreground layer called the *card* and a background layer called the *background*. When

FIGURE 4–5   A text field is a rectangular area for entering and displaying text on a card. HyperCard software is © 1987–1993 Claris Corporation. All rights reserved. HyperCard is a registered trademark of Claris Corporation.

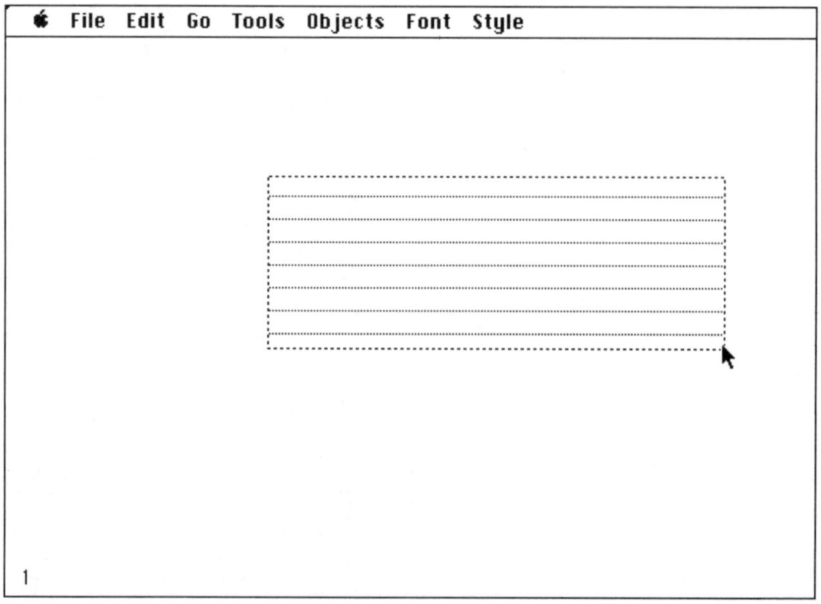

FIGURE 4-6   Using the Tools and Patterns palettes in HyperCard, sophisticated graphics can be created. HyperCard software is © 1987–1993 Claris Corporation. All rights reserved. HyperCard is a registered trademark of Claris Corporation.

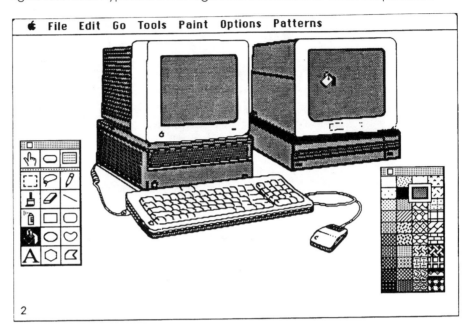

FIGURE 4-7   Graphics can be added to your HyperCard stack by copying pictures from the public domain collection of pictures available in Art Bits. HyperCard software is © 1987–1993 Claris Corporation. All rights reserved. HyperCard is a registered trademark of Claris Corporation.

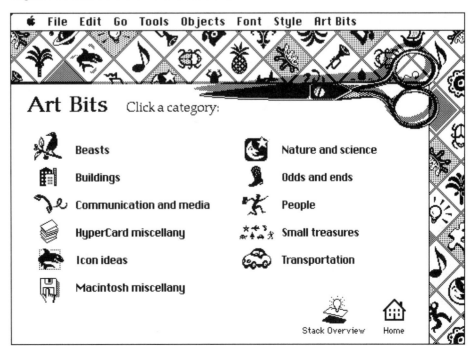

you start up HyperCard, you are immediately in the card layer. You need to intentionally select background in order to be in the background layer. Every object placed in the background will be on all the cards with that same background. For example, if a next card button is placed in the background, then this button will be accessible from every card sharing that background. However, objects placed in the card layer are only visible in that individual card. You may want to put a main menu in the card layer since the menu would appear only once in the stack. Therefore, the menu would be unique to one card and would not be seen from all other cards, as would the next card button. A stack can have many backgrounds. When it does, a group of selected cards then share the same background in that stack and another grouping of cards share a different background.

The HyperCard scripting language is called *HyperTalk*. Although an entire stack with graphics, buttons, and text can be created entirely with commands selected from pull-down menus and selections made from dialog boxes, HyperTalk scripting lets an author perform more complicated operations—for example, calling out to external programs, like an animation made with a specialized animation software product, such as Macromind Director. HyperTalk can be used to program cards, stacks, backgrounds, and buttons to perform specified actions and for external commands. Buttons are the most obvious objects to be programmed with HyperTalk. HyperTalk uses an English-like language, as evidenced in the following script written for a next card button:

```
on mouseUp
   go to the next card
end mouseUp
```

In this script, "on mouseUp" means when the mouse button is clicked on, then perform the following lines of code until an "end mouseUp" is encountered. "on mouseUp" indicates the beginning of the script and "end mouseUp" specifies the end. The second line of script "go to the next card" means just what it says. End-users, such as students, do not see the scripting. They see only the results of the scripting when they click on a button. For example, when the next card button is clicked on, the next card will be displayed. To create a previous card button, the second line of script would be replaced with "go to the previous card." As you can see, a HyperTalk script is easy to read and remember. Thus, it does not take long to learn how to write a script. However, it does take a considerable amount of scripting experience to perform complex operations.

Since HyperCard is so popular, there are many fine add-on products for multimedia work in animation, interactive video, and sound. AddMotionII is an add-on animation product for creating both path- and cell-based animations. The user simply drags the pointer across the screen to create the path for moving the graphic object. *Cell-based animation* is where the changes in moving something is done screen by screen, called *cells*. Little changes are made incrementally. In the end, all the cells are played back and an animation appears, much like flipping the pages in a flipbook. The Voyager Videodisc ToolKit 2.2, another add-on product, is an interactive videodisc product that works within HyperCard.

ToolKit lets your software control a videodisc player in playing back video segments selected by the user. ToolKit includes a variety of canned buttons that are already scripted to interface to the videodisc player. All you have to do is copy the videodisc buttons to your stack. You will be getting some experience with ToolKit later in the hands-on exercise.

Advantages

- A major strength of HyperCard is that it is so easy to use and learn. The on-line tutorial, called HyperCard Tour, is useful, as are the five user's manuals. A stack could be made entirely from commands selected from the many pull-down menus. Commands can also be programmed using the specialized HyperTalk scripting language. Selections may be made from the various dialog boxes and from using the various tools available in the Tools and Patterns palettes.

- HyperCard comes complete with many canned buttons, scanned graphics, clip art, cards, and stack templates that can be used in your own stack. Using these will make your stack look more professionally designed. Figure 4–8, shows some of the canned buttons available in HyperCard that can be copied to your stack.

- Typically, most software applications will fit on one 3.5" diskette that can be freely distributed in a class.

- The built-in Tools and Patterns palettes are easily accessible from the menubar. The Tools palette lets the author create sophisticated bit-

---

FIGURE 4–8　　In this picture, the previous card button is being selected and copied over to another stack. These are just a few of canned buttons available in HyperCard. HyperCard software is © 1987–1993 Claris Corporation. All rights reserved. HyperCard is a registered trademark of Claris Corporation.

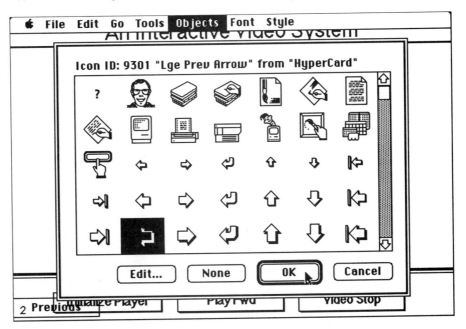

mapped graphics directly on the card. The Patterns palette offers an array of exciting patterns to use in your designs.

- HyperCard provides an excellent on-line tutorial and several stack examples, such as Graph Maker, which generates a graph of your choosing from numerical data and headings that you have entered.

- Various fonts, fontstyles, and fontsizes can be easily mixed within a field.

- Most commands listed in the pull-down menus have equivalent keyboard shortcuts. For example, instead of pulling down the File Menu and selecting Quit HyperCard, the user can simply press two keys to achieve the same effect: Command and Q. The keyboard shortcut for boldface lettering is Command and B, and to save is Command and S.

- HyperTalk uses an English-like programming code that is easy to remember and program in. HyperCard's scripting language is called HyperTalk.

- Using the Recent command, an author can quickly jump between cards or stacks without having to close the current stack. As illustrated in Figure 4-9, the Recent command displays miniature cards representing the most recent cards that the author has worked on. To jump over to another stack, the author simply clicks on a card from another stack displayed in the miniature cards. Immediately, that card from the other stack will appear on the screen.

FIGURE 4-9   Miniatures of cards that you have recently looked at are displayed on the screen by selecting the Recent command. The Recent command is used to jump back and forth among various cards within the same stack as well as in other stacks. HyperCard software is © 1987–1993 Claris Corporation. All rights reserved. HyperCard is a registered trademark of Claris Corporation.

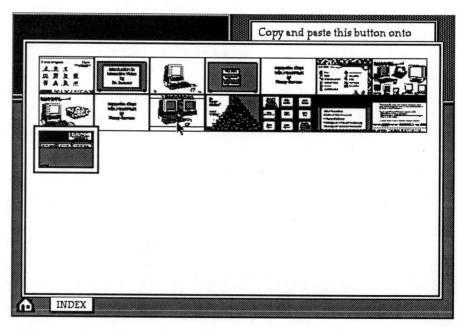

- Overall, actions performed by buttons—such as links to cards, linking to other stacks, and calls to a videodisc player—are immediate and fast.

- A stack can have several backgrounds. One group of cards can share one kind of background while another group of cards can share another.

- The size of a card in HyperCard can be changed. Cards can be as large as the full size of the screen.

- HyperCard stacks can be converted over to the MS/PC-DOS platform using an utility program called ConvertIt!. ConvertIt! translates HyperCard stacks into ToolBook books, which run under the Windows 3.0 environment. ToolBook is a popular authoring tool for the MS/PC-DOS computer, which is similar to HyperCard.

Disadvantages

- Although HyperCard is a monochrome program, external commands can be written to colorize HyperCard if you have a color monitor. In fact, a public domain tool called HyperCard Colorize can be used to add color to a black-and-white stack. A color version of HyperCard is planned to be released in the near future. By the time you read this, it will probably be available.

- When the user pulls down a menu, the mouse button has to be continuously depressed to display the pull-down menu. If the button is released, the menu will fly back up and disappear. The use of stay-down menus would have been more desirable.

- HyperCard provides only three types of text justification, as illustrated in the bottom left-hand corner of Figure 4–10. They are left, center, and right alignment. Many other authoring tools offer a fourth justification, called *justified justification*. Justified justification is commonly used in newspaper columns where both sides of the column are straight.

- Although HyperCard provides many useful buttons, card templates, graphics, clip art, and stack templates that can be incorporated into your own stack, these features are not directly available while you are working from within the current card or stack. To copy a ready-made button over to one's own stack, the HyperCard author must first switch out from her or his stack, open the HomeCard, find the desired button, copy it, switch back to her or his own stack, find the card that it will be pasted to, and then paste it. This operation involves many steps that could have been avoided with the use of a pull-down menu that would provide direct access to the buttons and some of the other public domain work.

- Although the level of user access can be changed from within a stack, this is not easily done. The level of user access is usually done by switching out of the stack. Since this can become complicated, it is best to set it from the onset when the stack is initially created from the Home stack. The user access level is set in the user Preferences' card or it can be changed by typing in a script into the message box. The first method is the easier method, which is chosen by beginner users. Typing some script into the message box is the method preferred by more advanced users who are already familiar with

FIGURE 4-10   Text characteristics can be selected in the dialog box. HyperCard software is © 1987–1993 Claris Corporation. All rights reserved. HyperCard is a registered trademark of Claris Corporation.

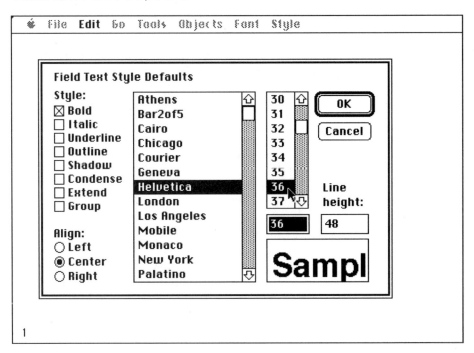

scripting. It would have made sense to have the level of user access be changed from within the stack just by selecting a command from a pull-down menu or by pressing one key.

- HyperCard does not provide an on-screen display of the user's current location within the stack. In order to find out where you are, you have to go up to the Objects Menu and select Card Info..., which will then display a dialog box full of detailed information about the card that you are currently working on. It would have been helpful to the user if HyperCard did provide a status line on the card itself that indicates the user's current location in the stack. For instance, it could say something like "card 1 or 5" to indicate that the HyperCard author is currently working on the card layer of card 1 in a stack containing 5 cards.

- Saving is done automatically by the HyperCard program itself. Thus, any changes that are made to a card are automatically saved, including mistakes. Although this auto-save capability can be viewed as a time-saving feature, it can also be viewed as an unforgiving characteristic of HyperCard because it does not let you revert back to an earlier version of the stack. It would have been more desirable to have the software author intentionally save the software application by selecting the save command from a pull-down menu.

- HyperCard automatically starts up in the card layer. To move to the background, the software author has to intentionally select this. From an instructional design perspective, it would be better to start off directly in the background. In the background, the author could establish all the features in common for the stack, such as the background pattern, placement of navigational buttons, and any other items shared by a group of cards. Then, the author would switch to the card layer where each individual card could be designed.

If you are interested in learning more about HyperCard, the following are some excellent introductory to intermediate books that you might want to purchase:

- An easy-to-read book on HyperCard version 2.1 is called *The Educator's Guide to HyperCard and HyperTalk* (1993) by George H. Culp and G. Morgan Watkins. It is published by Allyn and Bacon, 160 Gould Street, Needham Heights, MA 02194.
- Another book is entitled *HyperCard Authoring Tool* (1990) authored by Dennis Myers and Annette Lamb. It is published by Career Publishing, Inc., 910 N. Main St., Orange, CA 92667. (800) 854-4014.
- Another introductory to intermediate book is entitled *HyperCard 2 in a Hurry* (1992) authored by George Beekman. The publisher is Wadsworth Publishing Company, Belmont, CA 94002.

The Voyager Videodisc ToolKit 2.2

An add-on product to HyperCard that controls videodisc players is called The Voyager Videodisc ToolKit 2.2 by The Voyager Company in Santa Monica, California. ToolKit provides all the buttons and drivers to control a variety of common videodisc players. ToolKit is so easy to use that a nonprogrammer, such as a teacher or student, can create interactive video lessons within a short period of time. Figure 4–11 illustrates a card from ToolKit.

ToolKit is very popular primarily due to its reasonable price (compared to other products) of $99, its user-friendliness, and the fact that it runs within the HyperCard 2.1 authoring environment. ToolKit is context sensitive to the level of user, in that most users can use this authoring tool to some degree.

ToolKit runs within HyperCard; therefore, the end product is actually a HyperCard stack with some videodisc controls in it that were copied from ToolKit. Later in the hands-on exercise, when you work with ToolKit, you will be installing some videodisc buttons into your stack using ToolKit.

Using ToolKit, a novice can create a stack with some text, simple graphics using the built-in paint tools, and video buttons. Advanced users will be interested in writing their own scripts to control the videodisc player. Using HyperCard, the advanced author is also able to call up external programs created outside of HyperCard, such as animations written in C or created with AddMotionII or Macromind Director.

A version of ToolKit available for MS/PC-DOS computer is called The Voyager Videodisc ToolKit version 1.0. If you are interested in learning more about The Voyager Videodisc ToolKit, then you might want to read over the user's guide that accompanies the software.

FIGURE 4-11   This card from The Voyager Videodisc ToolKit is used to create software interfaces to a videodisc player. Courtesy of The Voyager Company.

Other Macintosh Authoring Tools

Authorware Professional

Authorware Professional by Macromedia is a high-level, powerful multimedia authoring system that is perfectly suited for creating educational applications. It is designed so that even a nonprogrammer, such as a teacher, can build a highly interactive multimedia application without scripting or programming. It is an icon-based, object-oriented authoring environment that treats graphics, buttons, and text as independent objects on the screen. When an object is changed, this change does not affect the whole program—it affects only the object being changed. As illustrated in Figure 4–12, an author creates a program by adding icons to a *flowline*. The icons can represent animations, places where the user responds, and interfaces to a videodisc player. In a sense, this flowline is an explicit flowchart that visually shows a map of the program's logic flow from top on down. Icons are selected from an icon palette and are easily added to the flowline with click-and-drag motions. An entire interactive video program can be created in this manner without scripting. You can modify the flowline at any time by rearranging the ordering of the icons, by adding more icons, or by deleting icons. You will instantly see the results of your changes. This feature helps in the instructional design process. Probably, all authoring tools should do this.

Authorware includes its own built-in audio digitizer and play-back tool, a sophisticated cell- and path-based animation tool, a variety of videodisc drivers, and a testing management component that allows you to keep track of how well students are performing.

FIGURE 4-12   Creating a program with the use of a flowline using Authorware Professional on the Macintosh. Authorware Professional screen used by permission of Macromedia.

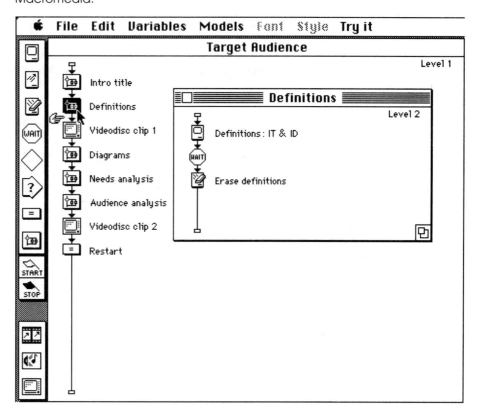

An MS/PC-DOS version is also available called Authorware Professional for Windows. For advanced, professional software developers, Authorware makes conversions between the Macintosh and IBM hardware platforms relatively straightforward.

A drawback to Authorware is its price. The educational pricing is approximately $1,000 per copy. Site licensing is available. Pricing for the corporate user of Authorware is much higher, starting at $2,500 per copy.

MediaText

MediaText is a relatively new product published by Wings for Learning, in Scotts Valley, California. MediaText is an enhanced word processor that allows text to be linked to a variety of media, including full-motion video clips from a videodisc, graphics, sound clips from a CD-ROM, and animation. MediaText is shown in Figure 4-13. Unlike so many other authoring tools, MediaText is made specifically for the development of educational applications. It is designed for creating interactive classroom lessons. Although the teacher's guide is brief, it is extremely useful.

FIGURE 4-13   This picture shows a screen taken from MediaText—an authoring tool for the Macintosh. MediaText © 1992 Constructive Instruments, Inc. Used with permission from Wings for Learning/Sunburst.

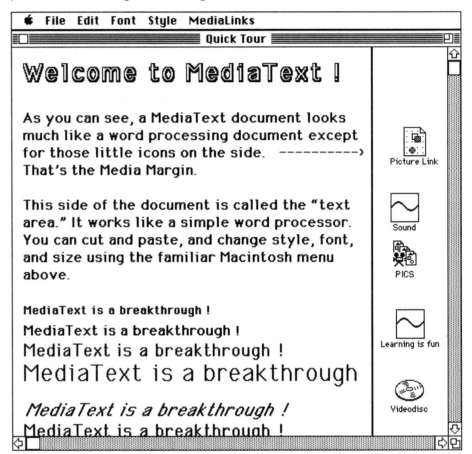

Authoring Tools for the Apple IIGS

For the Apple IIGS, there is a variety of products used in the schools, with HyperStudio by Roger Wagner Publishing being the most popular.

HyperStudio GS 3.0

HyperStudio for the Apple IIGS by Roger Wagner Publishing Inc. is reasonably priced around $129.95 and is easy to use. HyperStudio is illustrated in Figure 4-14, where the screen shows how a button is made. Authoring and scripting with HyperStudio is similar to HyperCard. Figure 4-15 illustrates how the script looks in HyperStudio. This script would make a button beep three times when it is clicked on. HyperStudio comes with an audio utility, including a no-slot sound-digitizing card, microphone, and a small amplified speaker. HyperStudio works with the Apple II Video Overlay Card. HyperStudio requires a 128K Apple IIGS with 1 MB of RAM.

FIGURE 4-14   A screen from the HyperStudio authoring tool for the Apple IIGS. This screen shows how a button named test is created. HyperStudio is published by Roger Wagner Publishing Inc.

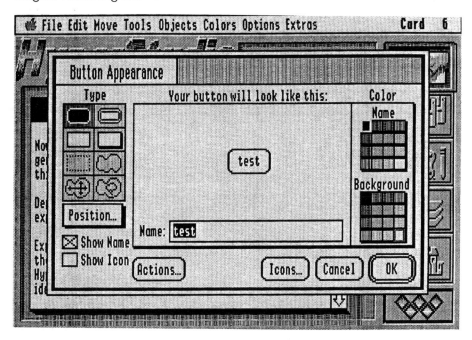

FIGURE 4-15   A script in HyperStudio. Each time the button that has this script is clicked on, three beeps will be heard. HyperStudio is published by Roger Wagner Publishing Inc.

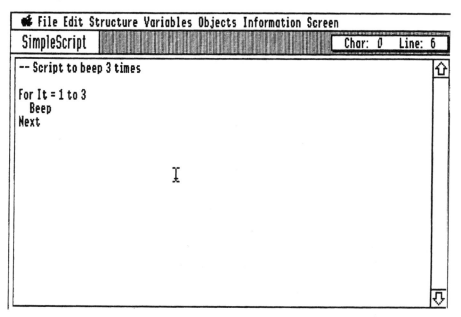

HyperCard 2.0 for the Apple IIGS

HyperCard 2.0 is available for the Apple IIGS. The only drawback to this tool is that it requires 4 MB of RAM, which is not a common memory configuration for most Apple IIGS computers whose users who are mostly teachers and students. There are many similarities between the Macintosh version of HyperCard and the one for the IIGS. In HyperCard, a screen is called a *card* and a grouping of cards is called a *stack*. An action spot on the card, which when clicked on performs a specified action, is called a *button*. Scripting in HyperCard for the Apple IIGS is different from the HyperTalk scripting language for the Macintosh. This has caused some problems for authors when they are already familiar with one version and are switching over to another platform.

Tutor-Tech

Tutor-Tech by Techware Corporation is another authoring tool used on the Apple IIGS. Tutor-Tech is shown in Figure 4–16. As its name implies, it is specifically designed for use by teachers and students. Tutor-Tech was one of the first Apple authoring tools. Using a mouse or joystick, a teacher can develop computer-based lessons, tests, courseware, multimedia presentations, and videodisc-based lessons. Tutor-Tech requires a 128K Apple IIe, IIc, or IIGS with a mouse or joystick. Tutor-Tech comes with a disk of 300 clip art pictures, a 200-page manual, and built-in videodisc drivers. The program itself is supplied on three 5.25" disks. Disk 1 contains the Teacher module for creating hypermedia stacks. The Teacher mod-

FIGURE 4-16   A page from the Tutor-Tech authoring tool for the Apple IIGS. Tutor-Tech and this stack are copyright 1993 by Techware Inc.

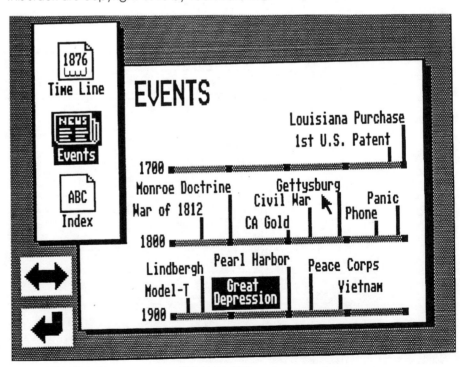

ule looks similar to a Mac screen with a menu bar across the top and a Tools palette for creating graphics. Disk 2 contains the Student module, which is for learning about Tutor-Tech. Disk 3, called the Samples disk, contains several sample hypermedia stacks and educational lessons.

In Tutor-Tech, a screen is referred to as a *page* and a grouping of pages is called a *stack*. An action spot on the page, which when clicked on performs an action, is called a *button*. Tutor-Tech comes with videodisc buttons that interface with a videodisc player. Techware provides ongoing support on Tutor-Tech and publishes a free quarterly magazine called *The Stack Exchange*, which offers tutorials, hints, tips, a list of new add-on products, and a question-and-answer column.

Hands-On Exercise: HyperCard 2.1

Publisher

Claris Corporation, 5201 Patrick Henry Drive, Box 58168, Santa Clara, CA 95052-8168

Introduction

In this exercise, you will be creating a HyperCard 2.1 stack to control a videodisc player, such as a Pioneer LD-V4200, LD-V2400, or LD-V2200. To do this, you will also need to use The Voyager Videodisc ToolKit 2.2 along with HyperCard 2.1. ToolKit runs within the HyperCard authoring environment.

Note that the following exercise is broken into many steps. Each step is a unique idea or technique.

Quitting

Since you are probably not quitting at this point, you can skip over this section—just remember that when you are ready to quit, you will need to come back to this section. If you need to quit before finishing the entire exercise, you can stop at anytime by selecting Quit HyperCard from the File Menu.

Starting Up HyperCard 2.1

Create a new HyperCard stack. To do this, start by launching HyperCard 2.1. HyperCard is launched or started up by double clicking on the HyperCard icon. The HyperCard icon looks like a stack of cards. It is in the top left corner of Figure 4–17.

Once the Home card appears, as in Figure 4–18, go to the user Preferences card, which is just before the Home card. To get there from the Home card, click on the previous arrow, which is in the bottom left-hand corner of the screen. Clicking on the previous arrow will display the previous card. (The previous arrow points to the left.) The user Preferences card looks like Figure 4–19.

In user Preferences, set the level of interactivity to 5 Scripting (if it is not already set there). You can do this by clicking once on 5 Scripting. When you do this, all five user levels should be highlighted in black, as in Figure 4–19.

FIGURE 4-17   Starting up HyperCard by double clicking on the HyperCard icon located in the top left corner of this picture. HyperCard software is © 1987–1993 Claris Corporation. All rights reserved. HyperCard is a registered trademark of Claris Corporation.

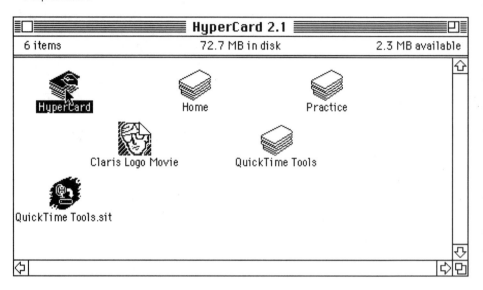

FIGURE 4-18   The Home card in HyperCard. HyperCard software is © 1987–1993 Claris Corporation. All rights reserved. HyperCard is a registered trademark of Claris Corporation.

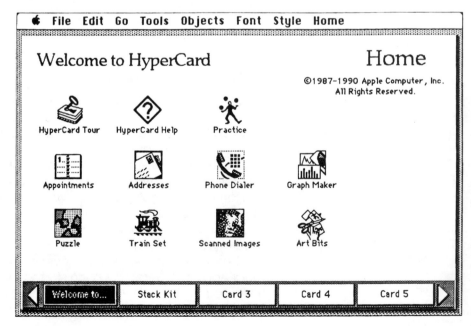

Creating a New Stack

Next, look at the menubar across the top of the screen. Move the pointer up to the File Menu. Then hold down the mouse button to see a pull-down menu. Keep holding the mouse down—do not let go. While the mouse button is being held down, drag the pointer down through the list till the pointer is on top of New Stack..., as in Figure 4–20. While your pointer is on New Stack..., it will be highlighted in black. Now, let go of the mouse button. This is how to select a command from a pull-down menu.

When the dialog box appears, type in a name for your newly created stack. Where you see an ɪbar flashing in the rectangle, type in a title or a name for your new stack. Do this from the keyboard. Type in a name like such as INTERVID, which will be short for interactive video. If you make a mistake, use the Delete key to erase the typo, then retype the change. If necessary, you may want to change directories. If so, click on the button labelled Drive or Desktop. You may need to click on it a few times if you are looking for a specific directory.

Make sure that the boxes before Copy current background and Open stack in new window are blank. In other words, you do not want to see an X in either one. If an X appears in either box, this means that this feature is selected. If an X appears in either box, you will need to "de-select" it. To de-select, place the tip of the pointer in the box and over the X. Click once and the X will disappear. When you are done, click once on New. This action will create a new stack for you. A blank white screen with the menu bar across the top will appear. You are now looking at the first card in your stack. Presently, it is blank because you

---

FIGURE 4–19   The user Preferences card. HyperCard software is © 1987–1993 Claris Corporation. All rights reserved. HyperCard is a registered trademark of Claris Corporation.

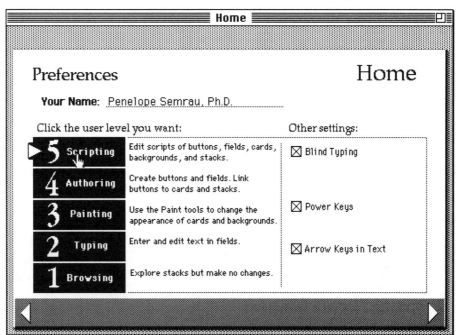

FIGURE 4-20   The pull-down File Menu. HyperCard software is © 1987–1993 Claris Corporation. All rights reserved. HyperCard is a registered trademark of Claris Corporation.

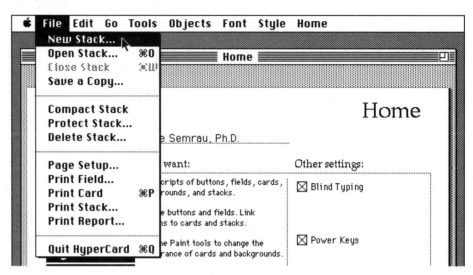

have not drawn or put anything on it yet. If your screen does not appear totally blank, then you need to go back to Starting Up HyperCard 2.1 and follow through the previous steps again.

Saving with HyperCard

As you work with HyperCard, you do not need to save your stack. The HyperCard program does this automatically for you. It saves as you work.

Making a New Card

Begin by making a simple stack of two cards (*card* means the same as *screen*). Card is the basic form of information. A collection or grouping of cards is a *stack*. The first card for your stack is already made—it is the blank white one that is in front of you.

Edit Menu   Create a second card by moving the pointer up to the Edit Menu and drag down to highlight New Card, as in Figure 4–21. The New Card command generates a second blank, white card. Each new card will be after the current card. So, if you are currently on the first card, then the new card will be put after this—it becomes the second card. At this time, both cards look identical. We will be changing that as we work.

Go Menu

Go up to the Go Menu and drag down to First, as in Figure 4–22. This action will display the first card. You will be using the Go Menu quite a bit to move around in the stack. From the Go Menu, select Next to move to the second card. Then, select First to go back to the first card in your stack. At this time, it is hard to tell the cards apart. You can also move to

FIGURE 4-21   The Edit pull-down menu of commands. HyperCard software is © 1987–1993 Claris Corporation. All rights reserved. HyperCard is a registered trademark of Claris Corporation.

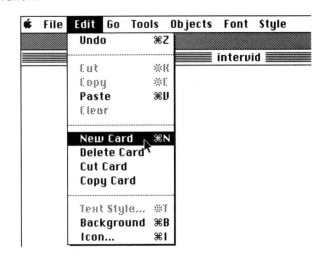

the next card by pressing the right arrow key on the keyboard. Use the left arrow key to move to the previous card.

Tools Palette

Since all the cards look the same, we will number them 1 and 2 to differentiate them. Make sure that you are on the first card. Use the Go Menu to move to the first card in your stack.

Go up to the Tools Menu and drag down to select the Paint Text tool, which is in the bottom left-hand corner of the Tools palette. It looks like

FIGURE 4-22   The pull-down Go Menu. HyperCard software is © 1987–1993 Claris Corporation. All rights reserved. HyperCard is a registered trademark of Claris Corporation.

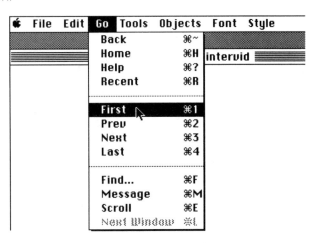

the letter *A*, as in Figure 4–23. Drag your pointer until it is on top of it. It should look selected—an outline around the *A* will appear. Then let go of the mouse button.

You will use the Paint Text tool to number the cards by typing in a number 1 on the first card. Move the pointer to the card. Notice that it looks like an I-bar. The I-bar stands for insertion of text.

Before you can start typing, you need to set the I-bar. Place the I-bar in the bottom left-hand corner and click once. This action sets the position for typing. Type in a number 1 from the keyboard. If you make a mistake while typing, use the Delete key on the right side in the top row of the keyboard or use the Eraser tool. The Eraser is the third tool down the center column of the Tools palette. It looks like a chalkboard eraser. Next, move to the second card to label it number 2.

Keyboard Shortcuts

Since the cards are now numbered you can see the differences between cards 1 and 2—even though they are blank. Go back and forth between the cards using the Go Menu commands.

Another way to go to the next card is with a keyboard shortcut. Command-3 is the keyboard shortcut for Next Card. The Command key is the first key to the left of the space bar. This key has an apple on it. The 3 key is in the top row of the keyboard. Try out Command-3 now. You'll need to keep the Command key depressed while tapping the 3 key. Each tap on 3 will display the next card. Pull down the Go Menu. You will notice to the right of each command is its keyboard equivalent.

Try the keyboard shortcut for Back, which is Command-~. ~ is the tilde key. The ~ key is either in the top left-hand side of your keyboard or it may be next to the spacebar, depending on the type of keyboard you have.

Creating a Text Field

Go to the first card. You will be putting a title on it that reads Interactive Video with ToolKit. To put text on the first card, you need to create a text field. A text field is a place where the text will be.

FIGURE 4–23   The Paint Palette and its various tools. HyperCard software is © 1987–1993 Claris Corporation. All rights reserved. HyperCard is a registered trademark of Claris Corporation.

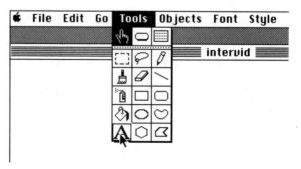

Objects Menu   Move the pointer up to the Objects Menu, as in Figure 4–24. *Note*: If the Objects Menu is not displayed in your menu bar, then you need to get the Browse tool—it looks like a hand with the index finger pointing up. It is the first tool in the left-most column in the Tools palette. Notice that the menu bar changes depending on the tool you are using. Now go up to the Objects Menu. Select New Field. A rectangular shape with ruled lines in it will automatically appear on the card. This is a text field.

Enlarging the Text Field   The current size and placement of the text field indicates where and how the text will appear on this card. You will want to change the size and placement of it since your title Interactive Video with ToolKit will be rather large and bold. To make the field larger, place the pointer in the bottom right-hand corner of the field. Then hold the mouse button down while dragging it diagonally out and down. Let go when it is about 2" high by 4" wide, as in Figure 4–25.

Moving the Text Field   To place the field in the center of the card, put the pointer directly in the center of the field. Then click and drag the field to the middle of the card. Let go when it is placed where you like it.

Text Properties   Now we will select the kind and size of text for the title. Place the pointer inside of the field and quickly double click the mouse button. A dialog box will appear. From the list of features in the right-hand column, select Transparent by clicking on it once, as in Figure 4–26. Next, click once on the button labeled Font... in the bottom left-hand corner.

You will see a collection of various fonts, as in Figure 4–27. From the assortment of fonts, click once on Helvetica to select it. In the Style column on the left, click once on Bold for boldface lettering. In the Align list at the bottom left, click on Center for center justification.

Now you will need to pick out a size for the lettering. Click once on a large size of font, such as 30. You may need to click on the up and down scroll arrows to see more sizes. Notice that the size of the sample lettering changes in the bottom right-hand corner. When you are done selecting

FIGURE 4–24   The Objects Menu. HyperCard software is © 1987–1993 Claris Corporation. All rights reserved. HyperCard is a registered trademark of Claris Corporation.

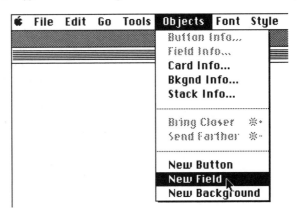

FIGURE 4-25   Creating a text field. HyperCard software is © 1987–1993 Claris Corporation. All rights reserved. HyperCard is a registered trademark of Claris Corporation.

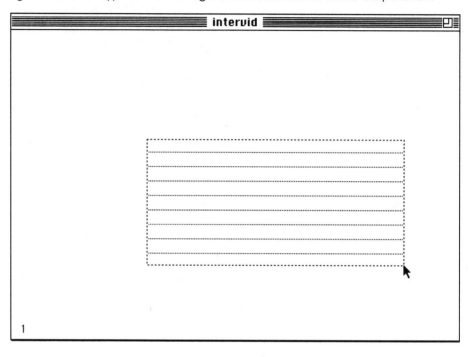

FIGURE 4-26   Setting the characteristics for a field. HyperCard software is © 1987–1993 Claris Corporation. All rights reserved. HyperCard is a registered trademark of Claris Corporation.

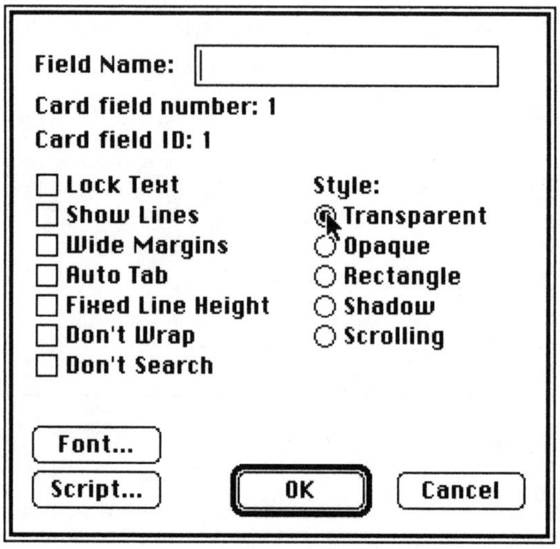

FIGURE 4-27   A dialog box showing the various text properties for a text field. HyperCard software is © 1987–1993 Claris Corporation. All rights reserved. HyperCard is a registered trademark of Claris Corporation.

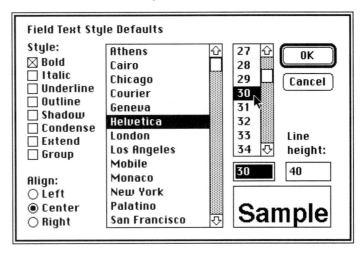

these properties, click once on the OK button, which is in the top right-hand corner.

Entering Text into a Field   Get the Browse tool from the Tools palette. You cannot enter text into a field with the arrow pointer. Next, move the Browse tool down to where the text field is suppose to be. Although you cannot see it because it is transparent, it is still there. As you move the Browse tool down, it will turn into an I-bar as soon as it reaches the field. When it turns into an I-bar, click once to set the I-bar. It should appear flashing in the center of your field.

Begin typing in the title from the keyboard. Type in Interactive Video with ToolKit, as in Figure 4-28. The computer will automatically do word-wrap as you type—*wordwrap* is when a word is too long to fit on a line, it will be pushed to the next line automatically. To push some words to the next line, place the I-bar in front of the word that you want to move and click once. Then press the Return key. Do the same with any other words.

Navigational Buttons

Let's put some buttons on each card that will allow you to move easily through the stack. A *button* is an object or hot spot on the card which, when clicked, will make something happen. A button performs a specific action when it is clicked on. You will use buttons to move back and forth among the cards instead of the Go Menu. You will be creating two buttons—a Previous Card and Next Card button.

Card Layer and Background Layer   Every card in HyperCard has two layers—a foreground layer called the *card* and a background layer called the *background*. You are going to be putting the navigational buttons in the background. Objects—such as buttons, text, and pictures—can be placed in either layer. Any item placed in the background will appear on all the cards in the stack. By putting the Next Card

FIGURE 4-28   Entering text into a text field. HyperCard software is © 1987–1993 Claris Corporation. All rights reserved. HyperCard is a registered trademark of Claris Corporation.

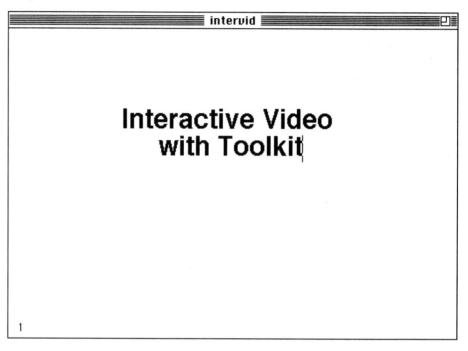

button there, it will automatically be visible on all the cards without having to copy it to the two cards in your stack. Put objects in the background that all the cards have in common. Put items in the card layer that are unique to that specific card. For example, you might want to put the title in the card layer because you probably would not want the title to appear on all the cards.

To move to the background, select Background from the Edit Menu. Notice that the menu bar looks like a marque with small ticks surrounding it. To move back to the card layer, select Background again. Try it out. Notice that the menu bar has changed. You can always tell if you are in the background by the look of the menu bar. Now move back to the background. There you will be creating a new button called Previous.

New Button   To make a new button, select New Button from the Objects Menu. Immediately, a button will appear in the center of your card.

Button Properties   Select Button Info... from the Objects Menu. A dialog box will appear. Change the name of the button from New Button to Previous. Do this by typing Previous from the keyboard (see Figure 4-29).

Make sure that Auto Hilite is selected. There should be an X in front of this item. Users like to receive feedback telling them that their click is received. If the button did not invert, then most users would probably continue clicking, since they are unaware it has been received by the computer.

FIGURE 4-29   Setting the button characteristics for the Previous Card button. HyperCard software is © 1987–1993 Claris Corporation. All rights reserved. HyperCard is a registered trademark of Claris Corporation.

```
Button Name: Previous
Bkgnd button number: 1
Bkgnd button ID: 2
⊠ Show Name              Style:
⊠ Auto Hilite            ○ Transparent
☐ Shared Hilite          ○ Opaque
                         ○ Rectangle
  [ Icon... ]            ⊙ Shadow
                         ○ Round Rect
  [ Effect... ]          ○ Check Box
  [ LinkTo... ]          ○ Radio Button
  [ Script... ]       [[  OK  ]]  [ Cancel ]
```

Make sure there is an X before Show Name. De-select Shared Hilite. For style, select Shadow, which is on the right side.

Scripting a Button   Now, let's enter in a program script for this button so that every time it is clicked on, the previous card will be displayed. A script is needed to make this action happen. Click once on Script..., which is in the bottom left corner, and the script window will appear. Everything starting from "on mouseUp" through "end mouseUp" is considered the script for the Previous button. By default, every new button is automatically given these two lines of code. You will be typing in a line between these two lines. Type in go to the previous card, as in Figure 4–30.

Then click on the Close box, which is in the upper left-hand corner. This confirms that you are done. When another dialog box pops up asking if you want to save the script changes, click on Yes.

Moving a Button   While the button is shimmering, place the pointer in the middle of it. Then click and drag it to a new location.

FIGURE 4-30   The script for the Previous Card button. HyperCard software is © 1987–1993 Claris Corporation. All rights reserved. HyperCard is a registered trademark of Claris Corporation.

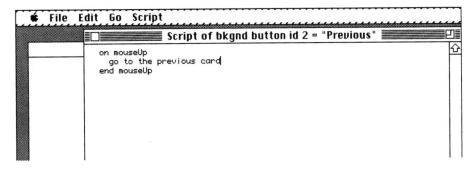

Trying Out the Button   Now let's try out this button. Switch back to the card layer by de-selecting Background from the Edit Menu. Notice that the menu bar has changed—there should not be any ticks around the menu bar. From the Tools palette, select the Browse tool. Click on Previous and watch what happens. It will quickly flash when clicked on. This is a result of selecting the Auto Hilite feature. When the button is clicked, the previous card is displayed. Notice that your button actually does appear on both cards. This is because it was placed in the background.

Next Card Button   Go to the background and make a Next Card button in the same way as the Previous Card button. To review, go back to the section of this chapter called New Button. This time, name this button Next and enter in the following line of script: Go to the next card. You could also abbreviate the script to simply Go next. Switch to the card layer and with the Browse tool, try out your new Next Card button. Your card should now look like Figure 4–31.

If you would like to take a break, this would be a good place to do it. To quit HyperCard, refer back to the beginning of this hands-on exercise. To restart HyperCard, refer to the section entitled Starting Up Your Own Stack, which is at the end of the next hands-on exercise called "The Voyager Videodisc ToolKit."

FIGURE 4–31   A finished card—Card 1. HyperCard software is © 1987–1993 Claris Corporation. All rights reserved. HyperCard is a registered trademark of Claris Corporation.

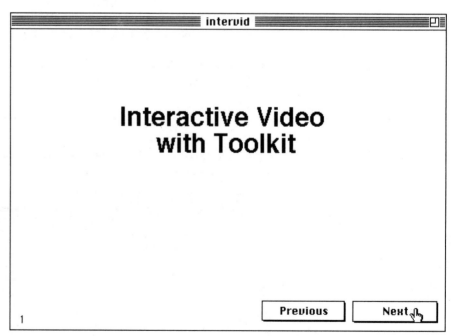

Hands-On Exercise: The Voyager Videodisc ToolKit 2.2

Publisher

The Voyager Company, 1351 Pacific Coast Highway, Santa Monica, CA 90401

Introduction

Videodisc ToolKit is another stack that you will be using in conjunction with your stack. You will be copying some buttons from ToolKit to your stack. The buttons will control the videodisc player.

Open Videodisc ToolKit

Let's switch over to Videodisc ToolKit. To do this, from the File Menu select Open Stack.... As in Figure 4–32, click on Drive or Desktop until you see the directory that ToolKit is in. ToolKit will need to have been previously installed on your hard drive. When you find it, click once on a stack by the name of Voyager VideoStack 2.2. It will appear highlighted to show that it has been selected. Then click once on Open.

Once the opening card appears, as in Figure 4–33, click once on the card. This will bring up the Main Index, as in Figure 4–34.

Turn on the power to your videodisc player. For this activity, we are using a Pioneer LD-V4200 player. Insert a CAV videodisc into the player. Turn on the video monitor.

As a new user of ToolKit, click once on Video Controllers. Select Mouse-Within Controllers, as in Figure 4–35. Simply move the mouse to control the videodisc player. Move it to the runner on the far right. You do not need to click. Watch what happens. Move it over the word *Still,*

FIGURE 4–32   Launching the Videodisc ToolKit stack. Courtesy of The Voyager Company.

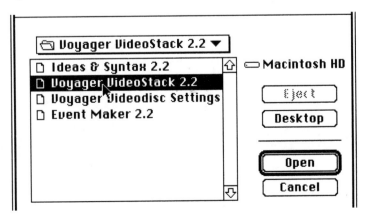

FIGURE 4-33   The opening card for Videodisc ToolKit 2.2. Courtesy of The Voyager Company.

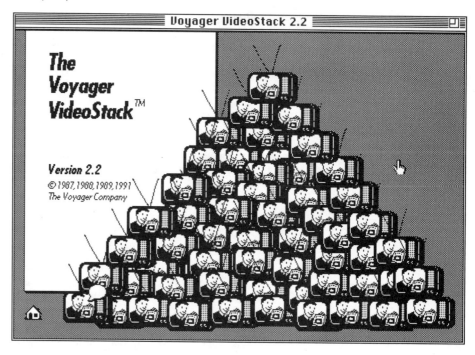

FIGURE 4-34   The Main Index from Videodisc ToolKit 2.2. Courtesy of The Voyager Company.

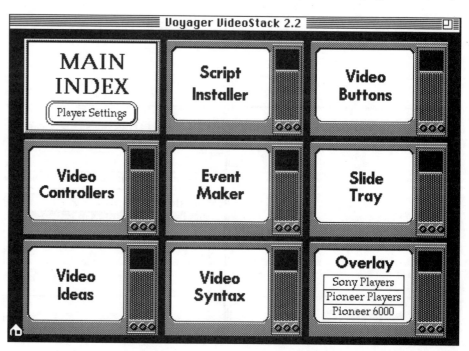

as in Figure 4–36. After you have experimented, go back to the Index by clicking on it once.

Select Video Controllers followed by CAV Controller. Click once on the right arrow next to Play. Then try out the Step button. Also try out the Display ON/OFF button, which will show the frame number on the monitor. Each side of a CAV videodisc can contain individual frames numbered from 1 to 54,000. When done, click on Index. Finally, select Video Buttons followed by Basic Video Buttons, as in Figure 4–37.

From the Basic Videodisc Buttons, try out Eject/Park Disc, as in Figure 4–38, and wait to see what happens. Then close the player tray. Next, try out Step Fwd. Try out some other buttons, too. When you are done, click on Index.

Videodisc Buttons

Using ToolKit, you will be putting three videodisc buttons into your stack. These buttons will control a videodisc player, such as a Pioneer LD-V4200, LD-V2200, or LD-V2400. These buttons will be placed in the card layer because we want them only to appear on card 2, unlike the Next and Previous buttons that appear on both cards.

Player Settings

To start, you will need to indicate the type of videodisc player you are using. From the Main Index, look in the upper left-hand box for Player Settings and click once on it. Read through the text displayed on the card, as in Figure 4–39.

FIGURE 4–35   A menu card from ToolKit. Courtesy of The Voyager Company.

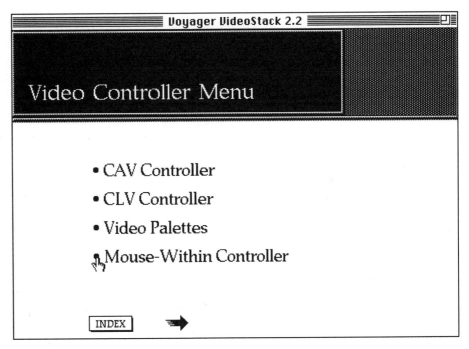

FIGURE 4–36   The Mouse-Within Videodisc Controller. Courtesy of The Voyager Company.

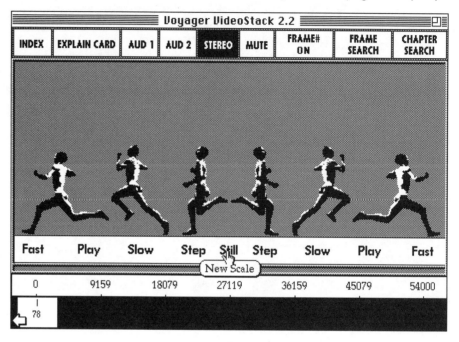

FIGURE 4–37   Selecting Basic Video Buttons from the Video Buttons Menu. Courtesy of The Voyager Company.

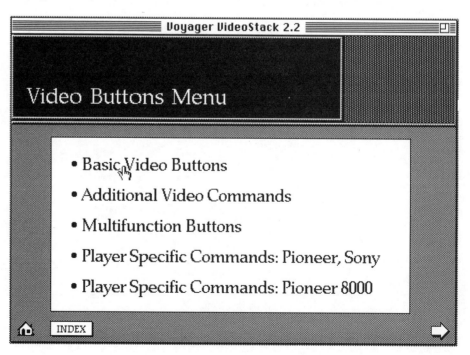

FIGURE 4-38   Basic Videodisc Buttons. Courtesy of The Voyager Company.

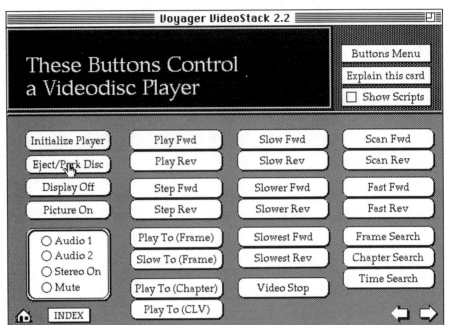

On-Line Help   Click once on the question mark in the bottom left-hand corner of the screen—the Help button. Once Help has been selected, the diamond surrounding the question mark will appear highlighted.

Selecting the Serial Port   Place your pointer over the button labeled Modem. Read through the help information. Press and hold the mouse button over the Modem button to display the two port choices—modem and printer. Highlight the serial port you are using to connect your Macintosh to the videodisc player. If you do not know which one, then select Modem, as it is the more commonly selected port.

Selecting the Videodisc Player   Slide the pointer over the button labeled PioneerPlayer. Hold down the mouse button and select the type of videodisc player you are using. In this exercise, we are selecting a PioneerPlayer. The brand and model number will be displayed on the front panel of your player.

Selecting the Baud Rate   Slide the pointer over the button labeled 4800. A common baud rate for transmitting information from your stack to the videodisc player is 4800. *Baud rate* is the speed at which the information is transmitted. A baud rate of 4800 means that 4800 bits per second are sent to the player. If you selected PioneerPlayer, then you will not need to change the baud rate. Before moving on, turn off the Help by clicking once on the question mark in the bottom left-hand corner. Now that you have designated everything, click once on the left bent arrow in the bottom left-hand corner.

FIGURE 4–39   Setting up the videodisc settings. Courtesy of The Voyager Company.

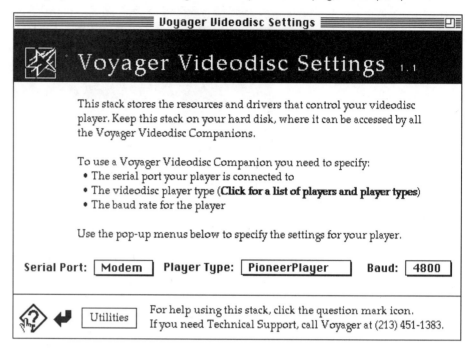

Script Installer   To make sure your stack "talks" to the videodisc player, your stack needs to have some special programming code in it. This code in HyperCard is called a _script_. HyperCard's scripts are written using the special HyperTalk scripting language. Scripting is much more simpler compared to programming in BASIC, Pascal, or C. The script you will be using in your stack utilizes the videodisc drivers that came with ToolKit. It lets your stack control the videodisc player. To place the script into your stack, click once on the box labeled Script Installer, which is at the top of the card. Next, when Figure 4–40 appears, click once on Install Video Scripts....

When prompted for your stack, search through the various directories by clicking on Drive or Desktop until you see your stack, as in Figure 4–41. If it is not highlighted, click once on it. Then click on the Open button. When the message appears, click once on Continue, which is at the bottom. Some messages will appear on the screen telling you how the installation is going. When the installation is completed, click on Cancel.

Copying Video Buttons to Your Stack

Now that your stack has the ability to "talk" to the videodisc player, let's give it something to say. Let's copy some buttons from this stack to yours. From the Main Index, click once on Video Buttons. Then click once on Basic Video Buttons.

You will be selecting and copying buttons from this collection to your stack. To copy the Play Fwd button to your stack, go up to the Tools Menu and select the Button tool, which is the top tool in the center column, to the right of the Browse tool. The pointer will not change when moved to the card—it is still a pointer. Move the pointer down to the

FIGURE 4-40   Installing a video script into your stack with ToolKit. Courtesy of The Voyager Company.

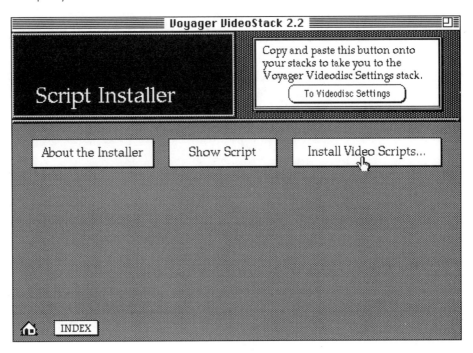

Play Fwd button and place the tip of the pointer directly in the center of the button. Click once on it to select it. The contour of the button will shimmer. Next, go up to the Edit Menu and select Copy Button. The copy will stay there until it is replaced with a copy of something else or until the computer is turned off.

Pasting Video Buttons to Your Stack   Now let's go back to your stack so that you can paste this button there. Do this by selecting Recent from the Go Menu. Then click once on a miniature representing your stack, as in Figure 4–42. This action links to your stack.

   When a dialog box appears asking you where the Voyager Video-disc Settings are, you need to search through your files and directories

FIGURE 4-41   Selecting your stack to install a script that will control a videodisc player. Courtesy of The Voyager Company.

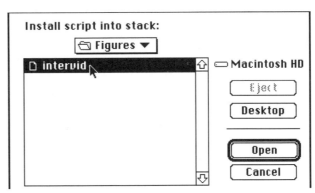

until you find the stack with this name (see Figure 4–43). Click once on it. Then click on Open. This action establishes the link between your stack and the videodisc drivers in ToolKit. Once your stack is up on the screen, go to the second card.

If the menu bar is not visible across the top of your screen, you can display it by pressing two keys: Command-spacebar. Now, go up to the Edit Menu and select Paste Button. The button will automatically appear in the center of the card. When you paste the button to your stack, the script automatically comes along. Move the button to the desired location, such as to the center of the card, as in Figure 4–44.

Let's paste another videodisc button to this card. Go back to ToolKit with the Recent command. Click on the miniature of the card contain-

FIGURE 4-42   The Recent command displays miniatures of cards that you have recently looked at. HyperCard software is © 1987–1993 Claris Corporation. All rights reserved. HyperCard is a registered trademark of Claris Corporation.

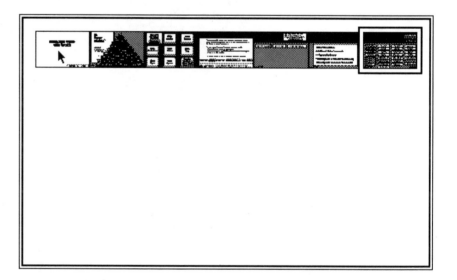

FIGURE 4-43   Finding the stack called Voyager Videodisc Settings. Courtesy of The Voyager Company.

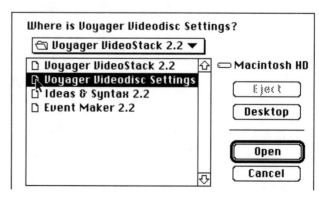

ing the Basic Video Buttons. Once the Basic Video Buttons card is up on the screen, look for the button labeled Video Stop. Go up to the Tools Menu and select the Button tool. Click once on Video Stop. Then select Copy Button from the Edit Menu. Go back to your stack using the Recent command. Once you are in your stack, go to card 2. Display the menu bar (if it is not already displayed). From the Edit Menu, select Paste Button. The button labeled Video Stop should now appear on your card. While it is shimmering, use the pointer to move it to the desired location, such as just below the Play Fwd button. Now let's try out your buttons. Get the Browse tool. Click once on Play Fwd. Then click on Video Stop.

When you are done trying out your buttons, select the Browse tool and go back to ToolKit with the Recent command. You will be selecting and copying one more button to your stack. The last button you will be copying is labeled Step Fwd. Follow the same procedure used above to copy this button to your stack. To start, you will need to select the Button tool for this. To try out your new button get the Browse tool. Your card should now look like Figure 4–45.

Now, let's quit HyperCard and restart our stack. Quitting is explained at the beginning of the hands-on HyperCard 2.1 exercise.

Starting Up Your Own Stack

Turn on the power to the videodisc player and video monitor. Insert a CAV videodisc into the player. From the various directories and files available on your Macintosh, find your stack labeled INTERVID. Place the

---

FIGURE 4-44   Pasting a videodisc button to card 2. HyperCard software is © 1987–1993 Claris Corporation. All rights reserved. HyperCard is a registered trademark of Claris Corporation.

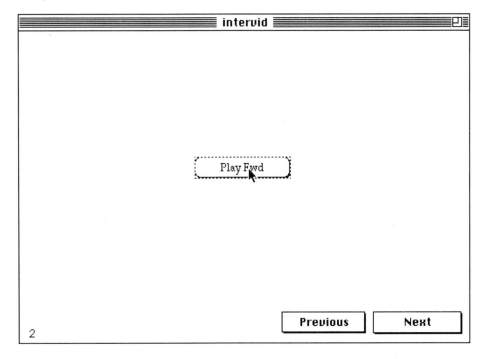

FIGURE 4–45   Card 2 with three videodisc buttons for controlling a videodisc player. HyperCard software is © 1987–1993 Claris Corporation. All rights reserved. HyperCard is a registered trademark of Claris Corporation.

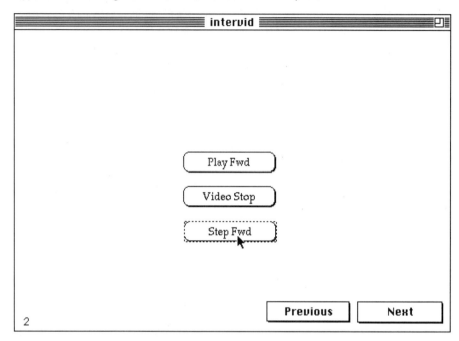

pointer directly in the center of it and double click. This will start it up. Once the first card is up on your screen, try out the Next button. While on card 2, try out Play Fwd. Then click on your other buttons. When done, select Quit HyperCard from the File Menu.

Using a 3.5" Disk

If you are keeping your INTERVID stack on a 3.5" diskette, you will need to copy another stack to it. To do this, quit out of HyperCard. Then find the stack called Voyager Videodisc Settings. Copy this stack over to your diskette. This way, you will be able to control a videodisc player directly from your own disk.

Now let's start up INTERVID from the 3.5" disk to see how it works. From your disk, launch INTERVID by double clicking on it. Turn on the videodisc player and monitor. Insert a videodisc into the player and then click on the Play Fwd button. Click on Video Stop button to stop the playing of the video. Then click on the Step Fwd button.

This completes this exercise on creating a stack for interactive video. Consult your HyperCard or The Voyager Videodisc ToolKit 2.2 User's Guides for more detailed information on creating buttons, text fields, pictures, and scripting. Have fun adding more buttons and cards to your stack. Why not try drawing some pictures on your cards with the Tools palette?

Conclusion

HyperCard is a very popular authoring tool used in education by both teachers and students. While teachers are using HyperCard to create their own customized lessons for the classroom, their students are developing multimedia presentations with it. An authoring tool should be so easy to use that programming is not required. Then, when HyperCard is combined with The Voyager Videodisc ToolKit, you will have the full potential to interface with a videodisc player. Creating your own interactive video lessons and presentations is very exciting. Interactive video merges the power of the computer with the full-motion video and dual audio tracks of a videodisc. Using ToolKit, your computer-based lessons can be interactive, dynamic, and bilingual.

In this chapter, you had the opportunity to compare and contrast various authoring tools for the Macintosh and Apple computers. You even had some hands-on experience with HyperCard 2.1 and ToolKit in creating a stack to control a videodisc player. In the following chapter, you will learn about authoring an interactive video lesson with an authoring tool on the MS/PC-DOS machine. To learn more about authoring tools, contact some of the companies listed in Appendix C and request some literature about their authoring tools. Appendix C provides an extensive listing of authoring tools available for a variety of computers, including Macintosh, Apple IIGS, MS/PC-DOS, and Amiga.

Suggested Learning Extensions
1. Create a mini-lesson for a particular subject area that consists of five or more cards and that uses a videodisc. Use an authoring tool like HyperCard with The Voyager Videodisc ToolKit.
2. Read two articles that discuss a particular authoring tool. Write a summary report of your findings.
3. Teach a student how to use an authoring tool such as HyperCard. Then let the student create a multimedia presentation using HyperCard and a videodisc. Show the class what your student has created.
4. On your own, learn how to use the Event Maker component of The Voyager Videodisc ToolKit. Then create a multimedia presentation using the Event Maker and a videodisc of your choice.

Chapter References and Additional Readings

Apple Computer, Inc. (1991). *Macintosh: Administrative and teacher productivity software guide.* 20525 Mariani Avenue, Cupertino, CA 95014. (408) 996-1010.

Barron, A., & Baumbach, D. (March 1991). Three ways to get hyper. *Multimedia & Videodisc Monitor, 9* (3), 22–24.

Beekman, G. (1992). *HyperCard 2 in a hurry.* Belmont, CA: Wadsworth.

Brader, L. L. (1990). Tools of the courseware trade. *Tech Trends, 35*(5), 10–17.

Claris Corporation. (1991). *HyperCard 2.1.* 5201 Patrick Henry Drive, Box 58168, Santa Clara, CA 95052-8168. (800) 628-2100.

Dana, A., & Mageau, T. (October 1989). Hypermedia hypermania. *Teaching and Computers, 7*(2), 16–17.

Farallon Computing, Inc. (1989). *MacRecorder.* Berkeley, CA. (415) 849-2331.

Goodman, D. (1988). *The complete HyperCard handbook.* New York: Bantam Books.

Goodman, D. (1988). *Danny Goodman's HyperCard developer's Guide.* New York: Bantam Books.

Heizer Software. (1991). *ConvertIt!* 1941 Oak Park Blvd., Suite 30, P.O. Box 232019, Pleasant Hill, CA 94523. (800) 888-7667.

Hertzberg, L. (November/December 1991). Multimedia authoring languages. *Electronic Learning, 11*(3), 30–32.

Jones, M., & Myers, D. (1988). *Hands-on HyperCard.* New York: John Wiley & Sons.

LaserDisc Corporation of America. (1989). *Encyclopedia of animals volume, reptiles and amphibians.* 200 West Grand Avenue, Montvale, NJ 07645.

Macromedia. *Authorware professional.* 600 Townsend, San Francisco, CA 94103. (800) 288-8108, (800) 288-2886, (612) 921-8555, (415) 595-3101, or (415) 252-2000. FAX: (415) 626-0554.

Macromedia. *Macromind director 3.0.* 600 Townsend St., San Francisco, CA 94103. (800) 288-0572, (415) 442-0200, or (415) 252-2000. FAX: (415) 626-0554.

Milheim, W. D., Haag, B. B., & Nichols, P. W. (November 1991). *Authoring options for developing computer-based interactive video programs.* Handouts presented at the 33rd International Conference of the Association for the Development of Computer-Based Instructional Systems.

Motion Works International, Inc. (1992). *AddMotionII.* 1020 Mainland Street, Suite #130, Vancouver, B.C. V6B 2T4. (604) 685-9975. FAX: (604) 685-6105.

Muller, D. G., Levy, L., Nelson, H., & Dean, D. (Summer 1988). The role of authoring systems in the development of interactive videodisc courseware. *Journal of Interactive Instruction Development, 1*(1), 16–24.

Munson, D. (1992). *Creepy critters.* A HyperCard stack created by Mrs. Diane Munson's class at Garfield Elementary School in Alhambra, CA.

Murray, R. B. (April 1991). Authoring for a multi-platform world on the Mac. *Medibytes, 6*(3), 3–7.

Myers, D., & Lamb, A. (1990). *HyperCard authoring tool.* Orange, CA: Career Publishing.

Paske, R. (September 1990). Hypermedia: A progress report part 2: Interactive videodisc. *T.H.E. Journal, 18*(2), 90–94.

Rode, M., & Poirot, J. (Winter 1989). Authoring systems—Are they used? *Journal of Research on Computing in Education, 22*(2), 191–198.

Roger Wagner Publishing, Inc. *HyperStudio GS 3.0.* 1050 Pioneer Way, Suite P, El Cajon, CA 92020. (619) 442-0522 or (800) 421-6526. FAX: (619) 442-0525.

Sanders, W. B. (1989). *HyperCard made easy.* Glenview, IL: Scott, Foresman.

Techware Inc. (1993). *Tutor-Tech.* P.O. Box 151085, Altamonte Springs, FL 32715. (407) 695-9000.

Voyager Company, The. (1991). *The Voyager Company videodisc Tool-Kit 2.2.* 1351 Pacific Coast Highway, Santa Monica, CA 90401. (213) 451-1383. FAX: (310) 394-2156.

Watson, J. A., Meshot, C. J., & Hagaman, W. H. (November/December 1988). Repurposing: The best chance for videodisc in education? *Instruction Delivery Systems, 2*(6), 11–14.

Watson, J. A., Nelson, C. S., & Busch, J. C. (November/December 1988). Getting hyper. *Instruction Delivery Systems, 2*(6), 8–10.

Wings for Learning. (1992). *MediaText.* 1600 Green Hills Rd., Scotts Valley, CA 95067. (800) 321-7511 or (408) 438-5502.

5

Authoring Tools for MS/PC-DOS Computers

Chapter Objectives

After completing this chapter, you will be able to:

❑ *Compare the features of two authoring tools—LinkWay and ToolBook.*

❑ *Use LinkWay or ToolBook to create your own interactive video application.*

❑ *Differentiate between the two layers of a page, such as the Background and Foreground layers in ToolBook, or the Base and Page layers in LinkWay.*

❑ *Copy videodisc buttons to your software application using LinkWay or ToolBook and The Voyager Videodisc ToolKit.*

Comparison of Two Authoring Tools: LinkWay and ToolBook

An *authoring tool* is an easy-to-use software program that allows even non-programmers the opportunity to develop their own customized software applications. Using an authoring tool, teachers as well as students can develop interactive multimedia presentations full of colors, animations, sounds, and action spots (called *buttons*). An introduction to authoring tools is provided at the beginning of Chapter 4. When an authoring tool is used to create a software application that runs with a videodisc, this activity is called *repurposing*. Repurposing is the act of modifying the purpose of an existing videodisc for another use. For example, a commercial videodisc containing a popular movie, such as "The Grapes of Wrath" could be repurposed to teach a lesson in a high school literature class. Repurposing is also explained in Chapter 1.

Two popular authoring tools used in schools today on MS/PC-DOS computers are LinkWay 2.01 and ToolBook 1.5. IBM is the publisher of LinkWay, which is marketed primarily to K–12 schools. Asymetrix is the publisher of ToolBook, which is directed at the higher educational and corporate user. An extensive listing of various authoring tools for MS/PC-DOS and other computers is provided in Appendix C. To obtain more information on authoring tools, please contact the companies listed in Appendix C for their product literature.

LinkWay Version 2.01

Publisher

IBM Corporation. P.O. Box 2150 (H05K1), Atlanta, GA 30301-2150. (800) IBM-2468. LinkWay is available from local IBM offices or through IBM resellers. IBM's toll-free hypermedia help line is (800) 627-0920.

Introduction

LinkWay operates in the MS/PC DOS 2.1 environment (or higher) and works best on IBM PS/2 computers with a minimum of 512K RAM. IBM is the publisher of LinkWay. With LinkWay, K–12 teachers can create interactive video presentations. Two of the components in LinkWay are LinkWay, the authoring tool, and LWPaint, the graphics, paint program. Although simple graphics, such as boxes and circles can be made from within the LinkWay authoring tool, LWPaint also offers such advanced graphic features as airbrush, fades, and mixed colors, which are common to paint and draw programs.

LinkWay is a page-based authoring tool in which the author creates a number of pages and links them together. An author starts by creating a *page*, which is the equivalent of one screen and is the basic unit in which information such as text, graphics, and buttons are entered. *Buttons* are objects which, when clicked on, enact an action associated with them. For example, buttons can link one page to another page, display a definition, play a sound effect, start up an animation, or show a video clip from a videodisc. Buttons can look like ovals labeled with Go to Next Page. They can also look more graphical by taking on the shape of an icon that looks like the activity it is to perform. An *icon* is a picture or symbol representing the action, such as a picture of a miniature printer would print the current page when clicked on.

Additionally, buttons can be transparent. Although the user is not able to actually see the invisible buttons, they are still there and, when clicked on, an action occurs. For example, transparent buttons can be placed over each of the 50 states in a picture of the United States. When the user clicks on California, a text field would appear listing the capital city, the total population, major industry, and so forth. In Figure 5–1, taken from the LinkWay tutorial, there are four buttons in the picture—a crab, a bird, a cow, and RETURN. When you click on RETURN another page is presented. When you click on an animal, a textual message is displayed telling you if you made the correct choice.

A *text field* is a rectangular shape where text can be entered and displayed. It can be used for entering titles, page headings, and such descriptive information as definitions, instructions, and state information (as in the above example). Text fields can be resized for less or more information and can be moved to other places on the page. In Figure 5–2, a text field is being moved to a new location on the page.

FIGURE 5–1   In this figure, taken from the LinkWay tutorial, there are four buttons—a crab, a bird, a cow, and Return. Courtesy IBM.

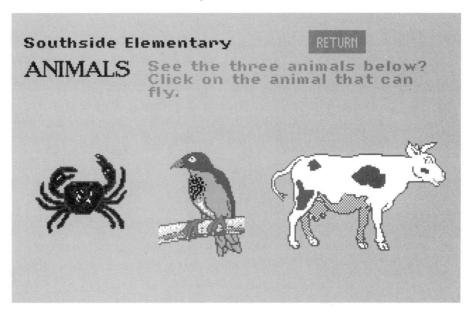

FIGURE 5–2   Moving the location of a text field in LinkWay. Courtesy IBM.

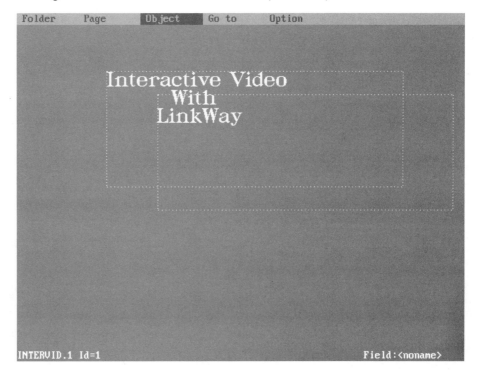

A completed LinkWay software application is a grouping of pages called a *folder*. Pages can be easily edited, added, copied, or deleted within folders.

Software applications can be created in LinkWay using a variety of pull-down menus full of commands and by making choices from pop-up dialog boxes that present various choices from which the user is to select. Figure 5–3 shows the commands available in the pull-down Draw Menu that is accessible in LWPaint—the LinkWay paint and draw tool. An entire interactive video presentation can be created using just the pull-down menus and dialog boxes and no programming. LinkWay also offers a simple type of programming language called a *scripting language*. The scripting language is used to create more complicated programs, such as transferring data back and forth with external applications. For example, real-time data can be imported from a spreadsheet program into a LinkWay folder where it is then displayed as a bar chart.

An enhanced version of LinkWay is called LinkWay Live!, which supports both analog video as well as digital video. Analog and digital information are discussed in Chapter 1. A typical source for analog video is the video coming from a videodisc. With the addition of a video overlay card like the M-motion Adapter for the MS/PC-DOS computer, the incoming analog video can be played back within a window in the computer screen using LinkWay Live!. In other words, video from a videodisc can be played back right on your IBM computer screen. *Digital video* is video that has been captured and then stored on a hard

FIGURE 5–3   The pull-down Draw Menu available in LWPaint—the LinkWay paint and draw tool. Courtesy IBM.

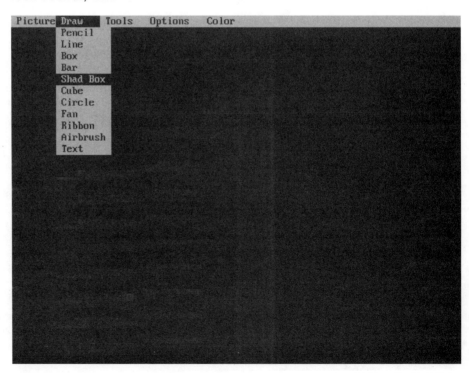

disk. LinkWay Live! is also capable of displaying digital video, such as DVI, which is discussed in Chapter 1.

Advantages

- A major strength of LinkWay is that it is easy to use. It is mostly a menu-driven and message box-driven system. Figure 5–4 shows how LinkWay displays messages to the user in the form of dialog boxes. Another user-friendly feature of LinkWay is the pull-down menus. When a pull-down menu is clicked on, it stays visible on the screen until the next mouse click.

- LinkWay runs in the DOS environment and requires only 512K of RAM. ToolBook, another popular authoring tool for MS/PC-DOS computers, requires a minimum of 4 MB of RAM because it runs in the Microsoft Windows 3.0 or higher environment. In fact, ToolBook will run much more efficiently and faster with 5 MB+ of RAM.

- LinkWay comes with a folder containing useful buttons, such as videodisc buttons that can be pasted to one's own folder. Figure 5–5 shows a page of videodisc buttons available in LinkWay. By comparison, videodisc buttons are not a standard built-in feature of Tool-Book. ToolBook requires an add-on product, such as Windows with Multimedia Extensions 1.0, The Voyager Videodisc ToolKit, or the ToolBook Multimedia Resource Kit.

FIGURE 5–4   In LinkWay, messages are displayed in boxes. In this figure, the user is asked "Start LWPaint program?" The user answers by clicking on either Yes or No. Courtesy IBM.

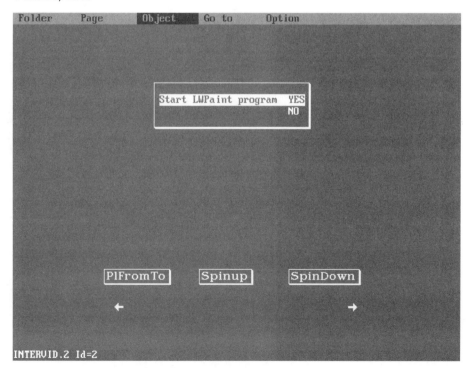

FIGURE 5–5   A page of various videodisc buttons available in LinkWay that can be used in your own folder to control a videodisc player. Courtesy IBM.

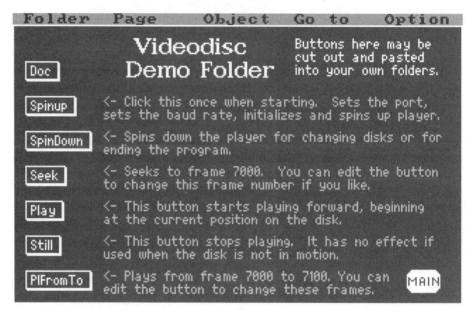

- LinkWay automatically starts up in the Base page, which is the background layer. Anything put in the Base page is common to the entire folder. For example, if the Base page is colored blue, then the background color for all the pages in the folder is blue. If the Previous Page and Next Page buttons are put in the Base page, then all pages in the folder will display these two buttons. To move to the foreground, the software author specifies this. From an instructional design perspective, starting in the Base makes sense because the software author would probably want to set up the overall design—that is, design everything that the folder has in common before moving to what is unique to the individual pages.

- LinkWay displays a *status* line in the bottom left-hand corner of the screen. The status line indicates what layer you are currently on. In Figure 5–6, a Next Page button is being created in the Base page. Because this button is being placed in the Base, it will be accessible from all the pages in the folder. The status line in the bottom left-hand corner notes that the author is currently working in the Base page. ToolBook also offers a status line called *Page Identification*.

- Saving a LinkWay folder is done intentionally by selecting Save. Thus, authoring changes are easily reversible in that nothing is permanent until it is actually saved. This is not a feature common to all authoring tools.

- A software author can quickly switch back and forth between the five levels of user access from within the authoring mode itself. In Figure 5–7, the Format Access Level is being selected in LinkWay. Although ToolBook offers only two levels of user access, switching can be easily done also.

FIGURE 5-6   In LinkWay, the status line indicating what page layer you are currently on is displayed in the lower left-hand corner of the page. In this figure, the Base page is shown. Courtesy IBM.

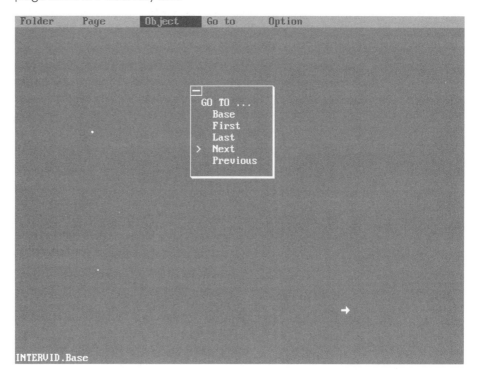

FIGURE 5-7   This figure shows a user selecting the Format Access Level, which is the most powerful and highest level of authoring in LinkWay. Courtesy IBM.

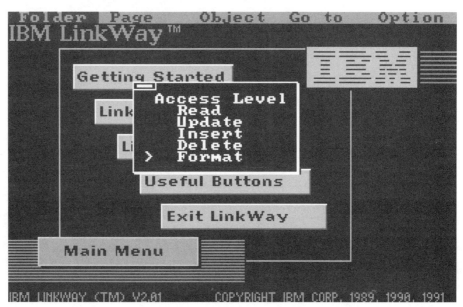

- The LinkWay graphics program called LWPaint is a very sophisticated drawing program for creating free-form shapes, lines, and even coils. Figure 5–8 shows a picture drawn free-hand with LWPaint.
- Runtime versions of finished folders can be freely distributed to other LinkWay users. On the other hand, a ToolBook author needs to purchase the ToolBook Author's Resource Kit 1.5 in order to distribute royalty-free runtime versions of ToolBook.
- LinkWay offers brilliantly colored screen displays.
- LinkWay provides an excellent on-line tutorial with a variety of example software applications.

Disadvantages
- Displaying pictures on a page is slow. LinkWay first imports the pictures and then displays them.
- LinkWay does not provide template designs for guiding the software author on how to make professional-looking pages. Guidelines on how to make professional-looking software would be helpful.
- LinkWay does not offer an on-screen Tools palette, as does ToolBook. The software author calls up the LWPaint tool from the Object Menu. This action essentially closes the LinkWay authoring mode and then opens LWPaint. Sophisticated graphics cannot be done right on the page, as would be done using the Tool palette in ToolBook. Figure 5–9 shows how the LWPaint tool is selected from the Object Menu in the LinkWay authoring mode. LinkWay does not offer a Patterns

FIGURE 5–8   A free-hand picture created using the paint and draw tools in LWPaint. Courtesy IBM.

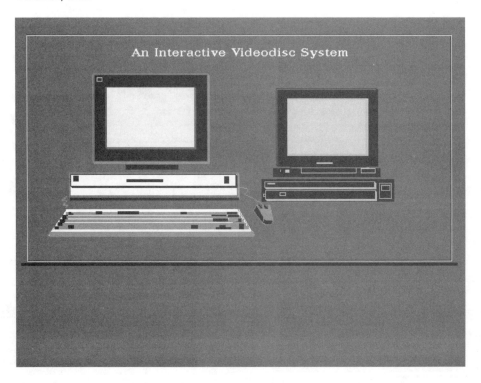

FIGURE 5-9   Starting up LWPaint from the LinkWay authoring mode. Courtesy IBM.

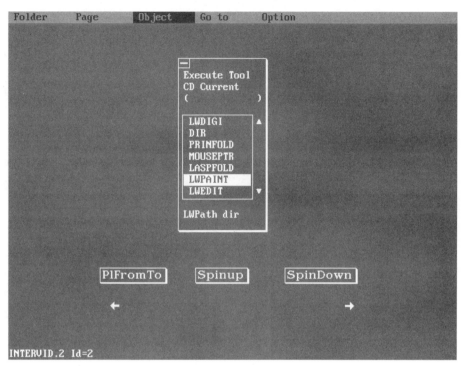

palette, as does ToolBook. Being able to draw directly on the page using drawing tools and patterns palettes would be an asset to LinkWay.

- Although you can do fades and mixing of colors with LinkWay, it is a cumbersome activity. It would be easier to select a fade from a Color palette with a mouse click, or mix a color by clicking on the two colors to be mixed from a Color tray, such as it is done in ToolBook.

- The LinkWay scripting language is very cryptic—it is not very English-like. Figure 5–10 displays some LinkWay script. It is not as simple to read as ToolBook's OpenScript. The syntax and commands in the LinkWay scripting language are harder to remember and thus make the scripting more difficult to accomplish.

- Only one Base page can be used throughout a LinkWay folder. A folder cannot have several distinct Base pages or backgrounds, as in ToolBook. Therefore, if a Base page is in blue, then blue will be the Base color throughout the entire folder. ToolBook lets you combine different backgrounds and colors within the same book, and this would be a great addition to LinkWay.

- A limitation to LinkWay is that fonts, fontsizes, and fontstyles cannot be mixed in the same text field. A *font* is the complete set of characters for one typeface, such as Helv (Helvetica). *Fontsize* is the point size describing the size of text characters. *Fontstyle* refers to text that is boldfaced, italicized, or underlined. ToolBook lets the user mix various fontstyles and fontsizes within the same field.

FIGURE 5–10   This figure shows how the LinkWay scripting language looks for a button called PlScene. Courtesy IBM.

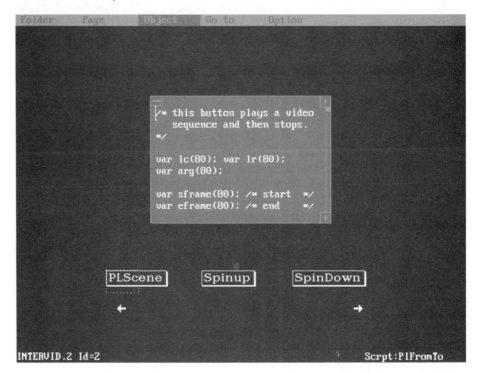

- There does not seem to be any keyboard shortcuts, such as the F1 key in ToolBook means save. LinkWay needs some keyboard short- cuts. Shortcuts save the author time by not having to constantly use the pull-down menus to activate commands.

- Use of terminology in LinkWay is inconsistent. For example, in the LinkWay Tutorial, the term *window* is used, yet in the user's manual *dialog box* refers to the same item. Also, the names of menus change, such as in LWPaint the Options Menu is a plural *Options* and in the LinkWay authoring mode it is singular as in *Option* Menu. Minor inconsistencies like these exist throughout.

- The size and orientation of a page in LinkWay cannot be changed. Pages are always the full size of the screen.

- Another disadvantage is that the LinkWay author has to exit the LinkWay authoring mode to access the Useful Buttons folder. The Useful Buttons folder contains the videodisc buttons. It would be convenient to have access to these buttons within the LinkWay authoring mode with the use of a pull-down menu. As is, a user has to quit the LinkWay authoring mode, go to Useful Buttons, cut the button, open the original folder where the button will be pasted, and then finally paste the button onto a page. This can become tedious, particularly when several buttons are being copied over to a folder.

ToolBook 1.5 for Windows

Publisher

Asymetrix Corporation. 110-110th Avenue N.E. Suite 717, Bellevue, WA 98004. (206) 637-1600 or (800) 624-8999

Introduction

Asymetrix is the publisher of ToolBook 1.5 for Windows. The Asymetrix Corporation is located in Bellevue, Washington—the same place where Bill Gates Microsoft Company is. In fact, the president of Asymetrix is a co-founder of Microsoft. This may explain why ToolBook runs within the Microsoft Windows environment. Windows is a Microsoft product. Tool-Book runs within the Windows 3.0 environment (or higher). By comparison, LinkWay 2.01 can run simply under DOS. Figure 5–11 shows the Windows environment.

Asymetrix describes ToolBook as a software construction set. Using ToolBook, you can develop your own software applications for a MS/PC-DOS machine without having to become a programmer.

Like LinkWay, a *page* is the basic unit of information in ToolBook. A grouping of pages is termed a *book*. There are three kinds objects that can be placed on a page—buttons, text fields, and graphics. Each object including graphics can be programmed with the special Tool-Book scripting language called OpenScript. ToolBook is very easy to use

FIGURE 5–11   This picture shows the Microsoft Windows 3.1 environment. Screen shot reprinted with permission from Microsoft Corporation.

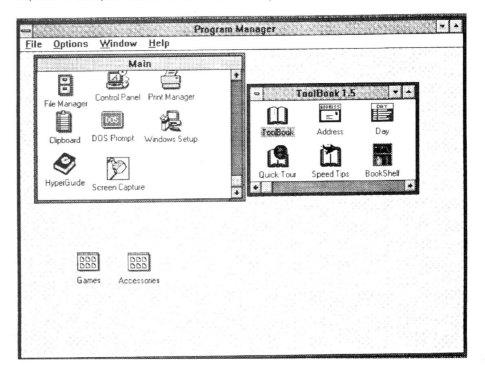

because its graphical user interface and object-oriented programming features make creating a software application almost as simple as using a paint program. Also, the pull-down menus full of commands attribute to its ease of use. To create a button, you would click on the button tool in the Tool palette, and then click and drag the pointer to place it on the page. Then the characteristics of the button are selected from those presented in a dialog box like the one displayed in Figure 5–12.

A feature of ToolBook is its similarity to the HyperCard authoring tool on the Macintosh. This similarity can help in transferring a software application created on one platform to another. If you are already familiar with HyperCard 2.1, then you will find that the Tool palette, pull-down menus, commands, and scripting in ToolBook 1.5 are similar. For example, the button script "on mouseUp" in HyperCard is written as "to handle buttonUp" in ToolBook 1.5. And the scripting command "wait" in HyperCard is called a "pause" in ToolBook. Transference of software applications between ToolBook and HyperCard has been made more efficient with the use of a utility program called ConvertIt!. ConvertIt!, published by Heizer Software in San Diego, converts finished ToolBook books to HyperCard 2.1 stacks. There is also a ConvertIt! version that does the reverse, going from HyperCard to ToolBook. Professional software developers have said that ConvertIt! is very reliable, with an 80 percent perfect conversion rate.

FIGURE 5–12   In this figure, a button called Next is being created. The characteristics for how the button will look and work are being selected from the various choices offered in the Button Properties dialog box. ToolBook 1.5 for Windows, Asymetrix Corporation. (ToolBook is a registered trademark of Asymetrix.)

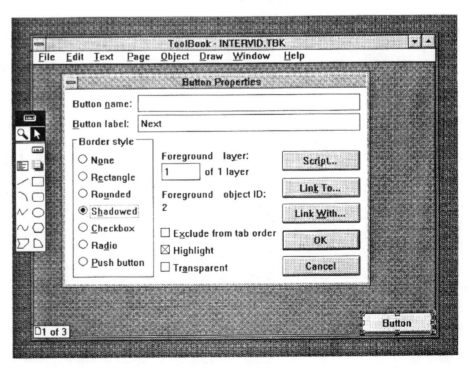

To create videodisc buttons, a specialized add-on product needs to be purchased and used in conjunction with ToolBook, whereas LinkWay itself includes many useful built-in video buttons to control a videodisc player. The Videodisc ToolKit by the Voyager Company contains over 60 buttons to perform a variety of actions and to control various videodisc players. The Asymetrix Corporation also makes available a collection of videodisc drivers and buttons. You can download these from the Asymetrix electronic bulletin board or by calling them. Additionally, Microsoft Windows 3.1 with Multimedia Extensions 1.0 provides the necessary drivers to control your videodisc player.

Advantages

- ToolBook 1.5 for Windows is easy to use and learn. ToolBook is both menu- and icon-driven, thus it is very user-friendly. The pull-down menus stay pulled down when they are selected for easy reading. Figure 5–13 shows the commands available in the Window pull-down menu and the tools available from the Tool palette located on the left side of the page.

- It is easy to change a button's properties, such as the colors and text. For changing the font style, simply select the button. Then, while it is selected, go up to the Text Menu and choose a font style, such as Bold. Immediately, the change in the button's text style appears.

- Another feature of ToolBook is *hotwords*—pieces of text which, when clicked on, tell ToolBook to access certain information. For example,

FIGURE 5–13   ToolBook offers a variety of commands in pull-down menus and tools in the Tool palette. ToolBook 1.5 for Windows, Asymetrix Corporation. (ToolBook is a registered trademark of Asymetrix.)

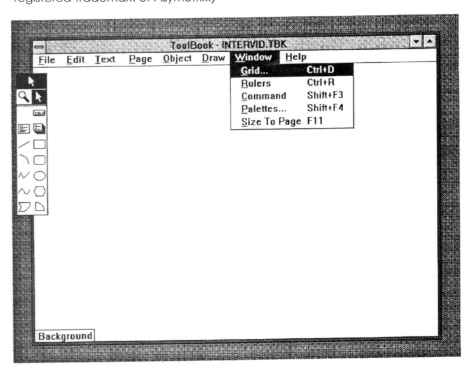

when a hotword is clicked on, a definition for that word could appear on the screen. A hotword has a script like a button. Hotwords are also known as *hypertext*. It is simple to establish a word as a hotword.

- A unique feature of ToolBook is that graphics can be scripted to perform actions. Graphics, which are objects, can be programmed just like a button to do a specified action. For example, when a graphic is clicked on, it could be scripted to move across the page as in an animation.

- Keyboard shortcuts are available, which are a time-saving feature for authors. For example, to switch between the Reader and Author levels of access, just press the F3 key. In Figure 5–14, notice the keyboard shortcuts to the right of each command. The keyboard shortcut for Next page is Ctrl+Right.

- There are two levels of user access—Author and Reader—that are accessible within the ToolBook authoring mode. To switch back and forth between the two user levels press the F3 key.

- ToolBook offers four kinds of text justification—right, left, center, and justify. Not all authoring tools offer justified justification, which is what is commonly used for newspaper columns.

- A graphics Tool palette is readily accessible from within the ToolBook authoring mode. Thus, sophisticated graphics can be drawn directly

FIGURE 5–14　An unique time-saving feature of ToolBook is keyboard shortcuts. This figure shows the keyboard shortcuts available in the Page Menu. ToolBook 1.5 for Windows, by the Asymetrix Corporation. (ToolBook is a registered trademark of Asymetrix.)

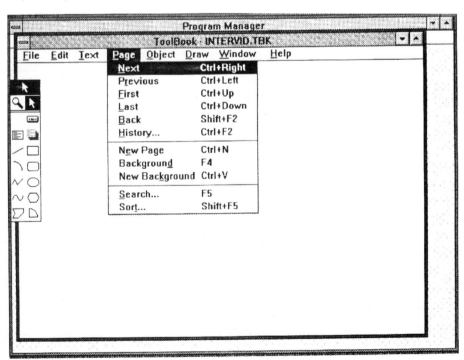

on the page. When ToolBook is launched, the Tool palette is automatically displayed to the left of the page, as in Figure 5–15. A Tool Palette is not available within the LinkWay authoring program.

- ToolBook is capable of importing pictures created with other graphic programs, such as PIC, PMX, TIF, GIF, and BMP (if done in 256 colors) pictures.

- Various fonts, fontsizes, and fontstyles can be mixed together in the same text field, unlike LinkWay.

- The scripting language, called OpenScript, uses a English-like language that is easy to use and remember. By comparison, LinkWay's scripting language is cryptic and difficult to remember.

- There are more fonts and sophisticated-looking buttons available with ToolBook than LinkWay, thus the screen designs tend to look more professionally designed. Figure 5–16 shows some of the fonts available with ToolBook. To select a font, simply click on it.

- ToolBook can display an exciting array of colors. On the other hand, finished ToolBook books will run faster when fewer colors are used, such as in the 16-color VGA mode. To select a color, simply click on a color displayed in the Color Tray, as in Figure 5–17.

- Books have to be manually saved by selecting Save from the File Menu. Thus, changes in a folder become permanent only after the author has intentionally selected the Save command. This is a feature that many authors appreciate because it gives them control over the saving process. If you make a mistake, it is not automatically

FIGURE 5–15   The Tool palette is automatically displayed to the left of the page when ToolBook is started up. ToolBook 1.5 for Windows, Asymetrix Corporation. (ToolBook is a registered trademark of Asymetrix.)

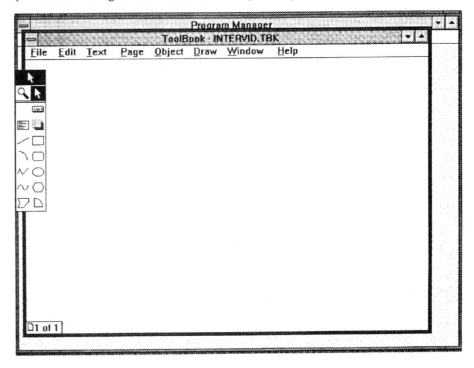

FIGURE 5–16   Selecting a font from a list of fonts available in ToolBook. ToolBook 1.5 for Windows, Asymetrix Corporation. (ToolBook is a registered trademark of Asymetrix.)

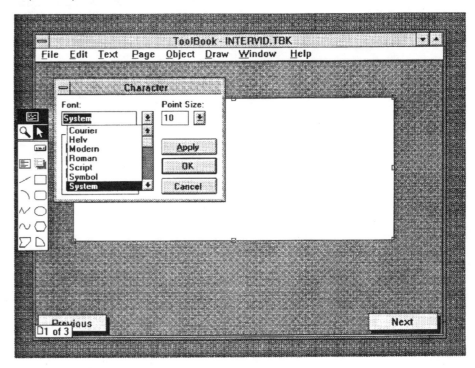

FIGURE 5–17   Colors for text, backgrounds, pictures, and buttons are selected by simply clicking on a color choice from the Color Tray. ToolBook 1.5 for Windows, Asymetrix Corporation. (ToolBook is a registered trademark of Asymetrix.)

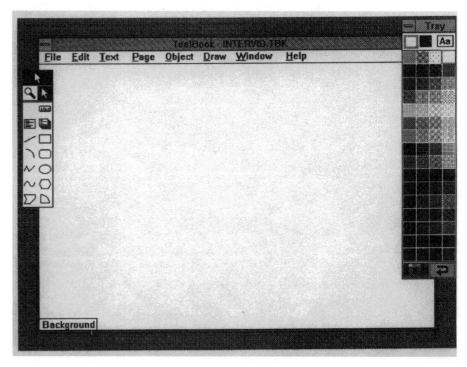

FIGURE 5-18   Books have to be manually saved with the Save or Save As commands in the
File Menu. ToolBook 1.5 for Windows, Asymetrix Corporation. (ToolBook is a
registered trademark of Asymetrix.)

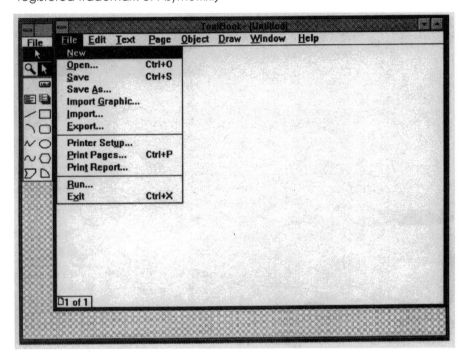

FIGURE 5-19   The page identification in the bottom left-hand corner of the page indicates
that the Background layer is currently accessed. ToolBook 1.5 for Windows,
Asymetrix Corporation. (ToolBook is a registered trademark of Asymetrix.)

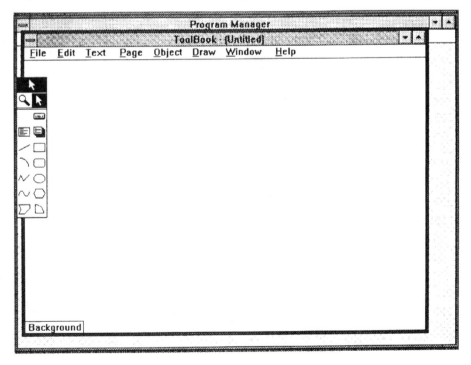

saved. Figure 5–18 displays the Save and Save As... commands available in the pull-down File Menu.

- ToolBook displays the page identification in the bottom left-hand corner of the page telling you what page you are currently on. In Figure 5–18, 1 of 1 means that page 1 in a book consisting of only one page is currently displayed on the screen. When you move to the background, the identification also states this, as in Figure 5–19. LinkWay also provides the page status.

- A folder can have several backgrounds in it, unlike LinkWay which will allow for only one Base page.

- ToolBook provides an excellent on-line tutorial with a variety of example software applications. Also, the tutorial addresses various levels of users, from novices to advanced scripters.

- The page size and orientation can be changed at any time in the Book Properties dialog box. Once selected, all of the pages in a book are the same size.

Disadvantages
- ToolBook 1.5 for Windows needs to run within the Microsoft Windows 3.0 or higher environment. The problem with this is that to run Tool-Book within Windows, a minimum of 4 MB of RAM and preferably

FIGURE 5–20   Pictures can be drawn directly on a page in ToolBook using the tools available in the Tool palette and commands in the pull-down Draw Menu. ToolBook 1.5 for Windows, Asymetrix Corporation. (ToolBook is a registered trademark of Asymetrix.)

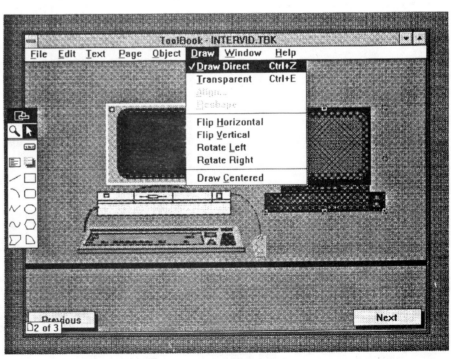

more (5 MB+) is required. All the way around, a ToolBook book runs slowly with just 4 MB of RAM. Actions from button clicks are slow in performing, animations appear jerky, and calls to a videodisc player are slow. Windows is a memory-intensive environment that directly affects the running of a ToolBook book. Creating everything within the same book rather than linking books can speed things up.

- Free-form lines, such as curly cable coils, cannot be easily done using the Tool palette. By comparison, coils can be easily done in LinkWay. Figure 5–20 shows a picture created in ToolBook using the Tool palette and Draw commands.

- In order to distribute royalty-free versions of finished books developed with ToolBook, an add-on product, called the ToolBook's Author's Resource Kit 1.5, needs to be purchased. LinkWay, by comparison, allows for free distribution of finished folders.

- Videodisc buttons are not a standard built-in feature of ToolBook. If you are creating an interactive video book, then an add-on product needs to be purchased, such as Windows 3.1 with Multimedia Extensions 1.0, The Voyager Videodisc ToolKit, or the ToolBook Multimedia Resource Kit. By comparison, LinkWay comes with all the necessary videodisc drivers and buttons. Later in this chapter, you will learn how to use ToolKit to add videodisc buttons to your book.

Other Authoring Tools for the MS/PC-DOS Computer

LinkWay Live!

Publisher

IBM Corporation, 4111 Northside Parkway, HO4L1, Atlanta, GA 30327. (800) IBM-2468

An enhanced version of LinkWay is called LinkWay Live!, which supports both analog video as well as digital video. A typical source for *analog video* is the video coming from a videodisc player. With the use of a video overlay card like the M-motion Adapter, the incoming video can be played back within a window on the computer screen. *Digital video* is video that has been captured and then stored on a hard disk. DVI, which is discussed in Chapter 1, is a form of digital video. LinkWay Live! is also compatible with all other versions of LinkWay.

InfoWindows Presentation System Version 1.0 (IWPS)

Publisher

IBM Corporation, 4111 Northside Parkway, HO4L1, Atlanta, GA 30327. (800) IBM-2468

For the higher education and business user, there is InfoWindows Presentation System Version 1.0 (IWPS). Although IBM is not supporting

IWPS anymore, IWPS was originally developed by IBM for applications involving touch screens. A *touch screen* is a visual display device which is the computer screen or is attached to it. It acts as an input device when it is touched. A touch on a word, message, or picture means the same as making a choice with a mouse or keyboard. For example, a choice can be selected from a main menu displayed on the screen simply by touching it. IWPS has built-in touch screen interfaces. Compared to LinkWay, which is also published by IBM, both AVC (which is discussed next) and IWPS are more powerful and sophisticated packages that generally are used by seasoned professional software developers. Like LinkWay, IWPS does not require anything special to run it. It will even run on a 286 MS-DOS-based machine with a minimum of 640K.

IWPS can be directly interfaced to a videodisc player. IWPS does not require any add-on products for controlling a videodisc player. Tool-Book, on the other hand, does require an add-on product, such as Videodisc ToolKit by The Voyager Company.

IWPS can import sound files. It also can perform data handling—that is, it can jump out to an external spreadsheet program to do calculations. It will then find the result of that calculation and bring the answer back into the IWPS authoring tool.

A disadvantage of IWPS is that it cannot be interfaced to a CD-ROM drive. Another limitation is that it does not include a built-in graphics program for drawing. You have to create all your pictures with a separate graphics program and then import the pictures into IWPS. IWPS is a complicated and time-consuming tool to learn.

AVC (AudioVisual Connection)

Publisher

IBM Corporation. 4111 Northside Parkway, HO4L1, Atlanta, GA 30327. (800) IBM-2468

Another authoring tool specifically developed with the higher education user in mind is AVC, meaning AudioVisual Connection. AVC is quickly replacing IWPS because IBM does not support IWPS anymore. AVC operates within the DOS 4.0 or OS/2 operating environments.

An advantage of AVC, compared to IWPS, is its user-friendliness. The user selects commands from menus and dialog boxes by simply clicking the mouse. It also provides a powerful authoring language called AVA (AudioVisual Authoring), used for importing and exporting data to external applications and programming languages and for advanced hypermedia effects. AVA commands are selected by clicking in the appropriate columns within the AVA statement table. For example, one column in the table is labeled AVA Statement, indicating the type of action that will be performed such as show picture, play music, or paste object. The second column indicates the type of visual transition to be performed such as a fade or wipe. In another column, the wait time between the various actions is specified. A videodisc player or even a VCR can be controlled using AVA commands. An IBM M-Motion Video Adapter is required for full-motion video. Full-motion video from a videodisc can be displayed in a variable-sized window, which can be synchronized to other events.

Hands-On Exercise: LinkWay Version 2.01

Start Up

Launch the LinkWay Version 2.01 for the IBM PS/2. If your computer is on a network, when the introductory LinkWay title screen appears, click once on the button labeled Program, which will start up the LinkWay authoring program. If your computer is not on a network, then wait until you see the LinkWay Main Menu. If you are prompted with a message, click once on With Default Start Options.

First-Time LinkWay Users

If you have previously used LinkWay, then skip over this section and start reading the section entitled Folder Menu. If you have never used Link-Way, then you will want to go through the LinkWay Tutorial followed by Getting Started. (Together, they take about two hours to go through.) From the Main Menu, place the pointer on top of LinkWay Tutorial, as in Figure 5–21 and click once. If nothing happens, you may need to click twice to get it going.

When you are done going through LinkWay Tutorial, select Getting Started from the Main Menu and go through that. These two modules provide an excellent discussion of the various menus and their commands.

FIGURE 5–21   The Main Menu in LinkWay. Courtesy IBM.

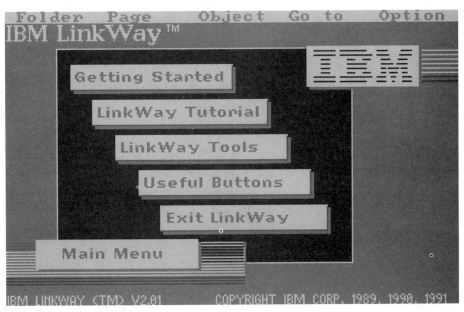

Folder Menu

From the Main Menu, move the arrow pointer up to the menu bar at the top of the screen. The Main Menu appears as in Figure 5–21. The menu bar displays the following commands across the top of the screen: Folder, Page, Object, Go To, and Option.

Place the arrow pointer on top of the command Folder, as in Figure 5–22. Click once on the mouse button. You will see a pull-down list of commands beneath Folder.

Quitting LinkWay

If at anytime you need to quit, select Exit LinkWay from the Folder Menu. To restart a folder that was previously made, follow the instructions in the section entitled Opening an Existing Folder.

Setting the Access Level

Go up to the Folder Menu and click once. From the Folder's list of commands, click once on Access Level. By doing this, you have just selected Access Level. Access Level lets you determine the level of interactivity. Refer to the on-line LinkWay Tutorial for a description of each of the Access Levels.

If you are prompted for a password, just press the Enter key. To set the Access Level to Format, which is the highest level, click once on Format, as in Figure 5–23. An arrow should appear to the left of Format, indicating that it has been selected. At the Format Level, you can create your own LinkWay folder. Then click once on the Close dot, which is the tiny rectangular dot in the top left corner of the Access

FIGURE 5–22   The Folder Menu of pull-down commands. Courtesy IBM.

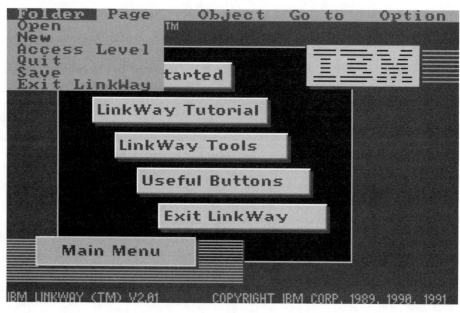

FIGURE 5-23   Setting the Access Level to Format. Courtesy IBM.

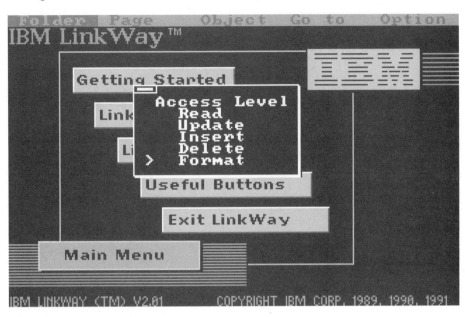

FIGURE 5-24   Creating a new folder with the name INTERVID. Courtesy IBM.

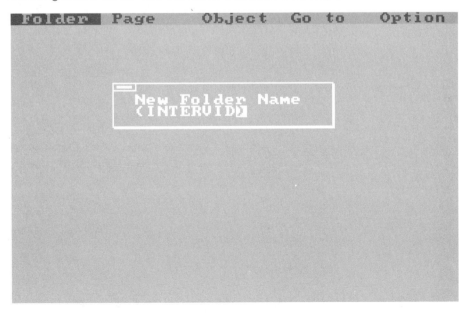

Level dialog box. Clicking on the Close dot will make the Access Level dialog box disappear. If the dialog box will not disappear, make sure that the very tip of your pointer is perfectly centered in the middle of the Close dot. Then click again.

Creating a New Folder

Go up to the Folder Menu and click on New. New creates a new folder for you. You will be working with this same folder throughout this exercise. When prompted for a name, type one in from the keyboard. As in Figure 5–24, type in a name like INTERVID (short for interactive video). If you make a mistake while typing, press the Backspace key to delete the typos. Then reenter the correct letters. When you are done typing, check to see if it is correct. If so, press the Enter key. Upon pressing the Enter key, a new folder is automatically created by the LinkWay program.

The name of your folder will appear in the bottom left-hand corner of the screen, as in Figure 5–25. Using LinkWay, you will be creating an interactive video folder consisting of two pages. The pages will contain text and buttons to control a videodisc player, such as a Pioneer LD-V4200, LD-V4400, LD-V2200, or LD-V2400 videodisc player.

The preceding steps are to be followed each time you want to create a new folder. If you want to use or change an existing folder, then you would not follow these steps. Instead, you would need to open an existing folder, which is described in the next section entitled Opening an Existing Folder. If you are not opening a folder at this time, then skip over the next section and start reading at Status Line.

FIGURE 5–25   The name of the newly created folder INTERVID appears in the bottom left-hand corner. This is the status line. Courtesy IBM.

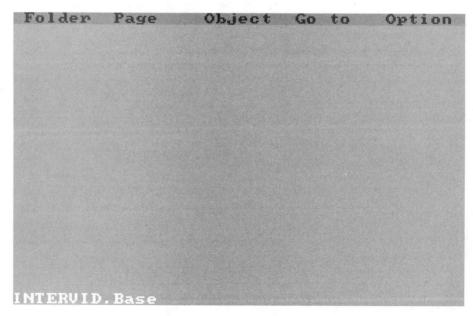

Opening an Existing Folder

To open an existing folder, select Open from the Folder Menu. A list of LinkWay folders will appear on the screen. If the desired folder's name does not appear, you may need to switch to a different directory. For example, to change directories from C:\ drive to A:\ drive, go up to the Option Menu and select Directory. Change the Directory to A:\ by typing this in from the keyboard. Then try out the Open command in the Folder Menu. From this directory, click once on the desired folder name. Then click once on the Close dot. Upon doing this, the Folder will appear on the screen.

Status Line

Notice that your new folder's name appears in the lower left-hand corner of the screen as INTERVID.Base. This is called the *status line*. INTERVID is the title of your folder and Base tells you that you are at the Base page.

Base Page

Every page has two layers—a Base page and a foreground. The *Base page* is the background for all the pages in the folder. The *foreground* is what is unique to a page. All objects that would not be repeated throughout the folder, such as an introductory title, are placed in the foreground. A *background* is what every page in the folder has in common, such as the same background color.

A folder automatically opens in the Base page. Notice that the status line indicates that the base is up on the screen.

Creating a New Page

Now let's start creating two pages for your folder. Go up to Page, as in Figure 5–26, and select New. When you do this, the status line in the lower left-hand corner of the screen has now changed from INTERVID.Base to read as INTERVID.1 Id=1. Id=1 means this is the first page. This is the foreground page.

Now, let's create the second page. From the Page Menu, select New. Notice that the status line now reads as Id=2, meaning this is the second page. Refer to Figure 5–27.

Go to Menu

You can move back and forth between the foreground and Base with the Go to Menu, as illustrated in Figure 5–27. To go to the Base, select Base Page. Notice that the page identification changes. To select the foreground, select First Page. To go to the second page, select Next Page.

Saving Your Folder

If you had previously set your directory to the desired drive and do not need to specify one now, then skip over to the next paragraph. If you need to change to a different directory because you want to save your

FIGURE 5-26 The Page Menu of pull-down commands. Courtesy IBM.

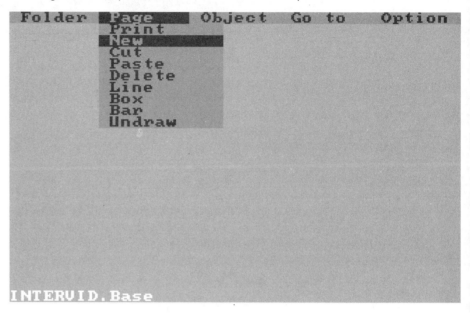

folder onto a floppy diskette in drive A:\, then select Directory from the Option Menu and type in the desired directory. Then, when you click on the Close dot, you are working and saving everything within that directory until another is specified.

Save your folder at this point by selecting Save from the Folder Menu. When the dialog box appears, as in Figure 5–28, click once on the Close dot. Save your folder periodically, such as every 10 minutes or so.

Setting the Base Color

Go to page 1 and then go to the Base page. You will be selecting the Base color for your folder. A *Base color* is a color that will appear in the background for all the pages in the folder. If you set the Base color to blue, then this is the color that will appear on all the pages. Only one Base color can be used.

To pick the Base color, go up to the Option Menu, as in Figure 5–29, and select Bg Color, short for background color. When prompted for a New Background, click on YES. When you do this, the color will automatically change on the screen. Click on YES again and the color will change once more. Cycle through the color choices by clicking on YES. Cycle through until you find one you like. Then set the color by clicking on NO.

The background color that you have just selected will appear as the Base color for both pages in this folder. Check this out by going to the Next Page. Go through both pages to confirm the fact that the Base color is the same throughout.

FIGURE 5–27   The Go to Menu of pull-down commands. Courtesy IBM.

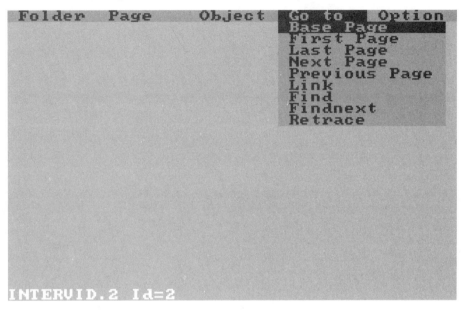

FIGURE 5–28   Saving a folder. Courtesy IBM.

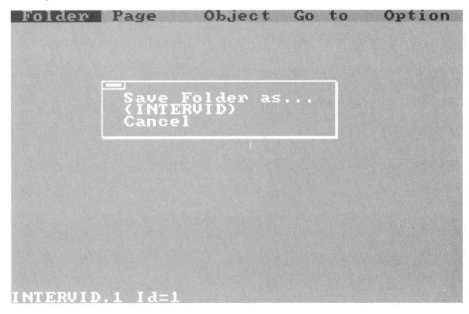

FIGURE 5–29   The pull-down Option Menu of commands. Courtesy IBM.

Creating a Text Field

Go back to page 1 where you will be entering in some text for the opening title screen. LinkWay considers text a type of object. In all, there are three kinds of LinkWay objects: text, pictures, and buttons. To create text, go to the Object Menu, as in Figure 5–30, and select New.

When prompted for the OBJECT TYPE, as in Figure 5–31, click once on Field. Then click on the Close dot to confirm your choice. A *field* is the place where the text will be typed. Notice that the arrow pointer has changed.

Next, let's establish the size and placement of the field. Do this by imagining where the text will appear on this page. The title you will be typing in will say INTERACTIVE VIDEO WITH LINKWAY. With your finger, point to the location of where you want the first letter in your title to begin. Now point to the spot where the last letter of the title will be. If you drew a diagonal line from the first spot to the second, this area is the text field. Now place the cursor at the beginning of the field where you first touched the screen. Click once to set the cursor. Move the mouse to the right and you will notice that a rectangle will appear on the page. Create a rectangle about 2" high by 4" wide, as in Figure 5–32. When you are satisfied with the size of the rectangle, click once to set it. The dotted bounding box shows the size and location of where the text will be on this page.

Next, you will see up on the screen, as in Figure 5–33, a variety of fonts and sizes to choose from. Click once on your choice. When the FIELD Information dialog box appears, notice that the size or length of the field in terms of the # of Characters and # of Lines is specified, as in Figure 5–34. This tells you how many letters and lines of letters can actually fit in the field. Make sure that the number of characters is equal

FIGURE 5–30   The Object Menu of pull-down commands. Courtesy IBM.

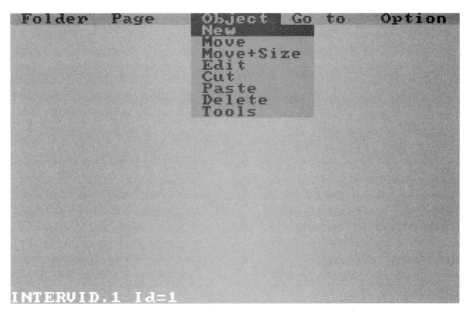

FIGURE 5–31   Creating a text field object. Courtesy IBM.

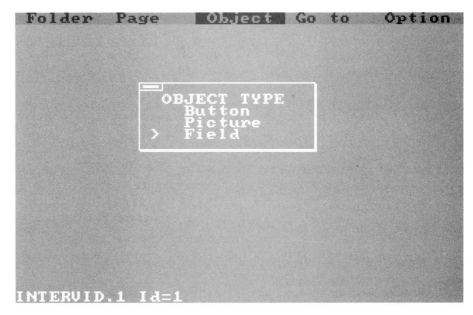

FIGURE 5-32   Creating a text field. Courtesy IBM.

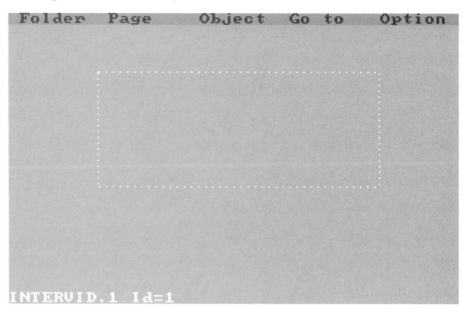

FIGURE 5-33   Selecting a font and fontsize for a text field. Courtesy IBM.

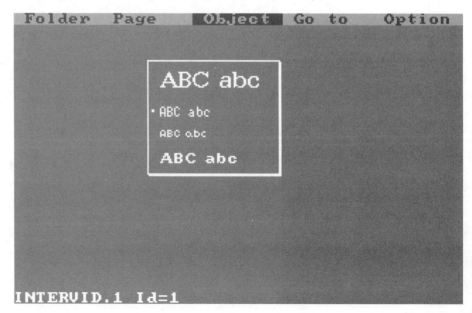

FIGURE 5-34   The Field Information dialog box for a text field. Courtesy IBM.

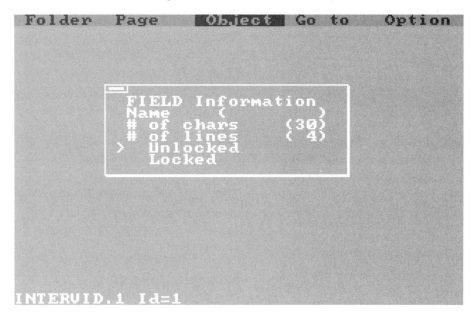

to at least 28. The title that you will be typing in consists of 28 characters. If it shows up as less than 28, click once on # of chars and type in 28. If you make a mistake while typing, use the Backspace key to delete the unwanted characters. Also, make sure that the number of lines is three or more. If it is not three, click once on # of Lines and type in 3. Then click once outside of the dialog box to confirm these changes. Select Unlocked by clicking on Unlocked (if it isn't already selected). When you are done, click on the Close dot to confirm your choices.

Next, pick a color for your lettering by clicking once on your choice. This will be the color of your text.

Entering in Text

Place the pointer in the left-hand corner of the rectangular text field and quickly double click on the mouse button. You always have to set the cursor somewhere within the field by double clicking before you can start to type.

From the keyboard, enter in INTERACTIVE VIDEO. Look over your typing for any errors. If you make a mistake while typing, use the Backspace key to delete backwards. Use the Delete key to delete one character at a time to the right of the cursor. To center-justify text, place the pointer in front of the letter *I* at the beginning of the line. Maker sure that the pointer is just inside of the field. Click once so it turns into an I shaped pointer. It will not work if you do not see the Ibar. Do it again until you see it. Then press the space bar to push the text to the right. You cannot specify center- or right-justification in any other manner than this. Text is automatically left-justified. You have to judge visually where the center is.

To move to the second line in the field, place your pointer at the end of the first line after the letter *o*. Click once. Press the Enter key to move down to the next line. On the second line, type in With. Again, center this line with the space bar. Move to the third line where you will type LINKWAY. Your finished title should look like Figure 5–35.

When you are done typing in the title, click once anywhere outside of the field and the field will be set. Notice that the dotted box surrounding the text field disappears.

Editing Text

If your title looks fine, skip over this section and go to Creating Buttons. To edit text after it has been typed in (as in correcting a misspelling), click once on the desired field to select it. Place the pointer in the space to the right of the error and double click. Use the Backspace key to delete one character to the left at a time, or use the Delete key to delete one character to the right at a time. Then type in the new, correct text from the keyboard.

To edit the color, size, and style of lettering (but not the actual characters themselves such as in correcting a typographical error), place the pointer where the field exists and click once. Notice that the rectangular text field appears. Go up to the Object Menu and select Edit. Click through the various information boxes, making whatever changes are necessary.

To move the text field to a different location on the page, place the pointer inside of the text field and from the Object Menu, select Move. Notice that the cursor has now taken on the rectangular shape of the selected field. Move the field-shaped cursor to the desired location. Click once to set it. The field will automatically move to the new location.

Don't forget to save your folder every 10 minutes.

FIGURE 5–35   Entering in text for a text field that will appear on the opening page. Courtesy IBM.

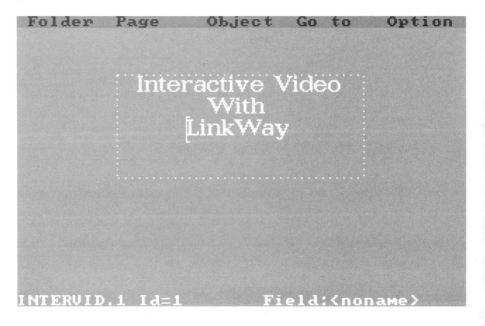

Creating Buttons

Next, let's add some buttons that will let you easily move back and forth among the pages. Buttons are like hotspots on the computer screen which, when clicked on with the mouse, perform a specific action such as going to the next page without having to use the Go to Menu all the time. Other actions performed by buttons include linking to a designated page not in sequence, playing a sound, displaying a picture, and playing a video clip from a videodisc.

The first button you will create is a Next Page button which, when clicked on, will present the next page. You will be creating this button in the Base page so it appears on all the pages in your folder. Go to the Base page by selecting Base Page from the Go to Menu. Your text should disappear, since the text was created in the foreground and not in the Base.

Like a text field, a button is also an object. From the Object Menu, select New. When prompted regarding the OBJECT TYPE, click once on Button. Then click once on the Close dot to confirm your selection.

Move the cursor to the lower right-hand corner of the screen about one inch up from the bottom edge and two inches in from the right side of the screen. Click once to set the placement of the top left corner of the button. Generally, a button takes the form of a rectangle. Move the cursor diagonally down to the right until you have a rectangle. Click again. This will set the size and placement of the button.

Next, a dialog box displaying various BUTTON Types will appear, as in Figure 5-36. From the selection, click on Go. Go indicates the kind of action that this button will do. Click once on the Close dot to confirm your choice. Now type in a name for your button such as NEXT. Click once on the mouse when you are done. Then click once on the Close dot.

FIGURE 5-36   The BUTTON Type dialog box. Courtesy IBM.

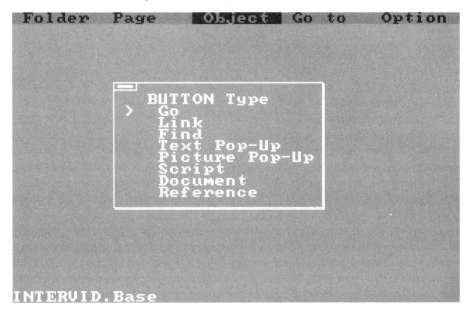

Next, let's choose an icon for your button by clicking once on a choice, as in Figure 5–37. Choose perhaps the right arrow since this best represents the concept of moving to the next page. To select the right arrow, click once on it.

When prompted with GO TO..., as in Figure 5–38, make sure Next is selected. An > arrow should appear before Next. If not, then click once on Next. Then click on the Close dot to confirm your choice.

Trying Out Your Button

To try out your new button, go to the first page. Place the pointer over the button. Notice that the cursor turns into a hand. Rapidly, double click on it and page 2 will appear. Double click on it again and page 1 will be presented. Double click once more and page 2 will appear. Going through the pages is circular—after the last page comes the first page.

Now it is your turn to create a button. Remember to start off in the Base page. Create a button named PREVIOUS. Place the Previous page button in the lower left-hand corner. Follow the preceding steps except select GO TO... Previous when the dialog box appears.

Now, let's try out your new Previous button. Go to the first page. Then double click on the new button. To edit the button, use the Object Menu commands. Save your folder.

Videodisc Buttons

Let's put some videodisc buttons on your pages. LinkWay comes with some useful video buttons that can be copied and pasted to your folder. Video buttons control the actions of the videodisc player.

FIGURE 5–37   Picking a button icon. Courtesy IBM.

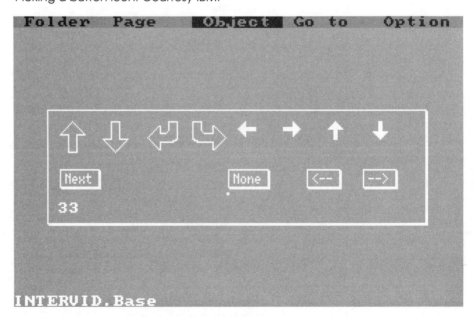

FIGURE 5-38   The GO TO... dialog box. Courtesy IBM.

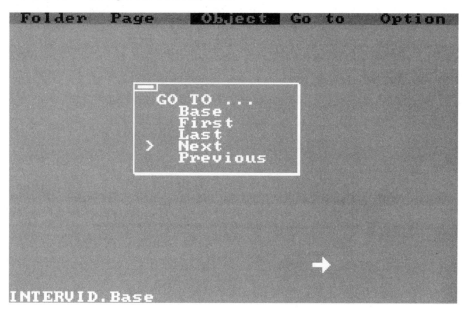

Now, from the Folder Menu, select Open. Then, when the dialog box appears, as in Figure 5–39, click on the down arrow until you see VIDEO. Then click once on VIDEO and click once on the Close dot. A replication of Figure 5–40 should appear on your screen.

The Videodisc Demo Folder contains an assortment of buttons for controlling a videodisc player. These buttons are canned, meaning they are already scripted with the correct programming code to control a videodisc player. All you have to do select and copy the ones you want to your own folder.

Turn on the power to the videodisc player and monitor. In this exercise, we are using a Pioneer LD-V4200 player. Place a CAV videodisc into the player. Start off by clicking once on the button labeled Spinup. When you are prompted for a baud rate, type in 4800 and press the Enter key. When prompted for a COM port, type in 1 and press the Enter key. Next, click once on the Play button. Then try out the Still button. These are the three buttons that you will be copying to your folder—Spinup, Play, and Still.

Copying a Button

Before selecting a button, recheck your Access Level. Go up to the Folder Menu and select Access Level. If a screen comes up asking for a password, just press the Enter key to go on. Make sure that the Access Level is set to Format. If not, click once on Format and then click once on the Close dot.

Next, select the button labeled Spinup by clicking once on it. The button should look selected. If an error message appears, then you will want to recheck the current Access Level and make sure it is set to Format.

FIGURE 5-39   The Open Folder dialog box for opening the video folder. Courtesy IBM.

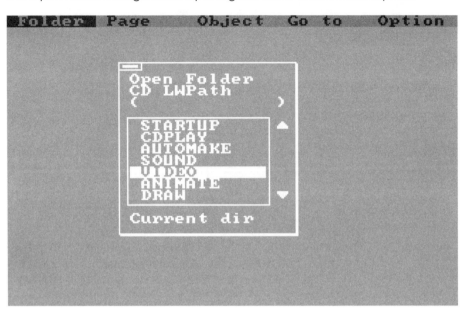

FIGURE 5-40   The Videodisc Demo Folder of useful video buttons that comes with LinkWay. These buttons control a videodisc player. Courtesy IBM.

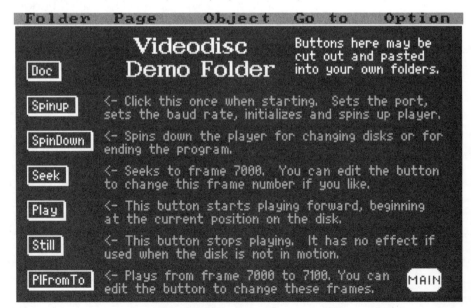

Now, let's copy the button to your folder. From the Object Menu, select Cut, which makes a copy of this button. Cut does not actually cut a button. When prompted for the directory, as in Figure 5–41, select SCRAP by clicking once on Scrap. If Scrap already appears between the parentheses, you may not be able to click on it to select it. Then click once on the Close dot to confirm this choice. When the message Cut Completed appears, just click once on the Close dot. Your cut is successful.

Pasting a Button

Now, let's go back to your folder, INTERVID, where you will paste the newly copied button. From the Folder Menu select Open. From the list of various folders displayed in the box, as in Figure 5–42, click once on your folder called INTERVID. If you do not see your folder listed, you will need to click on the down arrow to see the rest of the folders. Then click once on the Close dot.

Once your folder appears, go to page 2. Make sure you are not in the Base page. This is where you will be pasting the button. From the Object Menu, select Paste. When the dialog box appears, if SCRAP appears at the top, then just click once on the Close dot. If it does not appear there, you will need to click on the down arrow until you find SCRAP. Then click once on SCRAP and next click on the Close dot. Remember that when you had previously copied the button, SCRAP appeared. What had happened was that the button was copied and saved to a temporary folder called SCRAP (short for scrapbook). A copied button will remain there until it is either replaced by a copy of something else or the computer is turned off.

Note that the cursor now looks like a small rectangle. Place the rectangle in the center of the page. Click once to set it. Your page should look like Figure 5–43.

FIGURE 5–41   Copying a button. Courtesy IBM.

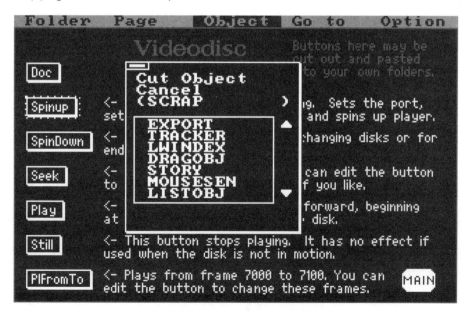

FIGURE 5–42   Opening your INTERVID folder. Courtesy IBM.

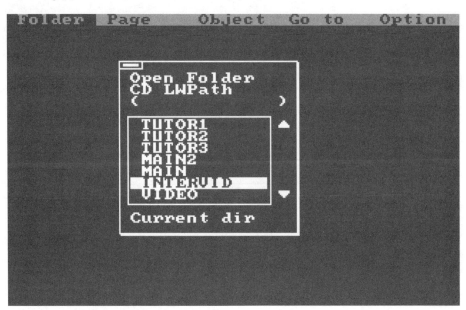

Moving a Button

If you need to move the button to a different location, click on it once to select it. Then use the Move command from the Object Menu. Place the rectangular cursor at a new location and click the mouse to set it. Save your folder.

Now, let's copy another button. Go up to the Folder Menu and select Open. From the list of folders in the dialog box, click once on VIDEO and then click on the Close dot. Click once on Play. Then, from the Object Menu, select Cut. When the dialog box appears, make sure SCRAP is selected. Click once on the Close dot. When the message Cut Completed appears, just click once on the Close dot. Finally, go up to the Folder Menu and select Open. Select the name of your folder INTERVID. Click once on the Close dot. Go to the last page—page 2 of your folder. Paste the button there by selecting Paste from the Object Menu. When the dialog box appears, make sure SCRAP is selected. Then click once on the Close dot. Place the rectangular cursor just beneath the Spinup button. Click once to set it. Save your folder. Now on your own, copy the Still button to here.

Trying Out the Buttons

Now let's try out the videodisc buttons. Make sure that the videodisc player is on and that a videodisc has already been inserted into the player. Also, turn on the power to the videodisc monitor. Go up to the Folder Menu and select Access Level. Set it to Read. Click on the Close dot. If you are prompted for a password, just press the Enter key.

First, click once on the Spinup button. When prompted to enter a baud rate, type in 4800 and press the Enter key. When prompted for a

FIGURE 5–43 Pasting a video button to a page. Courtesy IBM.

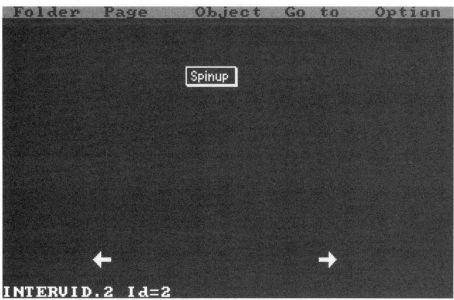

COM port, type in 1 and press the Enter key. After you do this, the videodisc player will start to hum. It is initializing. If nothing happens, try selecting COM port 2 instead of 1, or turn the videodisc over. Next, click once on the Play button, then click once on the Still button.

Exiting LinkWay

Save your folder. When you are done, go up to the Folder Menu and select Exit LinkWay.

Have fun working with LinkWay. Try copying some other videodisc buttons over to your folder. In addition, try making some graphics using LWPaint—a terrific drawing and paint program. LWPaint can be accessed by selecting Tools from the Object Menu. If you are interested in learning more about LinkWay, following are some excellent introductory books.

- An easy-to-read, introductory-intermediate book is called *IBM Link-Way Authoring Tool* (1993) authored by Annette Lamb. It is published by Career Publishing Inc., 910 N. Main St., Orange, CA 92667. (800) 854-4014.
- A quick way to get started with LinkWay is reading *Getting a Quick Start with IBM LinkWay*. This booklet is free from your IBM sales representative.
- Another excellent source is the user's manual that comes with the LinkWay program. It is entitled IBM LinkWay Version 2.00. The author is Larry Kheriaty at Washington Computer Services.

Hands-On Exercise: ToolBook 1.5 for Windows

Introduction

ToolBook 1.5 for Windows is a software construction set. With ToolBook, you can create applications for managing information, education, entertainment, hypermedia, and more. In this exercise, you will be using ToolBook along with The Voyager Videodisc ToolKit to create your own book with *buttons* to control a videodisc player. Buttons are objects on the screen which, when clicked on, an action occurs, such as the videodisc player starts playing a video clip.

Start Up

Launch Windows 3.1. From the Microsoft Windows Program Manager, find the folder icon labeled ToolBook 1.5. In Figure 5–44, it is in the bottom right-hand corner. Double click on the folder to open it up.

Next, find the program icon labeled ToolBook. It looks like an open book, as in Figure 5–45. Double click on the book icon. Double clicking on it will start up the ToolBook authoring tool.

Pull-Down Menus   Once ToolBook is up and running, the first thing to appear on your screen is a blank white page. At the very top is the title bar where the word ToolBook-(Untitled) appears, as in Figure 5–46. Just under that is the menu bar, listing a variety of commands such as File, Edit, Text, Page, and so on. Beneath that is the work area where you will

---

FIGURE 5–44   Opening the ToolBook folder in the Windows Program Manager. Windows is published by the Microsoft Corporation. ToolBook 1.5 for Windows is published by the Asymetrix Corporation. (ToolBook is a registered trademark of Asymetrix.)

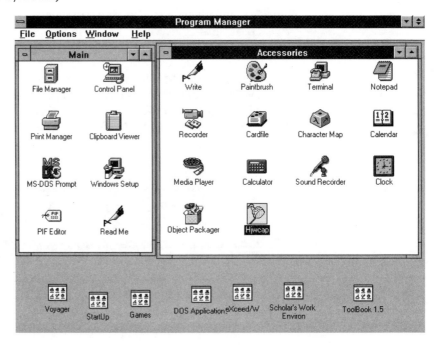

FIGURE 5–45   Starting up ToolBook by double clicking on the ToolBook book icon. ToolBook 1.5 for Windows is published by the Asymetrix Corporation. (ToolBook is a registered trademark of Asymetrix.)

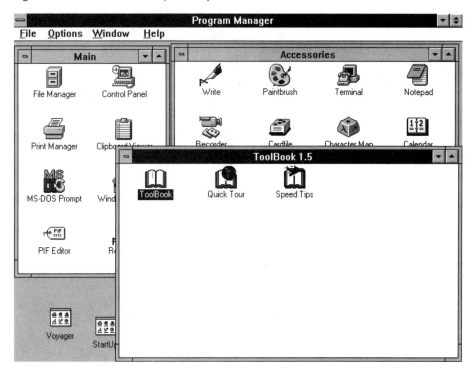

be creating your book. Take a look at the commands listed in the menu bar. Place the pointer over the menu item called File and click the mouse button once. A pull-down menu of commands should appear, as in Figure 5–46.

Slide the pointer to the right. Place it over Edit and click once. Look over all the editing commands available in the Edit Menu, as in Figure 5–47. Now, move one by one through the rest of the menu bar and look at their pull-down menus.

Help Menu

A feature of ToolBook is its extensive on-line tutorial. The ToolBook tutorial provides help for various levels of authoring competence—for beginning authors, intermediate authors, and advanced authors. Before we start to create anything, let's go through the tutorial. (This will take about one to two hours.) Move the pointer over to Help in the menu bar and click once to see the pull-down menu of commands. Figure 5–48 provides a list of all the Help commands.

Place the tip of your pointer over Tutorial. When its on top of Tutorial, click the mouse button once. Tutorial will be highlighted, indicating that you have selected it. This is how to select a command like Tutorial from the pull-down menu. Use this same procedure later for selecting any other commands from the menu bar. By clicking on Tutorial, you have

FIGURE 5–46   The pull-down menu of commands available in the File Menu. ToolBook 1.5 for Windows, Asymetrix Corporation. (ToolBook is a registered trademark of Asymetrix.)

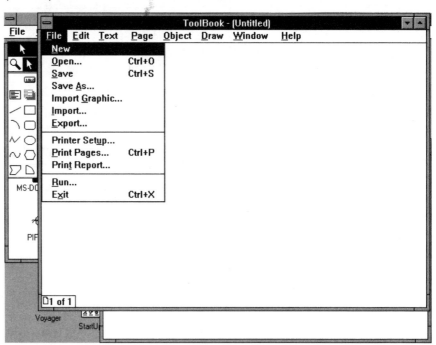

FIGURE 5–47   Edit Menu of pull-down commands. ToolBook 1.5 for Windows, Asymetrix Corporation. (ToolBook is a registered trademark of Asymetrix.)

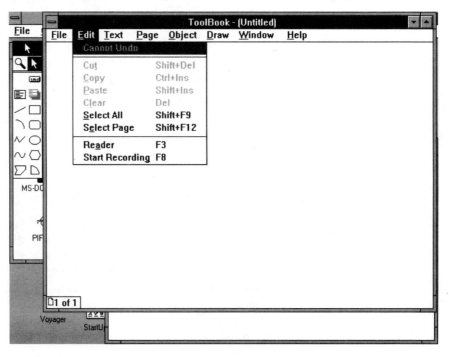

FIGURE 5–48　The pull-down commands available in the Help Menu. ToolBook 1.5 for Windows, Asymetrix Corporation. (ToolBook is a registered trademark of Asymetrix.)

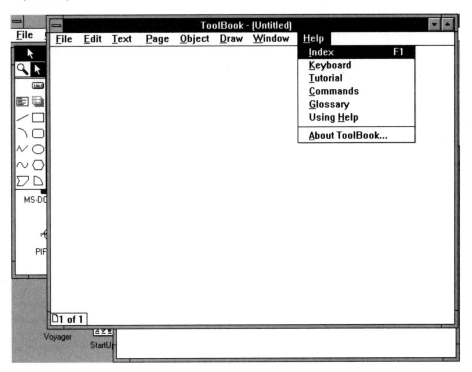

just launched Quick Tour—the interactive on-line tutorial for ToolBook. Figure 5–49 shows all the Quick Tour topics.

The menu is arranged into various levels of complexity. For example, the first topic—Taking the Quick Tour—is for first-time users of ToolBook. It explains how to move through the Quick Tour by using the pointer to click on the Forward and Backward buttons. This is where you should start. Place your pointer over Taking the Quick Tour and click once. A pop-up window will appear and describe what you can expect from this menu item.

Now quickly double click on Taking the Quick Tour to select it. This action will start it up. Follow along the tutorial by reading each page and doing whatever you are instructed to do. When you have finished Taking the Quick Tour, go through the second topic called Introducing ToolBook. Select Introducing ToolBook by double clicking on this menu item. Finally, go through the next two topics—The ToolBook Reader Tour and The ToolBook Author Tour. Leave The OpenScript Workbook for later—when you are more experienced.

Exiting Quick Tour　If at anytime during the tutorial you want to quit, select the Topics button in the bottom left-hand corner of the page. The Topics button looks like a small rectangle filled with horizontal bars of color, as in Figure 5–50. By clicking once on the Topics button, the Topics

FIGURE 5–49   Quick Tour topics—the main menu from the on-line interactive tutorial for ToolBook. ToolBook 1.5 for Windows, Asymetrix Corporation. (ToolBook is a registered trademark of Asymetrix.)

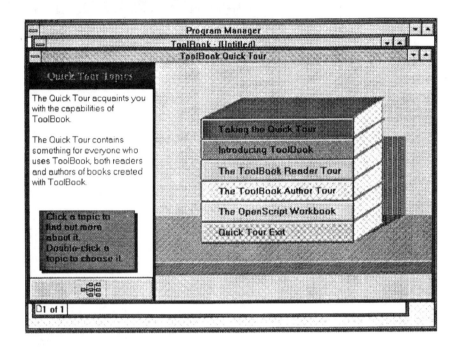

FIGURE 5–50   Exiting from Quick Tour by clicking on the Topics Menu button in the bottom left-hand corner. ToolBook 1.5 for Windows, Asymetrix Corporation. (ToolBook is a registered trademark of Asymetrix.)

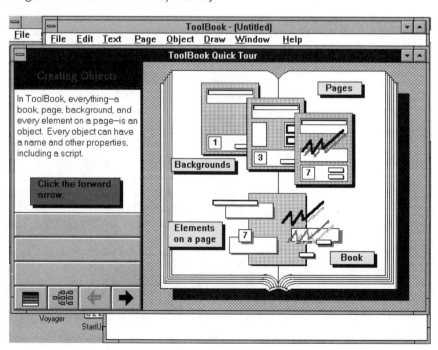

Menu will appear. If necessary, keep clicking on the Topics Menu button until you are back at the Main Menu for the Quick Tour.

Then, from the Quick Tour Topics, double click on the bottom choice called Quick Tour Exit. When prompted with the message "Are you sure you want to exit the Quick Tour?" click once on YES to confirm your decision. If you are prompted with "Leaving the Quick Tour—Save the checkmarks for the topics you visited?" click on YES. This message means that the next time you start up Quick Tour, you'll see where you left off. The topics that you have previously gone through will be checked. This way, you will know which ones you still need to cover.

Quitting ToolBook

If you are not ready to quit at this time, skip over this section.

At any point you can exit out of the ToolBook program. If you are in the ToolBook authoring program, go up to the File Menu and click once to see all the pull-down File commands. Look for Exit, which is at the very bottom of the pull-down menu. Refer back to Figure 5–46 for a listing of the File commands. If you want to quit at this time, you would click once on Exit. If a message box appears asking "Save current changes to:" then click on your choice. For instance, if you have made any changes and would like to save them, then click on YES. The current book will replace the previously saved book. If you click on NO, then you will exit out of ToolBook without saving. If you click on Cancel, you will not exit. Cancel does as it says—it cancels the selected menu item that was to exit. The message box will appear only if you have made changes to your book since the last time it was saved.

If you want to exit Windows, when the Program Manager appears, select Exit Windows from the File Menu.

Page

In ToolBook, the basic unit is a *page*. You view pages one at a time in a ToolBook window. A *window* is a rectangular area of the screen that displays information. Each instance of an application appears in its own window. For example, the ToolBook Help book appears in one window while the ToolBook program book appears in another window. A grouping of pages is called a *book*.

Foreground and Background

Every page has two layers—a Foreground and a Background. Whatever is put in the Foreground of each page is unique to that individual page. The Foreground contains objects (text, buttons, graphics) that are unique to the page. An example of Foreground objects would be some text for a title on an opening page. This text would only appear on that page—thus, it is unique to the page.

On the other hand, objects placed in the Background appear on every page in the book. Any number of pages can share the same Background. In the Background, objects appear in the same size, style, and position on every page that shares the Background. For example, you might want to place the Next Page and Previous Page buttons in the Background. By putting them there, they are accessible and visible from every page in the book. Each book can have one or more Backgrounds.

Page Identification In the bottom left-hand corner of Figure 5–51, you will see the page identification displayed as 1 of 1. There is also a tiny miniature icon of a page in front of 1 of 1, indicating that you are currently at the Foreground page layer. When ToolBook is initially launched, it starts up in the Foreground. You are currently looking at the first page in your book.

You have to intentionally switch to the Background to work on that part of the page. When the Background is up on your screen, the page identification will say Background. When you are in the Foreground, it will tell you the number of the page and the total number of pages in the book.

Switching between the Foreground and Background of a Page Now let's go to the Background by selecting Background from the pull-down Page Menu. Go to the Page Menu and click once to see the pull-down menu. Figure 5–51 displays the pull-down commands available in the Page Menu. Place the pointer over Background and click once to select it. Now that the Background is up on the screen, notice that the page identification in the bottom left-hand corner says Background, as in Figure 5–52.

FIGURE 5–51   The pull-down menu of commands available in the Page Menu. ToolBook 1.5 for Windows, Asymetrix Corporation. (ToolBook is a registered trademark of Asymetrix.)

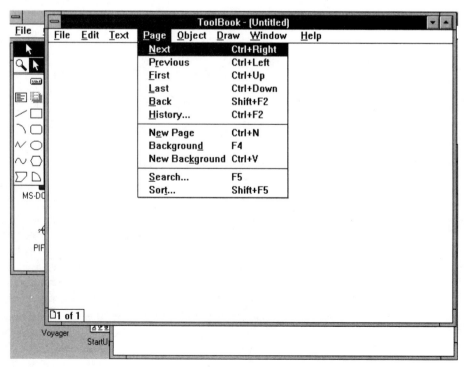

FIGURE 5–52   Displaying the Background layer of a page. ToolBook 1.5 for Windows, Asymetrix Corporation. (ToolBook is a registered trademark of Asymetrix.)

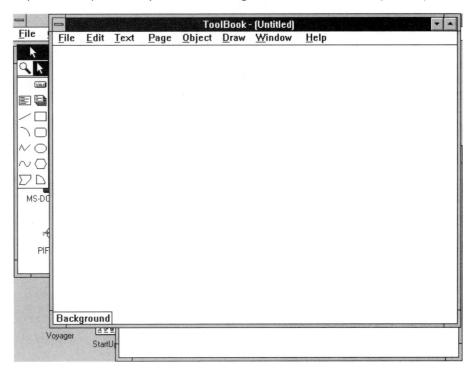

Go back up to the Page Menu and select Foreground. Notice that the page identification has changed back to 1 of 1. This is how to switch back and forth between the Foreground and Background of a page.

Another way to switch back and forth is with a keyboard shortcut. A *keyboard shortcut* lets you select a command from the keyboard rather than from a pull-down menu. One press on the F4 key and you are in the Background. The F4 key is in the very top row of your keyboard. Try it out. Another press and you are switched back to the Foreground. You can always tell when you are in the Background because the page identification will say Background. When you are in the Foreground, it will say something like 1 of 1.

All the keyboard shortcuts for the commands in the pull-down menus are actually listed in the pull-down menus. Click once on Page. Next to the Background command in the Page Menu, you will see F4 listed. The keyboard shortcuts are listed to the right of the commands.

Creating a New Page

Let's create a second page for your book. While in the Foreground, create another page by selecting New Page from the Page Menu. The page is automatically created as soon as the command is selected. The page identification now reads as 2 of 2, meaning this is the second page in a two-page book. You could have also created the New Page using its keyboard shortcut Ctrl + N.

Keyboard Shortcuts for Moving Around in a Book

To move around in the book, select Next from the Page Menu. Place your pointer over Next and click once. To go to the last page in the book, page 2, select Last from the Page Menu. To go to the previous page, select Previous. Also, try out First and Back.

As previously mentioned, another way to get around in a book is with keyboard shortcuts. By pressing the Ctrl key and "→" (the right arrow key), the next page after the current page will appear. You need to press these two keys together by first holding down the Ctrl key and tapping on the → key. Crtl + ← (the left arrow key) will take you to the previous page. The keyboard shortcut to go to the first page is Ctrl + ↑ (the up arrow key). Ctrl + ↓ (the down arrow key) is the shortcut to go to the last page.

If the menus pop down while using the keyboard shortcuts, then press the Num Lock key once. The Num Lock key is on the right-hand side of your keyboard in the top row of the numeric keypad.

Saving the Book

Now let's save the book before moving on. To save a book for the first time, select Save As... from the File Menu. The command Save As... is used only the first time to save a book. It is also used when you want to save the book under a different name. Since this is the first time in saving the book, you need to select Save As.... When the Save As dialog box appears, type in a name for your newly created book. Type the name where the blinking vertical bar appears after the word Filename:, as in Figure 5–53. The name can be up to eight characters long. Type a name like INTERVID (short for Interactive Video). After typing in the name, do not press the Enter key. What you just typed in will be the title for your new book. If you made a mistake, use the Backspace key to delete characters. The Backspace key is in the top right corner.

Next, make sure that the directory where you save your book appears after the label Directory. If you are satisfied with saving your book to the current directory, then skip over to the next paragraph. You can select a different directory by just clicking once on one of the directories listed in the bottom square of the dialog box. For example, if you click on (-c-), then your book will be saved on the hard drive—the C:\ drive. If you click on (-a-), then your book will be saved on the diskette in the A:\ drive. If you are saving to the A:\ drive, make sure that a formatted diskette is in there.

When you are done, click on the OK button. ToolBook will save your book under the filename you typed. Once it is saved, the title bar at the top will display the name of your book as ToolBook—INTERVID.TBK. TBK is automatically added to your filename, indicating that this was made with ToolBook.

Save As... is used to save a book the very first time or to save the current book in the active window under a different name. The Save command, which is also in the File Menu, is used to save whatever book is currently in the active window which will replace whatever book exists in that directory with the same name. Generally, while you are working, Save is a quicker way to save than Save As... But, since this was the first

FIGURE 5-53   Saving a book for the first time using the Save As... command. ToolBook 1.5 for Windows, Asymetrix Corporation. (ToolBook is a registered trademark of Asymetrix.)

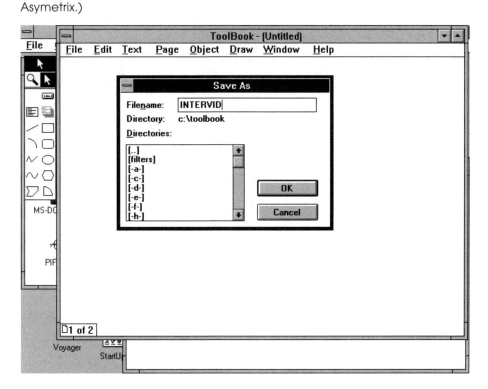

time for saving your book, you needed to use Save As... to specify the directory as well as to give the book a name.

Now that you have saved your book using Save As..., try out the Save command. Go up to the File Menu and click once on Save. See how fast it saves!

Setting the Background Color

Now go to the Background (if you are not there already). Use the keyboard shortcut—press the F4 key to go there. While in the Background, you will be selecting a color. When a color is placed in the Background, it will show up on all the pages in the book.

To set the Background color, go up to the Object Menu, as in Figure 5-54, and select Background Properties.... From the Background Properties dialog box, click once on the button labeled Colors, which appears on the right side. A Color Tray will appear on the right side of the screen. From this Color Tray, click once on a color choice that you would like to see as the background for all your pages. As soon as you click on a color, watch the color fill the page. To change the color, simply click once on another color. When you are satisfied with your color choice, click on OK to set the color.

FIGURE 5-54   Select Background Properties... from the Object Menu of pull-down commands to set the background characteristics such as the background color. ToolBook 1.5 for Windows, Asymetrix Corporation. (ToolBook is a registered trademark of Asymetrix.)

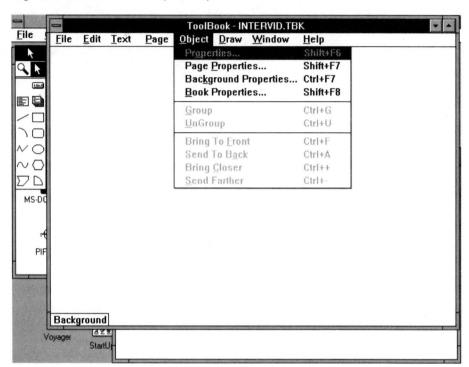

Making Navigational Buttons: Next Page and Previous Page

Go to the Background by pressing the F4 key (if you are not there already). You will be creating the Next Page and Previous Page buttons in the Background, which will take you back and forth through the book.

Author and Reader Levels   On the left-hand side of the screen, you should see a palette of tools. The Tool palette is visible whenever you are in the Author Level. There are two levels of user access available in ToolBook—*Author* and *Reader.* Being in the Author mode lets you author software, such as a book full of pages, color, graphics, text, and buttons. When you see the Tool palette, you will know that you are in the Author mode.

If you are in the Reader mode, your access is limited to reading it like a traditional book—by turning pages. Being in the Reader mode limits the access so that you cannot create a page or button. The Reader mode is what you will want your book to be in for the end-user (your students), because generally you would not want a user to make changes to your book—at least not without your approval.

To flip back and forth between the Author and Reader modes, go up to the Edit Menu and select Reader. You can also do this using the F3 key. When you are in the Reader mode, the Tool palette will not be available. To switch back to the Author mode, press the F3 key again.

Palettes   Palettes are used to make objects, such as buttons. You will be using the Tool palette to create buttons. The Tool palette is a collection of tools for creating objects. This is the main palette. It is always visible at the Author Level. It is used to create text fields with the Field tool, buttons with the Button tool, and graphics with the Drawing tools. Figure 5–55 illustrates the Tool palette on the left side of the screen.

At the top of the Tool palette are three items:

1. Selection Indicator: Located at the very top of the Tool palette, the Selection indicator is not a tool. It changes, depending on the tool or object you selected.
2. Zoom Tool: Located beneath the Selection indicator to the left, the Zoom tool is used to magnify your view of the page.
3. Selection Arrow: Located to the right of the Zoom tool, the Selection arrow is used to select an object.

Creating a Button   To create a button, be sure you are in the Background. Start by selecting the Button tool from the Tool palette. In Figure 5–55, the Button tool is the first tool in the right-hand column just beneath the Selection arrow. To select the Button tool, place the pointer over it and click once. You will know it has been selected because it will appear highlighted.

Move the pointer to the page and watch it turn into a cross hair "+." Place the cross hair at the location of where you want the Next Page

---

FIGURE 5–55   The Tool palette on the left side is used for creating buttons, text, and graphics. ToolBook 1.5 for Windows, Asymetrix Corporation. (ToolBook is a registered trademark of Asymetrix.)

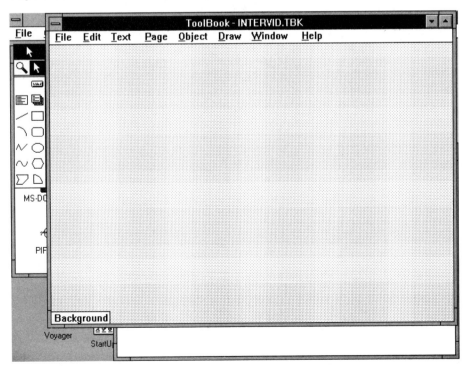

button to appear on your page. For example, place the cross hair about 1/2″ up from the bottom edge of the page and 1″ in from the right side of the page. Click and drag the cross hair diagonally down to the bottom right corner until the word Button appears, as in Figure 5–56. Then let go. If you are dissatisfied with the results, click once on the button and then press the Delete key. This will delete the button from the page. You will then need to redraw it.

Setting the Button Properties Now go back to the Tool palette and choose the Selection arrow by clicking on it once. Bring the arrow over to the page. Using the arrow, click once on the button to select it. Once the button is selected, an outline with handles appear. _Handles_ are small rectangular shapes that appear around the selected object. Handles indicate that the object is currently selected.

While it is selected, go up to the Object Menu and select Button Properties, which allows you to set the characteristics of a button. When the Button Properties dialog box appears, as in Figure 5–57, delete the label Button that appears after the heading Button label:. To delete it, place the arrow pointer directly over the word Button. When this is done, the pointer will look like a vertical bar. Quickly double click on top of the word Button. This will make it highlighted. While it is highlighted, press the

FIGURE 5–56   Creating a button in the bottom right corner of the page using the button tool from the Tool palette. ToolBook 1.5 for Windows, Asymetrix Corporation. (ToolBook is a registered trademark of Asymetrix.)

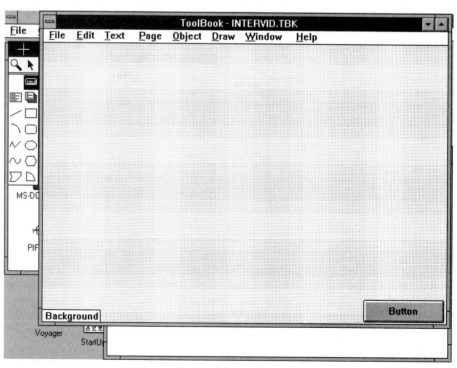

FIGURE 5-57   The dialog box for Button Properties lets you set the characteristics of a button such as the label, type, and style of font to appear on the face of a button. ToolBook 1.5 for Windows, Asymetrix Corporation. (ToolBook is a registered trademark of Asymetrix.)

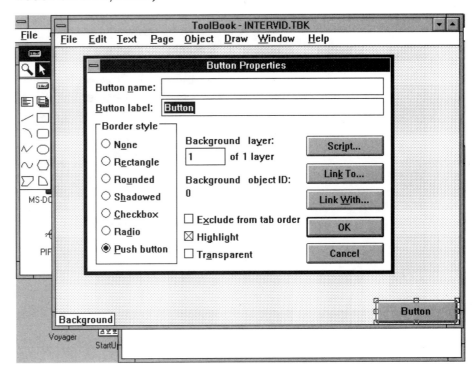

Backspace key. Now type in NEXT after the heading Button label:. This will be the label for your button. Select Shadowed from the list of border styles appearing on the left side of the box. Do this by clicking once inside of the circle or bullet appearing before Shadowed.

Entering Script for a Button   From the right side of the dialog box, click once on Script. Now you have to type in the script, which will happen each time this button is clicked on. You will want this button to go to the next page everytime it is clicked. Where you see the blinking vertical bar, type in the lines of script listed below. Type them just as they are listed below. Notice that everything except the U in buttonUp is in lower-case lettering. If you make a typo, use the Backspace key to delete the unwanted character. Then type in the correction. To move to the second line, where you will type in go to the next page, press the Enter key at the end of typing in the first line. After typing in the second line, press Enter to move to the last line. On the third line, type in end.

```
to handle buttonUp
go to next page
end
```

When you are done, go up to the Script Menu and select Exit/Update, as in Figure 5–58. The scripting box will disappear. These three lines of script will make the Next button display the next page every time that the mouse button is depressed while the pointer is on the Next button.

Close the Button Properties dialog box by clicking once on OK. Notice the immediate change in your button. It is shadowed and labeled Next. Save your book before going on by selecting Save from the File Menu.

To try out the newly created Next Page button, you need to switch from the Author Level to Reader Level. Try out the Next button. Place the tip of the pointer directly in the center of the Next button and click once. When you click on it, the button will blink to indicate that it is selected. When this is done, the next page will be displayed. In other words, if page 1 is currently displayed and you clicked on the Next button, then page 2 would be displayed because that is the page that comes after 1. Of course at this point both pages look identical—so you cannot tell them apart.

Let's create a Previous Page button. Switch from Reader to Author. Create the Previous button in the Background in the same manner as described earlier for the Next button, except that it should be labeled as Previous and it has a different script. The script for it is written in Figure 5–59.

FIGURE 5–58   Saving a button's script with the Exit/Update command. ToolBook 1.5 for Windows, Asymetrix Corporation. (ToolBook is a registered trademark of Asymetrix.)

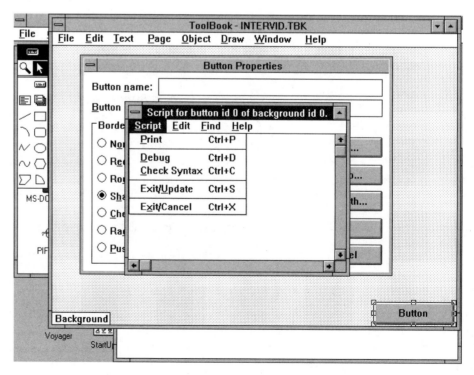

FIGURE 5–59   Typing in the script for the Previous Page button. ToolBook 1.5 for Windows, Asymetrix Corporation. (ToolBook is a registered trademark of Asymetrix.)

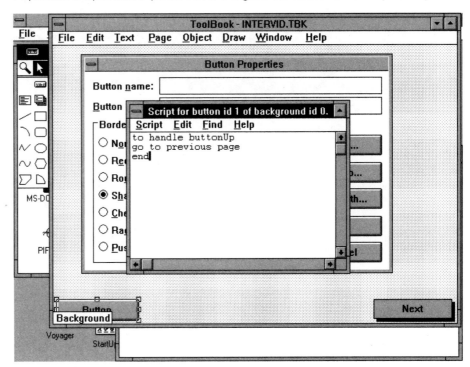

Once the button is created, go to the Reader mode to try out the button. Then click on the Previous button. Save your book before going on.

Creating a Text Field

You will need to be in the Author mode to do this. Go to page 1. You will be creating a text field on page 1. A *text field* is a place where text is displayed on a page. This field will be for the title of your book.

Switch to the Foreground if you are not there already. Select the Field tool from the Tool palette. The Field tool is the first tool beneath the Zoom tool in the left-hand column of the Tool palette. Click once. It should appear highlighted, signifying that it is selected. Notice that the highlighted icon at the top of the Tool palette is now a cross hair. The cross hair indicates that a text field can be drawn on this page. Move the pointer to the page. It should turn into a cross hair.

Making the Text Field   Place the cross hair about 1" in and down from the top left corner. Click and drag diagonally down to the right to create a rectangle that is 2" high by 5" wide, as in Figure 5–60. This is where your text will be.

Setting the Style and Size of Lettering   Let's set the characteristics for the lettering, such as its size and style. If your cursor does not look like a

FIGURE 5–60   Creating a text field. ToolBook 1.5 for Windows, Asymetrix Corporation. (ToolBook is a registered trademark of Asymetrix.)

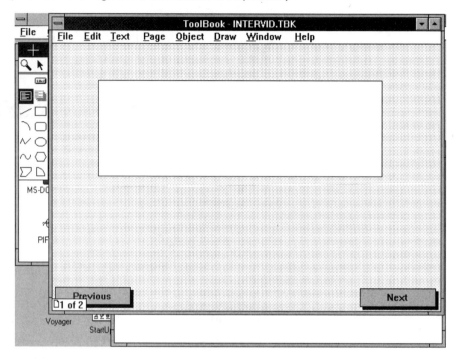

FIGURE 5–61   Setting the characteristics for text using the Text Menu. ToolBook 1.5 for Windows, Asymetrix Corporation. (ToolBook is a registered trademark of Asymetrix.)

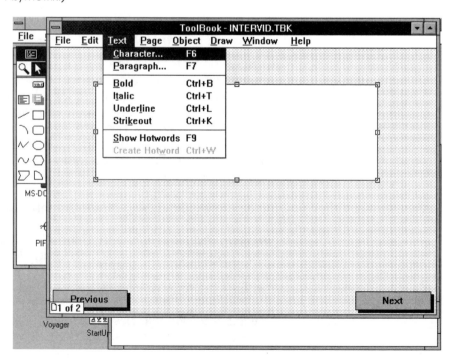

pointer at this time, then get the Selection arrow by clicking once on it in the Tool palette. Then, with the pointer, click once on the field to select it. The handles should appear to indicate that it is selected. Later, when you have several fields and other objects on your page, you will look for the handles to determine what is the currently selected object.

Select Character... from the Text Menu, as in Figure 5–61. Click once on the down arrow appearing to the right of System, as in Figure 5–62. A list of fonts will appear below System. You can move through the fonts by clicking on the up and down scroll arrows that are along the right side of the box. Click once on a font choice like Times New Roman. When you clicked on Times New Roman, notice that it now appears at the top—where the word System was.

Now you will change the size of the lettering to a point size like 18. Do this by clicking once on the down arrow just beneath Point Size:. A list of various point sizes should appear on the screen. Click once on 18 to select it. Next, from the Style choices on the left, click once on Bold to select a boldface style of lettering. When you are done, click on OK. As you type in the lettering, it will appear in the Times New Roman font, fontsize 18, and in boldface.

Entering in Text   If you have not already done so, get the pointer from the Tool palette by clicking once on the Selection arrow. Put the pointer inside the very top left corner of the rectangular text field. Quickly double click. A blinking vertical line will appear in the upper left-hand

FIGURE 5–62   Setting the characteristics of the text. ToolBook 1.5 for Windows, Asymetrix Corporation. (ToolBook is a registered trademark of Asymetrix.)

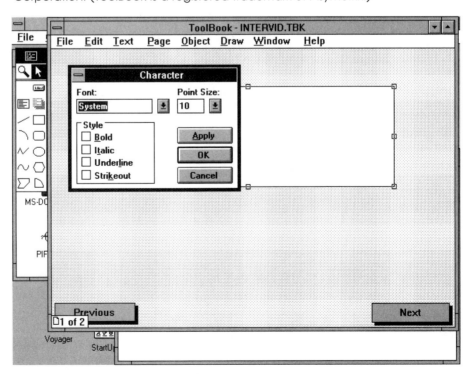

corner of the field. This line is called the *insertion point*, meaning the place to insert text.

From the keyboard, type in the following: Interactive Video. If you make a mistake, use the Backspace key to delete unwanted characters. Then type in the corrections. Press the Enter key to move to the second line. The blinking insertion point will appear there now. On the second line, type in with and press the Enter key to move down to the third line. On the third line type in ToolBook. Your title should look like Figure 5–63.

Justification of Text   Now, let's center the title. Get the Arrow pointer from the Tool palette. Place the Arrow pointer inside the field and click once to select it. The handles should appear. Select Paragraph... from the Text Menu. In the Paragraph dialog box, click once on Center, which is just under the heading Alignment, as in Figure 5–64. This will set the alignment to center justification. Click on the Apply button, then click on OK. You should immediately see the results of this change.

Exiting ToolBook and Starting Up Your Book

If you would like to quit, this would be a good time to do it. Refer back to the beginning of this hands-on exercise for directions on how to quit. First, save your book. Then, select Exit from the File Menu. To start-up your book, first launch ToolBook as you had previously done. The start-up instructions are at the beginning of this exercise. Once ToolBook is up

FIGURE 5–63   Typing in a title on page one. ToolBook 1.5 for Windows, Asymetrix Corporation. (ToolBook is a registered trademark of Asymetrix.)

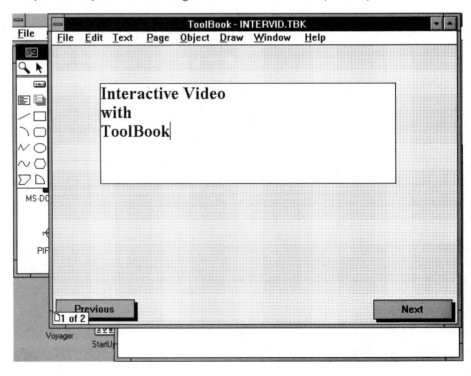

FIGURE 5–64   Centering the title. ToolBook 1.5 for Windows, Asymetrix Corporation. (ToolBook is a registered trademark of Asymetrix.)

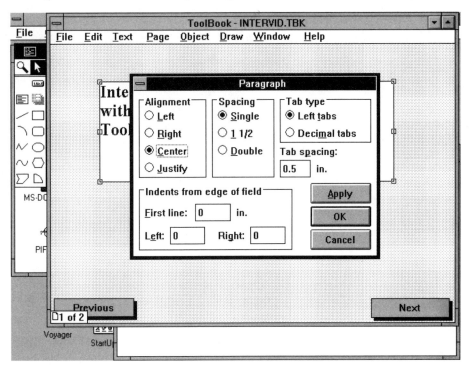

and running, from the File menu select Open.... Look through the directory until you find your book called INTERVID. Click once on it to select it. Then click on OK. This is the process for opening your book.

If you are interested in learning more about ToolBook, the following books will help you:

- The user's manuals that come with ToolBook are an excellent source of information.
- *ToolBook Companion* (1990) by Joseph R. Pierce is an intermediate-advanced book. It is published by Microsoft Press, One Microsoft Way, Redmond, WA 98052-6399.

The following hands-on exercise shows you how to add buttons to your book that will control a videodisc player. In the following, continue working with the book you just made.

Hands-On Exercise: The Voyager Videodisc ToolKit Version 1.0

The videodisc buttons that you will be putting into your book are from another book. You will be using The Voyager Videodisc ToolKit for the videodisc buttons. ToolKit contains over 60 ready-made buttons and controllers that you can copy into your own book.

Before using it, ToolKit must first be installed on your hard disk. Follow the instructions in the *User's Guide for ToolKit* on how to install it. If it is already installed, continue with the next section.

Starting Up The Voyager Videodisc ToolKit

If you have not done so already, turn on the videodisc player and monitor. Put a CAV videodisc into the player and close the door. Click once on the Program Manager button in the top left corner. It is in the left corner of the title bar. It looks like a square button with no label. It is just above the word File. From the pull-down menu, select Switch To..., as in Figure 5–65.

Then, from the task list, select Program Manager by clicking once on it. Click on the button at the bottom called Switch To. Look for the Voyager folder. In Figure 5–66, it is in the bottom left-hand corner. Double click on it to open it.

Double click on The Voyager Videodisc ToolKit to launch it, as in Figure 5–67. This action will start it up. An introductory setup screen will appear. The lights on the front panel of your videodisc player will blink. Read the text on your screen. If a message appears, click once on the appropriate button. After the introductory title screens, the Contents page will appear, as in Figure 5–68.

Let's start by familiarizing ourselves with some of the exciting capabilities found in ToolKit. Start off by clicking once on Ready-Made But-

---

FIGURE 5–65   Using the Switch To command from the File Menu. ToolBook 1.5 for Windows, Asymetrix Corporation. (ToolBook is a registered trademark of Asymetrix.

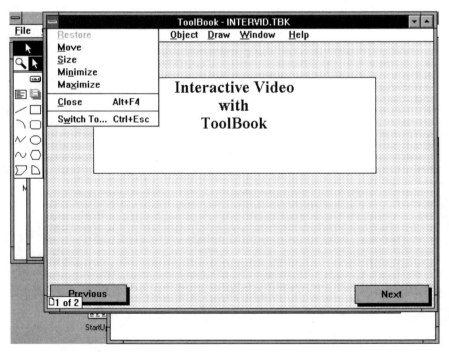

FIGURE 5–66   Opening the Voyager folder, which appears in the bottom left corner in this figure. This figure shows the Program Manager available in Microsoft Windows. Screen shot reprinted with permission from Microsoft Corporation.

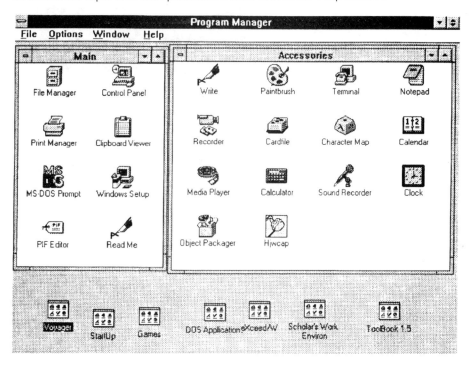

FIGURE 5–67   Launching The Voyager Videodisc ToolKit. ToolKit is published by The Voyager Company.

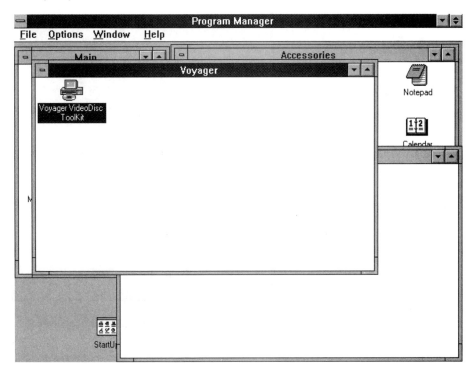

FIGURE 5-68   The Contents page from The Voyager Videodisc ToolKit Version 1.0. Courtesy of The Voyager Company.

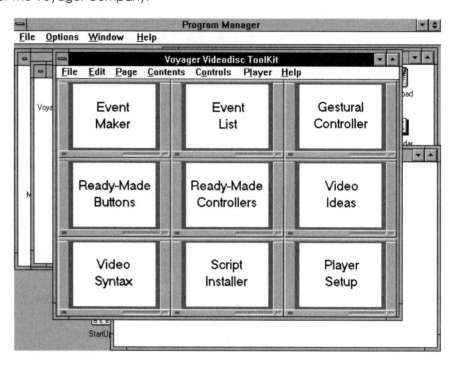

FIGURE 5-69   The menu for Ready-Made Buttons. Courtesy of The Voyager Company.

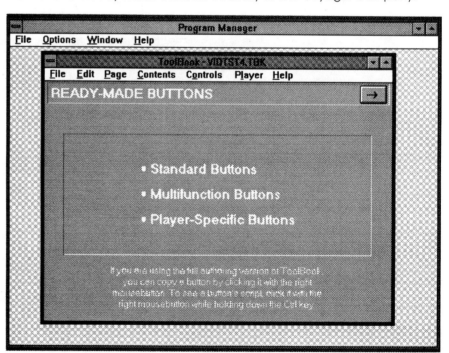

FIGURE 5-70   The pull-down Contents Menu full of commands. Courtesy of The Voyager Company.

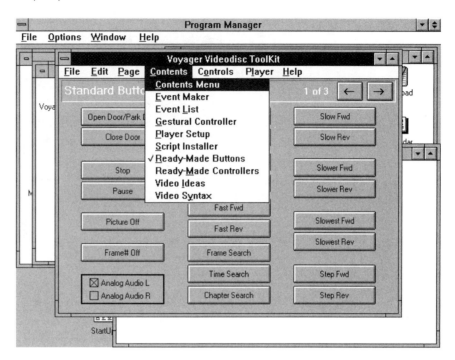

tons. From the Ready-Made Buttons Menu, as in Figure 5–69, click once on Standard Buttons. Click once on the Open Door/Park Disc button in the top left-hand corner. The door on your videodisc player will slide open. Then click once on the Close Door button. Try out some of the other buttons such as Play Fwd and Pause. Then try out Frame# On and Frame# Off. Also try Step Fwd and Step Rev.

To go back to the main Contents page, click once on Contents in the menu bar at the top of the page, as in Figure 5–70. From the Contents pull-down menu, click once on Contents Menu to go back.

Next, from the main Contents page, select Ready-Made Controllers. From the Ready-Made Controllers menu, select Universal Controller. From the Universal Controller page, as in Figure 5–71, click once on the Play > button (play forward). Try out the Stop button and the Step > button (step forward). Then click on Frame# On. Try the < Scan button (scan reverse), as well as some other buttons. After you are done trying the Universal Controller Buttons, go back to the Contents page. Do this by clicking once on Contents at the top of the page. Then, from the pull-down menu, click once on Contents Menu.

Next, from the main Contents page, select Gestural Controller. If a message appears, click on Don't Change. Now place the pointer on top of the runner on the right side of the screen just above the word Play. You do not need to click the mouse. When it is placed there, the videodisc will start playing. Move the pointer over to the word Slow. Notice that you do not need to click. The current frame number is being displayed at the bottom of the page. To try out some of the other

FIGURE 5-71   Buttons available in the Universal Controller page. Courtesy of The Voyager Company.

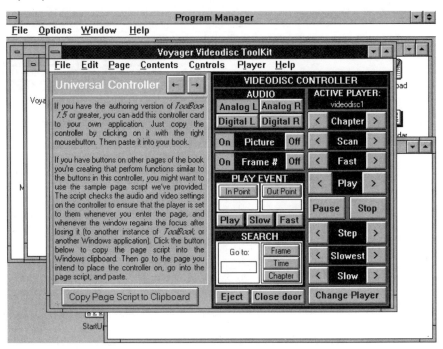

FIGURE 5-72   The Gestural Controller. Courtesy of The Voyager Company.

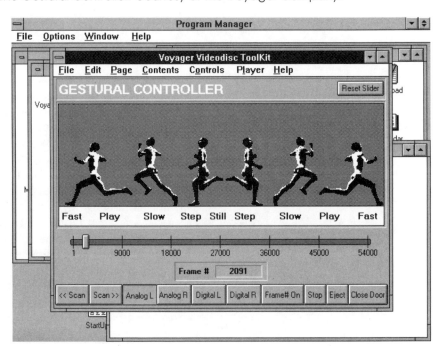

buttons, all you need to do is to place the arrow pointer over either a runner or a command beneath the runners. Just slide the arrow there and it will control the videodisc player. Figure 5-72 shows the Gestural Controller. You do not need to click the mouse button to select a command. When you are done experimenting with Gestural Controller, go back to the Contents page.

Now that you are familiar with some of the features of ToolKit, let's start working with our book.

Installing the Videodisc ToolKit Script into Your Book First, you will need to copy the Voyager Videodisc System Book called VidSys.TBK into the same directory that your INTERVID book is in. If you are working on a diskette or in a different directory, you will need to copy VidSys.TBK over to the directory that you are working in.

Second, you will need to make the appropriate link between your VidSys.TBK and with your book using the Script Installer. Click once on Script Installer. Next, click once on Install Scripts into Existing Book. Then, from the dialog box, click once on the directory that INTERVID is in. If it is in the (-c-) directory, then click on this. Otherwise, if it is in C:\toolbook, then type in C:\toolbook where you see *.TBK after the word Filename:. Then click on OK. This action will change the directory. From the list of files on the left side, as in Figure 5-73, click once on intervid.tbk to select it. Then click on OK. This will immediately begin the installation process. When the installation is done, a message will appear on the screen stating "Installation Successful!" To go on, click on OK.

FIGURE 5-73   Installing the video script into your book using the Script Installer. Courtesy of The Voyager Company.

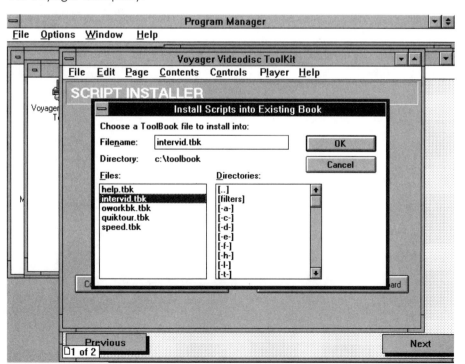

Copying Video Buttons   Go back to the main Contents page and select Ready-Made Buttons. Click once on Standard Buttons. You will be selecting three buttons from page 1 to copy to your book. You can copy a button from this page by clicking it with the right mouse button. For example, using the right mouse button, click once on the button labeled Play Fwd. Only one button at a time can be copied.

Now, switch back to your book INTERVID. Go up to the Program Manager button and select Switch To. From the list of filenames, select the name of your book by clicking on it once. Then click on the Switch To button. This will bring it to the front. Make sure you are in the Author mode. Go to page 2 in your book (if you are not there already). Then select Paste from the Edit Menu. The Play Fwd button with handles will instantly appear on your page. You can move a button by placing the Arrow pointer directly in the center of the button. Then click and drag it to a new location.

Let's copy another button over to your book. Switch over to ToolKit. Go to page 1 of Standard Buttons. Find the button labeled Pause. Using the right mouse button, click once on this button. Switch over to your book. Make sure you are in the Author mode. Then, from the Edit Menu, select Paste. Pause should instantly appear on the page. Now switch back to ToolKit and copy the button called Step Fwd to your book. Your page will probably look something like Figure 5–74.

Finally, let's test out the buttons. Go to the Reader mode. Click on the Play button and try out the other buttons. If your buttons work, skip over to the next paragraph. If they do not work, read on to restart your

FIGURE 5–74   Three videodisc buttons copied from ToolKit to your book. ToolKit is published by The Voyager Company.

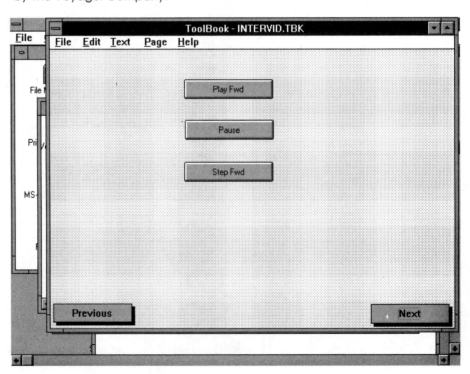

book. While in your book, select Exit from the File Menu. Then, when ToolKit appears, select Exit from the File Menu. Restart ToolBook. Select Open from the File Menu and open your book. Now go to page 2 of your book. While in the Reader mode, try out your buttons.

Finally, paste some other buttons in the same manner that you copied and pasted the other buttons. Perhaps you might want to paste an Open Door/Park Disc button. Then try out your newly pasted buttons. Remember to switch to the Reader mode with F3 in order to try them out. Be sure to save your folder before quitting.

This completes this exercise. If you are done working for now, select Exit from the File Menu. If the ToolKit is still up and running, you need to select Exit from the File Menu when it appears on the screen. When the Windows Program Manager appears, select Exit Windows from the File Menu.

Opening Your Book

First, turn on the power to the videodisc player and monitor. Insert a CAV videodisc into the player. Launch Microsoft Windows 3.1. Once Windows is running, from the Windows Program Manager, open the ToolBook folder by double clicking on it. Then launch ToolBook by double clicking on its open book icon. Select Open from the File Menu. ToolBook will display the Open dialog box. Click once on your book INTERVID and then click on OK. Select Reader from the Edit Menu. Go to page 2 of your book by clicking on the Next button. Click on your Play Fwd button. Try out your other buttons. Good work!

In this exercise, you learned how to create pages filled with a background color, text, and buttons—including videodisc buttons. The next step in working with ToolBook would be to learn how to create graphics. You must be in the Author mode to do this. ToolBook has a built-in paint and drawing program that lets you design some wonderful pictures. To start drawing, try out some of the tools available in the Tool palette, such as the rectangle tool. Later, try out some of the commands in the Draw Menu. Have fun working with ToolBook and ToolKit.

Conclusion

From this chapter, you will have realized that although both LinkWay and ToolBook can control a videodisc player, there are some unique differences between how they do it, how they work, and how they look. ToolBook requires that its videodisc buttons come from another package—a videodisc-specific tool, such as The Voyager Videodisc TookKit or Microsoft Windows 3.1 with Multimedia Extensions. Also, the overall appearance of a page created with ToolBook looks more sophisticated than pages in LinkWay. ToolBook's pages appear professionally designed, whereas LinkWay's pages look simple, blocky, and elementary. This difference may be due to the fact that LinkWay is being directed toward the K–12 educational market. Thus, the screen designs come out looking as if they are intended for the early elementary grades. ToolBook, on the other hand, is being marketed to the higher educational and corporate user. In many ways, when ToolBook is combined with

ToolKit, it is much easier to use for creating videodisc buttons than LinkWay. To create a button using ToolKit, simply point and click. Also, the scripting in ToolBook is so easy that if you are already familiar with scripting in HyperCard, you will find ToolBook simple to learn. However, scripting in LinkWay is awkward, cryptic, and difficult to remember.

In trying to select between ToolBook and LinkWay, remember who your audience is. If you are an elementary classroom teacher, then seriously consider LinkWay because of its simple presentation of pages, reasonable pricing, and the fact that everything needed to drive a videodisc player is bundled within LinkWay. You do not have to purchase anything in addition to LinkWay, whereas you will with ToolBook.

Now that you have been introduced to authoring on the MS/PC-DOS computer, have fun authoring your own customized software programs with LinkWay and ToolBook.

Suggested Learning Extensions

1. Construct a list of criteria to use in evaluating an authoring tool.
2. Compare and contrast two authoring tools and write a summary of your evaluation.
3. Review several articles on authoring tools. Write a report of your findings.
4. Contact one of the companies listed in Appendix C. Obtain a preview copy of the authoring tool. Review it and write an evaluation.
5. Using one of the authoring tools discussed in this chapter and a videodisc, create an interactive video lesson of 5 pages for a particular topic and grade level.

Chapter References and Additional Readings

Amthor, G. R. (1992–93). Getting started with multimedia: A practical tutorial. Multimedia Source Guide—Supplement to *T.H.E. Journal*, 40–49.

Asymetrix Corporation. (1991). *ToolBook 1.5 for windows*. 110-110th Avenue N.E. Suite 717, Bellevue, WA 98004. (206) 637-1500.

Asymetrix Corporation. (1991). *ToolBook author's resource kit 1.5*. 110-110th Avenue N.E. Suite 717, Bellevue, WA 98004. (206) 637-1500 or (800) 624-8999.

Bork, A. (March/April 1989). Production of technology-based learning material tools vs. authoring systems. *Instruction Delivery Systems, 3*(2), 22–24.

Brader, L. L. (1990). Tools of the courseware trade. *Tech Trends, 35*(5), 10–17.

Burtness, L. (1989). A look at IBM LinkWay. *HyperLink Magazine, 2*(3), 26–31.

BYTE. (February 1992). Asymetrix multimedia resource kit. *BYTE*, 218.

Coffee, P. (September 9, 1991). Asymetrix defies critics and captures honors. *PC Week*.

Crowell, P. (March/April 1989). Authoring systems: Genesis through relevations. *Instruction Delivery Systems, 3*(2), 19–21.

Egeland, Wood, & Zuber. (July/August 1991). Multimedia tips & techniques. *Multimedia Solutions, 5*(4), 32–33.

Greenfield, E. (August 1990). Authoring systems focus on new structure and users. *T.H.E. Journal, 18*(1), 7–10.

Hein, K. J. (August 1990). Multimedia package sparks students' imagination. *T.H.E. Journal, 18*(1), 34–35.

Heizer Software. (1991). *ConvertIt!* 1941 Oak Park Blvd., Suite 30, P.O. Box 232019, Pleasant Hill, CA 94523. (800) 888-7667.

Hertzberg, L. (November/December 1991). Multimedia authoring languages. *Electronic Learning, 11*(3), 30–32.

Hillelsohn, M. J. (Summer 1984). Benchmarking authoring systems. *Journal of Computer-Based Instruction, 11*(3), 95–97.

Huntley, J. S., & Alessi, S. M. (July–August 1987). Videodisc authoring tools: Evaluating products and a process. *Optical Information Systems,* 259-281.

IBM Corporation. *AVC.* 4111 Northside Parkway, HO4L1, Atlanta, GA 30327. (800) IBM-2468.

IBM Corporation. *Infowindows presentation system version 1.0.* 4111 Northside Parkway, HO4L1, Atlanta, GA 30327. (800) IBM-2468.

IBM Corporation. (1990). *LinkWay 2.01.* P.O. Box 1328-W, Boca Raton, FL 33429. (404) 238-3245. For educator's discounts on LinkWay or IBM hardware, call (800) IBM-2468.

IBM Corporation. (1992). *LinkWay live!* P.O. Box 1328-W, Boca Raton, FL 33429. (800) IBM-2468.

IBM Corporation. (1991). *Getting a quick start with IBM LinkWay.* P.O. Box 1328-W, Boca Raton, FL 33429. (800) IBM-2468.

Kheriaty, L. (1991). *IBM LinkWay version 2.0.* Bellingham, WA: Washington Computer Services.

Lamb, A. (1992). *IBM LinkWay creativity tool.* Orange, CA: Career Publishing Incorporated.

Lo, R., Locatis, C., Ullmer, E., Carr, V., Banvard, R., Le, Q., & Williamson, M. (February 6, 1992). *Developing a database of authoring system software.* National Library of Medicine/National Institutes of Health, Betheseda, MD 20894. (301) 496-6280. Handouts presented at the Association of Educational Communications and Technology Conference held in Washington, DC.

Locatis, C., & Carr, V. (Spring 1985). Selecting authoring systems. *Journal of Computer-Based Instruction, 12*(2), 28–33.

Locatis, C., & Carr, V. (Winter, 1988). Using a lesson-element keystroke oriented approach for estimating authoring tool efficiency. *Journal of Computer-Based Instruction, 15*(1), 23–28.

Locatis, C., Ullmer, E., Carr, V., Ranvard, R., Lo, R., Le, Q., & Williamson, M. (January, 1992). *Authoring systems.* U.S. Department of Health and Human Services, Public Health Service, National Institutes of Health, National Library of Medicine, Lister Hill National Center for Biomedical Communications, Bethesda, MD 20894. Lister Hill Monograph LHNCBC 92-1.

MacKnight, C. B., & Balagopalan, S. (Autumn 1988). Authoring systems: Some instructional implications. *Journal of Interactive Instruction Development, 1*(2), 18–24.

MacKnight, C. B., & Balagopalan, S. (Winter 1990). An evaluation tool for measuring authoring system performance. *Journal of Computing in Higher Education, 1*(2), 104–120.

Maule, R. W., Gregg, A., & Petry, J. (Fall 1991). An analysis of IBM's hypermedia authoring platforms. *Journal of Hypermedia and Multimedia Studies, 2*(1), 18–21.

Merrill, M. D. (Autumn 1985). Where is the authoring in authoring systems? *Journal of Computer-Based Instruction, 12*(4), 90–96.

Michel, S. (November/December 1991). Multimedia authoring systems: Windows makes the grade. *NewMedia*, 39–41.

Microsoft Corporation. (1992). *Windows 3.1 with multimedia extensions 1.0*. One Microsoft Way, Redmond, WA 98052-6399.

Milheim, W. D., Haag, B. B., & Nichols, P. W. (November 1991). *Authoring options for developing computer-based interactive video programs.* Handouts presented at the 33rd International Conference of the Association for the Development of Computer-Based Instructional Systems.

Monkey Tree Computer Services. *Laserlink driver*. 2707 Jefferson St., Bellingham, WA 98225. (206) 671-2545.

Murray, R. B. (April 1991). Authoring for a multi-platform world on the MAC. *Medibytes, 6*(3), 3–7.

Park, O., & Seidel, R. J. (September 1989). Evaluation criteria for selecting a CBI authoring system. *T.H.E. Journal, 17*(2), 61–68.

Pierce, J. R. (1990). *ToolBook companion*. Redmond, WA: Microsoft Press.

Pioneer Communications of America. *LD-V4200 laserdisc player*. 600 E. Crescent Ave., Upper Saddle River, NJ 07458. (201) 327-6400.

Sales, G. C. (June 1989). Repurposing: Authoring tools for videodiscs. *The Computing Teacher*, 12-14.

Tyre, T. (October 1989). Authoring packages continue to mature. *T.H.E. Journal, 17*(3), 10–18.

Voyager Company, The. (1991, 1992). *Videodisc ToolKit version 1.0*. 1351 Pacific Coast Highway, Santa Monica, CA 90401. (213) 451-1383. FAX: (310) 394-2156.

Washington Computer Services. *Vman: The LinkWay video disc manager*. 2601 North Shore Road, Bellingham, WA 98225. (206) 734-8248.

6

Creating an Interactive Video Program

Chapter Objectives

After completing this chapter, you will be able to:

❑ *Discuss the five stages in making a videodisc.*

❑ *Describe the role of scriptwriting for a videodisc.*

❑ *Describe what a storyboard is.*

❑ *Explain what a flowchart is.*

❑ *Identify the key personnel involved in the development of an interactive video product.*

❑ *Discuss the role of the educator in making a videodisc.*

❑ *Identify various activities where software programs can be of help in the creation of an interactive video program.*

Introduction

In the previous chapters, you read about interactive video as it is used in the classroom. Hopefully, you have even sat down and worked with some quality educational videodiscs. Even though you may never actually produce your own videodisc, you are probably wondering how one is made. In this chapter, you will learn about the process for making an interactive video product from beginning to end. The term *interactive videodisc* will be referred to as *IVD* for short. An IVD is a level 3 videodisc that comes with software. The software lets the user select the video segments to be played back from the videodisc. At various points in the software, the user may be given several choices to select from, as in a main menu. Depending on which choice is selected, a different video clip is played back. For an explanation of level 3 interactivity, refer back to Chapter 1. Also, look through Appendix A, which provides an extensive listing of various sources for buying IVDs.

Making an IVD—Five Stages

Similarities to Videotape

In many ways, making an IVD is similar to producing a videotape. Like a videotape, an IVD can contain full-motion video, stills, and audio. Any kind of media that can be put on a tape can also be mastered to an IVD. A major difference, though, between the two formats is that an IVD is interactive. Basically, *interactive* means that the user can select which video clips are being played from the videodisc. In Chapter 2, you worked with a variety of level 3 IVDs. Remember how you used the software to select the particular videodisc sequence to be played back?

Differences from Videotape

The major difference between a videotape and an IVD is that an IVD is interactive and a videotape is not. An IVD is usually accompanied by software, which is what makes it interactive. A videotape is considered linear in format—that is, a videotape is played back in a continuous linear fashion starting at the beginning and running through until the end. Therefore, the making of an IVD is different because of its interactivity.

Another difference is that a videodisc can have up to four independent audio tracks, whereas a videotape has only one. Most videodiscs today take advantage of only two audio tracks. Each audio track can contain different information, such as track 1 could be a narration in English while track 2 is in Spanish.

The Five Stages

Making an IVD involves five stages. They are:

- Analysis
- Design
- Development
- Production
- Evaluation

Analysis, design, and development are considered preproduction activities because they occur at the start of the project—at the planning, proposal, and design level. During the production stage, the video is produced, the software is programmed, and the video is mastered as a videodisc. Although evaluation is ongoing throughout the IVD project, it is more intensely conducted during postproduction, when the videodisc comes back from the mastering company. Figure 6–1 diagrams the sequence of stages in the IVD project.

Educators today are being called on more frequently to consult on IVD projects for the classroom. Educators can be involved in both preproduction and postproduction activities where they consult on the effectiveness of various learning activities, the quality of the screen designs, the appropriateness to the grade level, and all evaluation

FIGURE 6-1   The five stages in an interactive videodisc (IVD) project.

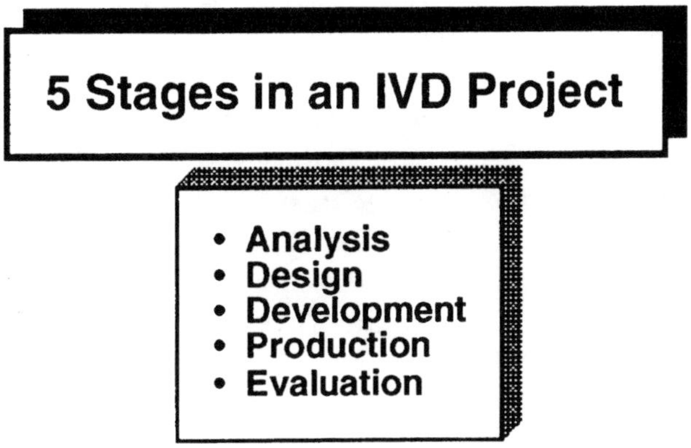

5 Stages in an IVD Project

- **Analysis**
- **Design**
- **Development**
- **Production**
- **Evaluation**

activities that occur while the IVD is being developed, as well as afterwards. Generally, educators are not involved in the actual development and production of the videodisc and software. This is typically done by professional software programmers and video producers.

Stage One: Analysis

During analysis, the following preproduction tasks are completed:

- The audience is determined. The audience consists of those individuals who will be the primary end-users of the IVD—such as your students. Once determined, the audience is analyzed in terms of its behaviors, attitudes, and preferences.
- The learning objectives are written. Objectives describe what will be accomplished by the audience as a result of using the IVD.
- The subject matter is thoroughly researched.
- Various treatment ideas are explored for how to present the content and story.
- An investigation is made of the various available audiovisual media that could be put on the videodisc.
- The delivery platform is determined. *Delivery platform* is the hardware that the IVD will be used on, such as a an IBM PS/2 computer and a Pioneer videodisc player.
- A schedule and budget are proposed.

Understanding Your Audience

Audience analysis is carried out by an instructional designer or a team of instructional designers. An *instructional designer* is responsible for the design of instruction presented in the IVD. In determining what kind of instruction will be on the IVD, the instructional designer will compose a profile of who the typical user is. To do this, demographic data about the audience are collected, such as where the user will use the IVD, the age range or grade of the users, as well as their sex, ethnic backgrounds, and occupations. Following are some ways to gather data about the target audience:

- Conduct written surveys with the audience.
- Interview the audience. The interview itself could be recorded on videotape or an audio cassette tape.
- Personally observe typical users, such as students as they work on their assignments in the classroom. The observation could be photographed or videotaped.
- Read articles on both local and national levels concerning issues related to the audience and their interests.
- Conduct a *needs analysis.* Find out what the audience already knows and is able to perform, and what they should know and be able to do. Determine what their needs are—what they need to know and do.
- Assess your audience's entry-level skills and prerequisite knowledge. (what the learner already knows prior to learning the lesson).
- Determine any psychological factors influencing the users' learning. In addition to observable factors, internal unobservable factors—such as math anxiety and test anxiety—are key in understanding the audience.
- Analyze the audience's preferences toward learning. Do the users prefer particular colors or a particular learning style, such as hands-on applied learning? What kind of music do they enjoy?
- Determine any cultural factors that could influence the users' learning. Cultural anthropology defines *culture* as the values, attitudes, and beliefs shared by a group of people. Certain ethnic, professional, or regional groups (such as the Pennsylvania Dutch) share certain rituals, beliefs even music, and common styles of dress. Teenagers from an inner-city culture may use certain jargon, music, or ways of dressing that could be incorporated into the IVD—if these teenagers will be the intended audience.
- Assess the audience's physical needs. Are there any disabilities that need to be considered? Perhaps a larger-sized print needs to be used on the computer screen if the program is being used with people who have visual impairments.
- Examine the audience's access to the IVD. Will they have all the time in the world to work with the IVD?
- Determine how familiar the audience is with technology. Will they need any kind of training to be able to operate the IVD hardware?

Defining the Learning Objectives

In determining what the audience will learn, the instructional designer writes out *learning objectives.* Objectives describe the learning that will take place or what the user will be expected to know, do, or feel after using the IVD. For example, "By the completion of the IVD, the users who are preservice teachers will be able to write lesson objectives that include the following parts—a description of the audience, the expected behavior, any conditions affecting the learning, and a degree of measurement that can be used to assess the learning." As identified in this example, there are four parts to an objective:

- Audience: The objective includes a brief description of who the audience is (such as fourth-graders).
- Behavior: The objective describes the kind of behavior the audience will be able to perform after working with the IVD. For example, will the learner solve a mathematical problem, write an essay, design a spreadsheet, diagnose a particular kind of engine problem, or differentiate between different furniture styles?
- Conditions: An objective will identify any conditions that may affect how well the audience performs, such as if there is a time restriction, if there is limited access to the videodisc hardware, or if certain materials are unavailable. Some example conditions are "given 30 minutes" or "given HyperCard ver. 2.1."
- Degree: An objective also specifies the degree of how well the learning was accomplished. A degree measures the performance by the audience. A statement about degree can be written as "How much of the task is finished? How correct is it? How well was it done? How safely was it performed? How long did it take to complete?"

Objectives are set up from the start of the IVD. Then, as the IVD is developed, they are continually referred to for assessment. They are used to evaluate the effectiveness of how the content is presented in the IVD. After the IVD has been finalized, objectives are a way of assessing the audience's performance to see what learning occurred. If the audience learned what was specified in the objectives, then the IVD is considered a success.

Exploring Various Treatment Ideas

Once the audience is determined and the objectives are clarified, a *treatment* is written to describe how the content will be presented in the IVD. A treatment is a narrative description of the IVD's design. It tells the story and who the major characters are. At the analysis stage, a group of people will brainstorm various ideas for the treatment. Generally, scriptwriters are primarily responsible for coming up with a treatment. Sometimes, the instructional designer and producer will also get involved. Once an idea is agreed upon, the scriptwriter will write a rough treatment of how the content will be presented—the overall story, who the main characters are, and basically how the IVD will work (that is, what will be on the computer screen and what will be played back from the videodisc). A treatment is like telling a friend about a movie, where you briefly summarize the plot and theme, describe the personalities and roles of the main characters, provide a few examples that are key to understanding the nature of the movie, and conclude with the movie's ending.

At this time, the treatment is considered a starting place for discussing the idea. The treatment gives the look and feel of the IVD. Figure 6–2 shows two pages from a treatment. Although this treatment was devel-

FIGURE 6–2   Two pages from a treatment created by Bob Mohl and Margo Nanny, courtesy of Aurora Media. After the treatment is developed, a script is written. (Refer to Figure 6–6 for the corresponding script.)

Objective:

To learn about:
   a)   planet order
   b)   size of planets and planetary distances
   c)   relative scale of planets and orbits
   d)   relations between distance and time (and speed)
   e)   interesting information about the various planets in the form of data and images.

To develop an intuitive understanding based on *experiencing* scale model travel rather than emphasizing facts and numbers.

To achieve two general pedagogical principles:
   a)   learn about the concept of "Model"
   b)   learn the value of research and planning

Methodology:

The sun has been shrunk down to 8 feet in diameter and the solar system has been layed out on a desert highway—making Pluto the size of a peanut and putting its orbit 6.5 miles down the road.

There are two ways to use the program:
   1)   as a database:
        Images/data of planets are arranged in order. You access information in a way very similar to the Visual Almanac Collection. The end of each planet section includes the Planetary Highway images of scale size, the road size sign, and the footage along the road to the next planet.
   2)   as a role-playing game:
        You play the role of an interplanetary taxi driver picking up passengers and taking them to destinations around the solar system. To be successful, they have to learn about the order of the planets, the time and distance between them, and some interesting facts about different planets.

Time and distance are crucial core concepts. To add to the challenge, there are built-in time/distance limits in playing the game.

Game Goal:

Complete missions by traveling along a scale model of the solar system.

You have a taxi and pick up passengers who are real characters (i.e., unreal characters) and drop them. Unfortunately, they never seem to be able to specify their destination precisely. They have a mission in mind. To help them find a solution, you have to use/discover the core concepts of Planetary Taxi—planet order, relative size, scale and distance, as well as some of the most characteristics of various planets. You may want to consult the information database to verify certain relationships before actually embarking on a trip of several years.

Your ultimate goal is to complete as many missions as possible before your cab falls apart (at 10 trillion miles). Your "score" is based on total tips collected from satisfied passengers.

Caveats:
There are a couple of liberties that the simulation takes that have to be clearly acknowledged:
1) Planets are (almost) never lined up the way they seem to be on the Planetary Highway, which really marks the orbits rather than the actual planets. It is a fortuitous time when all the planets have lined up (in the year 8797987987).
2) Going from the scale model to the actual NASA photos mixes the metaphor.

This title will apply to 2nd grade through 8th grade. The reading level and interface will be optimized for 4th and 5th grades.

Features:
Speed and Time:
You always travel at rocket speed. Traveling from the sun to Pluto in "taxi time" will clock 17 years on your meter. In "real time," it will take 22 seconds.

Communications always travel at the speed of light. Transmission time will be displayed as minutes in "taxi time." In "real time", the distance to Pluto will be covered in a couple of seconds.

Characters:
A lot of personality and humor is added by characters in the form of "interplanetary passengers." They are weird-looking cartoon aliens with funny monologs. (Still graphic plus audio.)

Levels:
You will be able to play at three different levels:
Driver Training School
Rookie
Expert

In Driver Training School (for first-time users and youngest kids), you will be introduced to the fundamental concepts:
What is a scale model?
What are the relative order, distances and sizes of the planets?
How do you use the basic interface in your cab?
No score is kept. You are not racing against the clock.

As a Rookie, you will go pick up passengers and go on missions. Score is kept. The game does not have an overall time/distance limit (though individual missions might.)

As an Expert, you will try to find the most efficient solutions to your passengers' requests. You are trying to complete as many missions as possible before time/distance run out.

Missions:
Missions—Driver Training School (no clock, no score):
1) *How Big?*
The sun has been reduced to 8 feet. How big are the rest of the planets? Think about it. Imagine. Write down your guesses on a piece of paper. Ready? OK. Here's your " mission": Find out which scale model picture (vegetable) matches each planet. {*Is there a goal??*}
2) *What Is the Order?*
Here, the planets are listed in alphabetic order. But which one comes first in the solar system? You will need to know this to drive passengers to their destinations. Ready to see..

oped for an interactive CD-ROM entitled "Planetary Taxi," a treatment for an interactive videodisc would be written in a similar manner. In writing a treatment, a difference between a CD-ROM and an interactive video program is that the visuals from a CD-ROM are displayed on the computer screen. The visuals from a videodisc, on the other hand, can be displayed either on the computer screen or on a separate monitor, depending on how the program is initially designed and developed. The treatment would be similar for both if the visuals are being displayed in a window on the computer screen.

Researching the Content

The *content* is the subject matter, theme, or topic. Here, the instructional designer is researching, writing, and determining the content. In researching the subject matter, the instructional designer will review articles, manuals, books, and even audiovisual media (such as software, filmstrips, slides, audiotapes, films, and videotapes) that are on the topic. The instructional designer may also want to seek out *subject matter experts (SME)*—individuals who unquestionably are recognized as authorities or experts on the subject. The SMEs can tell you what instructional strategies have been more effective with their students and will keep you abreast of the latest research, theories, and methodologies being used in the field. Educators may consult in this phase of the project as the SMEs. The instructional designer will also need to determine why an IVD is the best medium for the topic. In other words, a rationale needs to be developed to justify the strengths of using an IVD over other kinds of media, since an IVD is probably the most expensive medium to produce.

After the content is researched, the instructional designer will put together a content report outlining the major and minor ideas. A content report is like a table of contents for a textbook, outlining all the major topics or chapter headings that will be in the IVD.

Creating an Inventory of Various Available Audiovisual Media

If you are on a limited budget, knowing what resources are available might affect the storyline. Check out various public domain sources for media, such as the NASA computer animations of Mars available from the Jet Propulsion Lab. Examine these resources for their quality and usability in the IVD.

Determining the Delivery Platform: The Hardware

The *delivery platform* is the hardware (computer, videodisc player, monitor) that will be used to deliver the IVD. The basic components of an interactive level 3 IVD are a videodisc player, video monitor, and computer. Some additional components that may be considered are: Do you need a color monitor? Or will a black-and-white monochrome monitor suit your needs? Do you need a system capable of displaying everything on one screen? Or are two screens acceptable where the videodisc sequences are displayed on a video monitor separate from the computer screen? The differences between a single- and multiple-screen setup are described here.

Single-Screen Setup   A single-screen setup is where the videodisc sequences are displayed on the same screen as the text and graphics from the computer software.

Multiple-Screen Setup   A multiple-screen setup involves two separate monitors—a computer screen as well as a separate video monitor for playing back the video clips coming from the videodisc. Information from the software—such as menus, text, animations, and any places requiring the user's input—are all presented on the computer screen. The second monitor displays all the videodisc-based sequences coming from the videodisc.

Is touch input needed? Another consideration in determining the delivery platform is the kind of interaction occurring between the user and the IVD itself. A typical input device is a keyboard or mouse; another is a *touch screen.* Figure 6–3 shows a typical touch screen called TouchWindow by Edmark. TouchWindow is available for the Ap-

FIGURE 6–3   A touch screen is an input device that allows the user to make choices by simply touching the screen, as shown here. The touch screen displayed in this figure is called TouchWindow by Edmark. TouchWindow photo courtesy of Edmark Corporation.

ple II, PC/MS-DOS, Macintosh, and Amiga computers. With a touch screen, the user makes choices by touching the computer screen with her or his finger. For example, to make a choice from the main menu, the user simply touches it. A touch screen eliminates the need for a keyboard or mouse.

A level 3 IVD requires the use of a computer. How do you determine which computer to use? The best choice is to select the one with which the user is already familiar. The most popular computers in schools are Apple IIGS, Macintosh, and MS-DOS computers. Once the computer is selected, other decisions need to be made, such as how much RAM to add to the computer or if external speakers are needed.

IVD Delivery Platform Checklist Following is a checklist of considerations for determining the type of delivery platform:

- Types of Computer Hardware: Macintosh IIsi, Macintosh Performa IIfx, Macintosh LC, Apple IIGS, Amiga 3000, IBM PS/2 Model 55, IBM PS/2 Ultimedia Model 57 SLC, Tandy Sensation!, MS/PC-DOS compatible, or other types

- Special Hardware Needs: Additional memory requirements, such as 8 MB of RAM, video card, audio card, video motion adapter card, video capture cards, video overlay boards, cables, a VGA graphics card to display high-resolution graphics, 20 MB hard disk, cable to videodisc player, and gender changer

- Types of Display: Single-screen or multiple-screen setup, color or monochrome computer screen, touch screen, the size of the videodisc monitor (13", 21", etc.), a projection unit for whole-class instruction such as a LCD projection pad, and the type of graphic resolution for an MS/PC-DOS computer such as CGA displays graphics in low resolution and VGA displays them in high resolution

- Types of Videodisc Player: Some level 3 players include the Pioneer LD-V2200, CLD-V2400, LD-V4200, LD-V4400, and LD-V8000 player or the Sony MDP-1100 and LDP-1450 (the more expensive the player, the faster the access time to play back a desired video frame; level 3 videodisc players are discussed more thoroughly in Chapter 1).

- Peripherals: Printer, speakers, image scanner, CD-ROM drive, digitizer for audio input, microphone, videotape player/recorder, camcorder, audio cassette deck, stereo receiver, compact disc player, and TV

- Types of Input Devices: Mouse, keyboard, touch screen, voice-activated, touch control panel, special keypad, barcode reader, hand-held remote control, computer software, and control panel on front of videodisc player

The best way to determine the delivery platform is to use something with which your users are already familiar. Making the wrong decisions about hardware can be costly and result in not accomplishing the learning objectives.

Establishing a Project Schedule and Budget

Before an IVD is undertaken, a budget and time schedule are set. In many ways, the budget will determine the level of sophistication that can be considered for the video production. For example, a simple panning of a photograph may achieve the same effect at a lower cost than a complicated on-location shot with hired actors.

The *project manager* is the person who manages the schedule, people, and money. Sometimes, the producer and project manager are the same person. The project manager locates, organizes, arranges, and schedules the talent, equipment, locations, and any other materials pertinent to the production. After setting up the schedule and budget, and hiring the personnel, the project manager then goes about managing the video production to assure that it is completed within budget and on schedule.

Project management software can be very useful in organizing the schedule, personnel, and completion dates, referred to as *milestones*. Using project management software, the entire production can be organized and viewed in terms of hours, days, weeks, quarters, or years. Project management software is an integration of various programs, including spreadsheets, calendars, report and memo generators, and chart creators. A project can be mapped out graphically with charts, schedules, budgets, time lines, graphs, project reports, and calendars. Project management products for the Macintosh are MacProject Pro, Microsoft Project and FastTrack Schedule. Time Line for Windows, Super-Project for Windows, Microsoft Project for Windows, and On Target are project management packages for the MS/PC-DOS machine with Windows.

Evaluating at the Analysis Stage

Due to the huge investment of money, time, and creative energies, it is absolutely essential that the quality of the IVD project be evaluated from the start. At the analysis stage, the project manager and producer can assess the various written materials, called *deliverables*. Following is a list of deliverables that are produced during the analysis stage:

- Written audience profile
- Written treatment
- Written objectives
- Description of delivery platform
- Written content outline
- Proposed personnel assignment (actors, software programmers, scriptwriters, camera operators, editors, etc.)
- Printed project management schedule and budget proposal

The deliverables—such as the written treatment, objectives, audience analysis, and content outline—can be judged for their overall quality. Are the ideas exciting and motivating? Do the objectives fit the state curricular framework for the specified subject matter? Does the treatment promote cooperative learning and multidisciplinary learning?

Is the amount of detail in the content outline appropriate for teaching the lesson? Are the characters believable? Is the storyline appropriate for the specified age level of the audience? Will the storyline accomplish the learning objectives? Were the deliverables produced on time and within budget? The evaluation can start off with a "walk-through" of the treatment, which basically means that the treatment is read out loud and then discussed in terms of its strengths and weaknesses. Then the objectives can be read out loud to see how well they coincide with the storyline described in the treatment. The producer may want to involve several key personnel in the walk-through, such as the scriptwriters, instructional designers, SMEs, as well as some educators. Recommendations are then made and given back to the scriptwriters who will then revise the treatment based on this input.

Stage Two: Design

At the design stage, the following activities are completed:

- The instructional strategies are determined.
- The scope and sequence of the content are specified.
- The visual and audio media are selected.
- The treatment is finalized.
- A draft IVD script is written.

The design phase transforms the written documents produced during the analysis stage—such as the objectives, content report, audience profile, and treatment ideas—into a structured plan of development.

Determining Instructional Strategies

Instructional strategies are ways to teach the content effectively. Usually, it is the job of the instructional designer to determine the appropriate instructional strategies. Educators can make wonderful contributions here since they know from personal classroom experience what motivates students to learn. Various instructional strategies include case studies, scientific demonstrations, simulations, comparisons of concepts, hands-on applications of knowledge, summarizations, introductions, and reinforcement of learning.

Following are some instructional design guidelines that can help the instructional designer make decisions about the design of the IVD.

User Control   Users should be actively selecting which paths they want to take through the instructional content. In order to do this, the instructional designer must think through all the possible moves that the users could make at every point of the program. The users should be able to step forward, backward, back to the beginning of the sequence, exit out to the main menu, quit out of the program, and link to other related content areas in the program that provide greater detail, such as definitions and maps. Users should be able to control the pace and speed at which the instruction is presented. They should also be able to repeat the information, if needed.

The IVD program should provide for various levels of users. Advanced learners should have the opportunity to skip topics with which they are already familiar and start with the ones that they want to learn. An effective IVD lets the users take responsibility for their own learning by letting them make their own decisions.

Reinforcement When the user responds to a question with the correct answer, acknowledge this with reinforcement. Learners need positive reinforcement, telling them that they are on the right track. Positive reinforcement serves as a source of motivation and as a reward for a job well done. If the user inputs the wrong answer, provide guidance on why it is wrong and what needs to be done to make it correct.

Feedback Simple *feedback* occurs when you press the wrong key and hear a beep. The program is telling you that this is not an appropriate choice and you need to press another key. An IVD should also provide feedback regarding where the user is in relation to the total program. Users like to know their location in the total program. They want to know how much of the instructional content has been completed and how much more needs to be done. Figure 6–4 shows a visual map of a student's location within a program.

Direct Address *Direct address* is a video technique where an actor breaks from the scene to turn around and talk directly into the camera. The actor appears to be having a one-on-one conversation with the viewer (Awardy & Gayeski, 1989). Direct address is sometimes referred to

FIGURE 6–4 A map showing the current location of where a student is within the total program is a helpful device. This picture is from the Help section in HyperCard 1.2.5, which is published by the Claris Corporation. HyperCard software is © 1987–1993 Claris Corporation. All rights reserved. HyperCard is a registered trademark of Claris Corporation.

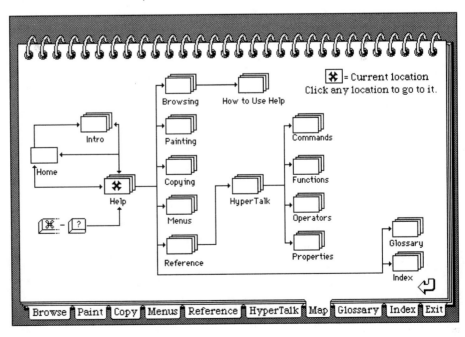

as a *cut-away shot*. Direct address personalizes the nature of the IVD and reduces the feeling of being "talked at," as in a lecture. Use direct address whenever possible.

Show Motion   As a result of watching TV programs, videos, and movies, today's audiences expect to see full-motion video played back from the videodisc. There are a variety of ways to show motion. For example, the camera can zoom in on an interesting part of the scene. Or the camera can change its angles from straight on, to looking down, up, and over someone's shoulder, as if the scene is seen from this person's eyes. A lengthy motion sequence can be broken into shorter sequences. When using a still—such as photograph, poster, diagram, or artwork—create motion by panning the camera over the still.

The information presented on the computer screen should also show motion to keep the user motivated. Some techniques for showing motion on the computer screen are the following:

- Highlighting: When the user selects an item presented on the computer screen, change its color, highlight it, or dim it. This flash between color tones indicates that the item has been selected. This is an effective yet simple way to provide feedback to the user.

- Color Banding: Use color banding when presenting a menu. *Color banding* is the sequential cycling through of various colors on the computer screen. The colors continue to cycle through the menu choices like a moving rainbow. This cycling stops when a choice is made.

- Simple Movement: Important points can be brought to the user's attention with moving lines, flashing colors, flashing patterns, and blinking. For example, a new term can be emphasized by having a simple white rectangle quickly drawn around it. The user's eyes will immediately be drawn to the movement.

- Flying Titles: *Flying titles* are lines of text that quickly fly onto the screen line by line.

- Computer Animations: Use computer animations to illustrate concepts visually and to simulate physical events. For example, bar charts can grow in front of the user's eyes, comparing a bank's increased profits over the previous year. In Interactive NOVA: Animal Pathfinders by Scholastic Software, the user assumes the role of an investigative reporter in a graphically rich computer-based simulation. In the Activities section, the user searches for clues about why loggerhead turtles are disappearing at such an alarming rate. The investigation begins in the office of noted reptile scientist Dr. Eltrut. The user starts by opening a desk drawer with a mouse click. A videotape is found inside of the drawer. A click on the VCR plays the videotape. A mouse click on the attaché case shown in Figure 6–5 opens it so that a clue can be put inside. Animations such as the opening of the attaché case let the user see the immediate results of her or his actions. Also, the animations make the interactions more life-like.

Narration: In addition to showing motion in the video and on the computer screen, the narration can also be stated in an uplifting and moving manner. The narration needs to be stated enthusiastically, as in an

FIGURE 6-5   Interactive NOVA: Animal Pathfinders by Scholastic Software is a computer-based simulation filled with graphically rich animations.

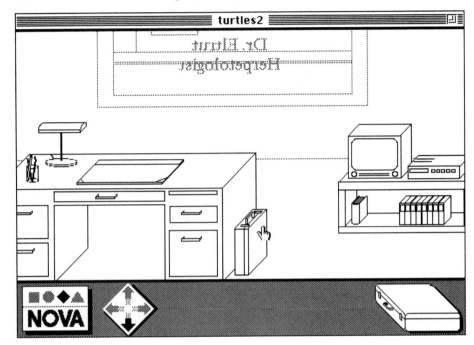

everyday conversation, rather than in a formal, academic lecture style. The following are some narration techniques:

- Select a voice that the audience can relate to. If the IVD is for the primary grades, select a child or a familiar personality, such as a sports figure.

- Change the narrators for variety as well as for differentiating among the various topics. The voice of the narrator can be switched from a male to a female voice or to a different voice tone and style. Perhaps one narrator could introduce the topic, another could discuss everyday applications of the topic, and a third could summarize the major ideas. Possibly, different narrators could address different menu items.

- Use On-Camera Narrators: The use of on-camera live narration is far more effective than voice-overs. Viewers like to see the face of the person talking. They want to relate to the narrator.

- Mix the Narration with Background Music: There is no doubt that music can create a mood. Different audiences relate to different kinds of music. The right choice of music can motivate the user and make the instructional content more inviting. Use music to enhance the overall presentation of the instructional content.

Use of Humor   Find ways and places to interject humor. Humor helps alleviate the stress the user might be feeling. When humor is used appropriately, users are better able to retain the information. For example, Interactive NOVA: Animal Pathfinders (discussed in Chapter 2) has effectively used games and humorous cartoons in teaching significant concepts about wildlife protection to children.

Determining the Scope and Sequence of the Content

Scope and sequence determine how the instructional content is organized and presented. *Scope* is what and how much is taught. In determining the scope, the instructional designer will answer the question, What does the user need to know or do in order to effectively accomplish the objectives? *Sequence* indicates the sequential order in which the content is presented. Some concepts need to be taught before others.

Specifying the Audio and Visual Media

Earlier in the analysis phase, a list of all the available audio and visual media was compiled. From this list, the media elements that will actually be used in the final IVD need to be identified. Any media elements that will need to be produced from scratch are also described at this time.

Finalizing the Treatment

At the design stage, the treatment is revised by incorporating the instructional strategies and how the audio and video elements fit in. This activity is done by the scriptwriter. The instructional designer may also consult on this task. The treatment assembles all the information, including descriptions of the stories and characters, interactions with the computer, instructional strategies to be applied, and the various audio and visual elements. Following are some guidelines for finalizing the treatment:

- Writing a treatment for an IVD differs from traditional video productions because an IVD is interactive. The final IVD treatment consists of independent scenarios, segments, or events. Each event is a specific set of videodisc frames, usually containing sound and motion, played back as one video segment. At various points in the software, the viewer may be given a choice of options from which to select. For example, a user may be given a main menu that presents four options. When the user makes a choice, then the software links to the selected event and the corresponding video segment from the videodisc is played back. In this example, there would be four video segments correlated to the four menu options.
- The IVD treatment describes in detail each video event as it will appear on the monitor. The written treatment is supplemented with artist sketches, called a *storyboard,* illustrating the video events. A storyboard is a series of small consecutive sketches highlighting key movements in the video. Each sketch describes the action and camera shots. The sketches are arranged sequentially, like a comic strip, matching the development of the storyline.
- The treatment describes the kind of instructional strategies used. The treatment also indicates the kind of menus, exercises, simulations, problem-solving exercises, and quizzes.

After the treatment is finalized, analyze it carefully for the following:

- How well does it meet the original objectives?
- Is the sequencing of instructional content effective?
- Is the storyline continuous?
- Are the characters convincing?
- Is the overall mood projected in the storyline successful?
- How effectively do the instructional activities match the needs of the audience and the teaching of the content?

A finalized treatment is like a blueprint for everything that follows. All video production activities that follow are based on the finalized treatment produced here.

Drafting an IVD Script

Scriptwriters write scripts. If you are an excellent writer, then you might be called on for writing the script. A *script* is a written account of the video recording. Later, the director will follow the script in shooting the video. The emphasis of a script is the dialog or audio. Usually, the scriptwriter writes the words first and then fits the video images to the words. An IVD script is different from a traditional script because of its interactivity. Figure 6–6 illustrates a script written for an interactive CD-ROM product. The user gets to respond to questions presented on the computer screen. (A script for an interactive video program would be similar to the one presented in Figure 6–6.)

After the script is written, auditioning of talent begins. In the script is specified the dialog, which is termed the *copy*. Copy is what the actors say on camera and what is read outloud by the narrators. The script also identifies the exact kind of music to be played, any sound effects (SFX), where the voice and music would be mixed, fade-ins and fade-outs, and the specifics of the other audio tracks.

In the script, each event is described, noting the direction and angle of the camera, the type of shots (such as a close-up), the setting, how the event/scene starts, and the location for the shooting (such as on location in front of the university library's main doors). Sets and props are described in the script. The length/time of each event is given. Skilled scriptwriters know the kind of actors they need and will actually write the words to match their personalities. Instructions regarding the character's feelings are discussed, such as the actor is sad, depressed, and tired looking. Any special actions such as waving, turning, or yawning are noted.

Each event is labeled with an identifying number, which will be referred to later in the storyboard and *flowchart*—a software diagram representing the way the software works. As revisions are made to the script, a new version number is given and perhaps the date of the change. Software, such as the Interactive Video Design Toolkit (IVD Toolkit) by Electronic Vision Inc., can be used for scriptwriting. Figure 6–7 illustrates an example script created with IVD Toolkit.

The most important goal of a script is in determining the final look, feel, and quality of the IVD program. A well-conceived script is what

FIGURE 6–6   A script written by Bob Mohl, courtesy of Aurora Media, for an interactive CD-ROM called "Planetary Taxi." (This script corresponds to the treatment presented in Figure 6–2.)

Preliminary Sample Mission Scripts

Note: "Hint" is going to disappear. It will be imbedded in the Failure Result. So, it looks like a special HINT BUTTON will not be needed.

Bob: Here is some preliminary copy. There is a lot of audio. We will try to have a minimum of text displayed which will function to accompany and summarize the audio.

High Jumper

Audio
I have just set the world record for the high jump: 7 feet 2 inches! (proudly) Now I want to find new heights to scale. How about the Interplanetary Record? Where can you take me to make the all-time high jump? Take me to the planet I can jump the highest on. And we have to get there in less than 10 years. Otherwise I'll be past my prime.

Text
My world high jump record is 7' 2".
Your mission: to help me set the Interplanetary record
Which Planet????

Hint
The lower the gravity, the higher I can jump.

Result
Failure: Oh no. This is even worse than I did on earth. Thanks (sarcastically). Please try somewhere with less gravity.
Failure: Hmm. This is the same as on earth. Where on earth did you take me?? Please try somewhere with less gravity.
Partial Success: Not bad. Not bad. This is higher than my jump on earth—even though it's not a interplanetary record. Mission accomplished. Here's a little tip.
Almost Success: Fantastic. Look at that height. If this isn't the record, I bet it is very very close. Good job choosing this planet. Mission accomplished. Here's a big tip.
Success: Unbelievable! The all-time Interplanetary Record. I did it. And you did it. You got me here. Mission accomplished. You have earned a big tip.

Caveat
Of course, no one could really high jump here.
   It's too hot to survive.
   You couldn't breathe.
   etc. (need explanations to cover all situations)

Shortest Year
Audio
Every year I make New Year's Resolutions. And every year I break them after about three months. I have good intentions. If only the year were shorter, I know I could keep from breaking my New Year's Resolutions. Take me to a planet where the year is less than three months long.

FIGURE 6-7   An example of a script for an IVD created using Interactive Video Design Toolkit by Electronic Vision Inc. Software such as this can help you keep track of all the elements that go into an IVD project.

INTRAVENOUS THERAPY SCRIPT		Page 1	2/4/93

Chapter 3 Scene 5	Audio 1	Audio 2
Video Close-up of order that reads "Start IV of 1000cc 5% Dextrose in Water. Infuse at 100cc/hour.	Determine the need to start the IV. You may not need an order to restart an IV that was discontinued because of complications.	

Chapter 3 Scene 6	Audio 1	Audio 2
Video Close-up of the order	The elements of the order include Type of solution, amount of solution, and rate of infusion.	No, you must consult the Physician's orders to begin setting the rate

eventually moves the audience to laugh, think, and be inspired. The script should motivate, challenge, and excite the audience.

Evaluating at the Design Stage

During the design stage, two of the most important deliverables to be created in the total IVD project are examined—the final treatment and the script. In evaluating the quality of the script and treatment, ask the following questions:

- Does the script successfully tell the stories and present the instruction in the most effective manner?

- How well does the script and treatment meet the original objectives and the needs of the target audience?
- Are the script and treatment written at the correct level for the target audience?
- Does the dialog fit the characters as well as the storyline?
- Is music used effectively to motivate learners and hold their attention?
- Are graphics on the computer screen frivolous or are they supportive of the learning that is taking place?

The treatment and script are the master plan for the entire IVD production. Errors that go undetected at this phase end up being very costly and time consuming during the video production. If these deliverables pass the test, move on to the next phase—the development stage.

Stage Three: Development

During the development stage, the following activities are completed:

- Draw a storyboard.
- Write a production script.
- Create a flowchart representing the software interface to the videodisc.
- Develop a production database.
- Produce original artwork, computer graphics, and animations.
- Conduct a rehearsal.

During this preproduction stage, all the preparation for the video production is developed.

To start, the producer will hire a *director* who will then assemble a camera crew and cast. The director works closely with the producer and project manager to keep within the budget and schedule. The director directs the camera crew on the camera shots. The director also directs the actors—telling them how to act, what to say, and what to do. In shooting the video, the director follows the script. Yet, the director may deviate from the script in applying her/his own interpretation.

Before the cameras start rolling, sets are built, props are prepared, and all the equipment is brought to location. Any computer graphics, animations, or video graphics are also developed at this time.

Drawing a Storyboard

A *storyboard* is a graphic representation of all the visual elements described in script, such as stills, full-motion video, computer graphics, animations, text on the computer screen, menus, Chyron-generated text overlays, and special effects. Figure 6–8 shows a storyboard page drawn by Bob Mohl and Margo Nanny of Aurora Media for an interactive CD-ROM product called "Planetary Taxi." Because this is for a CD-

FIGURE 6-8   A storyboard page drawn by Bob Mohl and Margo Nanny of Aurora Media for an interactive CD-ROM product called "Planetary Taxi." Refer to Figure 6–6, which shows the script written for this product. Also, look at Figures 6–9, 6–10, and 6–11 for the written explanations corresponding to the screens depicted in this storyboard. Courtesy of Aurora Media.

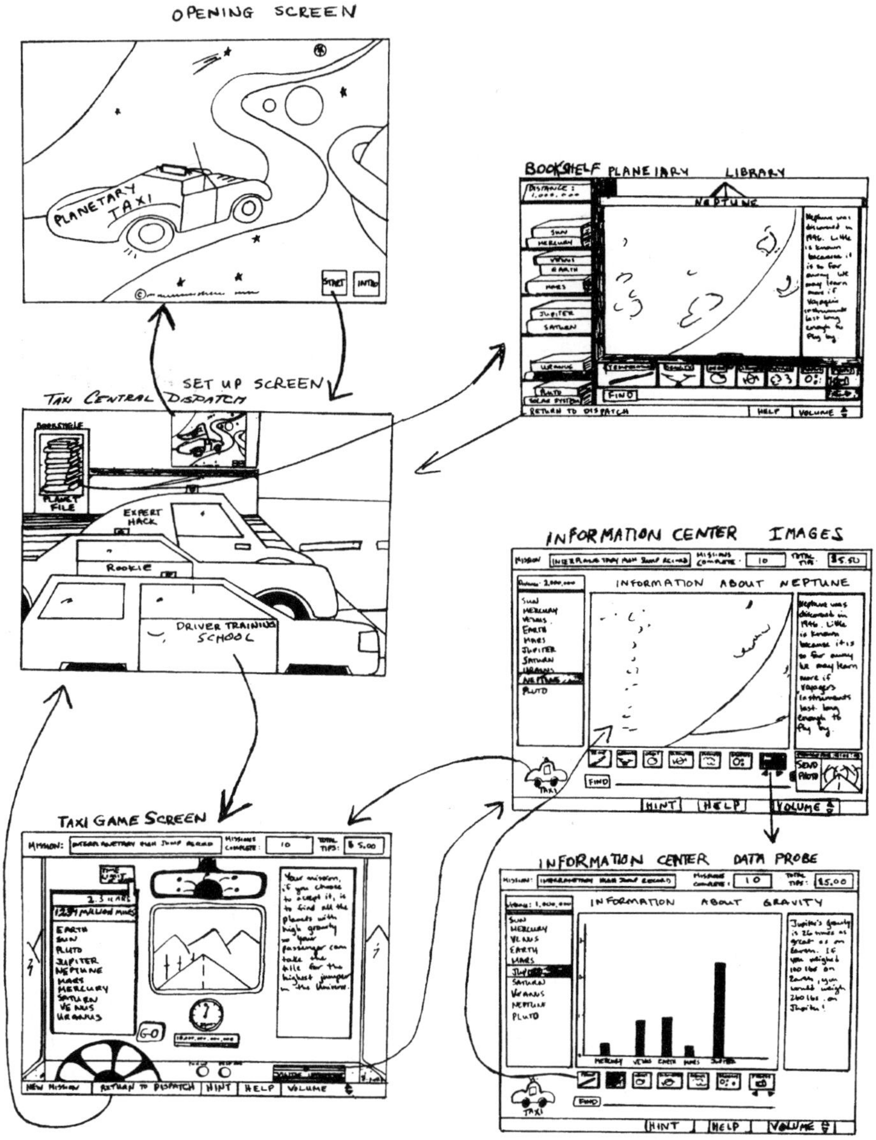

ROM, digitized video such as QuickTime appears in a window on the computer screen. Figures 6–9, 6–10, and 6–11 show the corresponding written descriptions explaining what is going on in the storyboard.

The storyboard is considered the visual half of the script because it shows what the visual elements will look like. Typically, an instructional designer creates the storyboard. Although the instructional designer is responsible for completing the storyboard, several key personnel—including SMEs, artists, software programmers, and the producer and/or

FIGURE 6-9   A description for the Opening Screen shown in the top left-hand corner of the storyboard designed for a CD-ROM entitled "Planetary Taxi." Courtesy of Aurora Media.

SCREEN 1: OPENING SCREEN

Links:
   from: SET-UP SCREEN—TAXI CENTRAL DISPATCH
   to: SET-UP SCREEN—TAXI CENTRAL DISPATCH

Graphics:
   Playful scene (identical to packaging) with Taxi Cab on ribbon of road winding through the "solar system," snaking past representations of planets, disappearing into a vanishing point where pinpoint stars are visible. The sun is not shown, but its presence is felt by the strong glow coming from the left and the long shadows cast by the cab. Text includes: Visual Almanac Series, Voyager Logo, Planetary Taxi, by Bob Mohl and Margo Nanny. The INTRO button is a QuickTime window (like in the CountDown CD-ROM).

Buttons:
   INTRODUCTION—launches QuickTime movie: INTRO
   START—starts Taxi game with TAXI CENTRAL DISPATCH

QuickTime Movies:
   INTRO—Linear explanation of concept of Planetary Highway Scale Model and Taxi Game. Shows the sun shrunk down to 8 feet in diameter and the signs for the orbits of the planets. Voiceover explains the idea of "scale model." It also acknowledges certain scientific liberties taken in the game—for example, that the planets don't normally line up. It explains the goal of the game—to learn how to drive a cab in Driver Training School and then to go out picking up passengers and figure out where to take them.

project manager—may also review the storyboard and provide input. Following are some of the specifications that are sometimes covered in a storyboard:

- A storyboard needs to be well drawn.
- The storyboard will show a sketch of what appears on the computer screen. If a single-screen setup is used, then everything will be shown using one screen as in Figure 6–8. If a multiple-screen setup is used, then what appears on the computer screen will be shown in one drawing and what appears in the videodisc monitor will be shown in another drawing.
- A storyboard may list any special directions for authoring the software that would be read by the software programmers. The storyboard will show a sketch of the computer screen pointing out any special locations on the screen as for buttons, action spots, touch screen areas, places for the user's input, and the use of function keys.

FIGURE 6–10   A description for the Setup Screen, which is shown in the middle of the left column of the storyboard shown in Figure 6–8. Courtesy of Aurora Media.

SCREEN 2: SET-UP SCREEN - TAXI CENTRAL DISPATCH

Links:
from: OPENING SCREEN
             TAXI GAMES and LIBRARY FILE
to: LIBRARY FILE
             TAXI GAME
                DRIVER TRAINING SCHOOL
                ROOKIE MISSIONS
                EXPERT "HACK" MISSIONS

Graphics:
Graphic look of "Taxi Central" with taxi(s) indicating 3 different levels (Driver Training School, Rookie, Expert), signposts pointing out to road indicating NEW MISSION.

Buttons :
    LIBRARY FILE—links to LIBRARY FILE (non-game planet database)
    INTRO—links to OPENING SCREEN
    DRIVER TRAINING SCHOOL—links to DRIVER TRAINING CAB
    ROOKIE—selects ROOKIE level, links to ROOKIE CAB
    EXPERT—selects EXPERT level, links to EXPERT CAB

{NEXT MISSION, LIST OF MISSION (or PICK YOUR OWN) AND RESET GAME have been axed.}

QuickTime Movies:
    None

SCREEN 3a: TAXI GAME SCREEN—DRIVERS TRAINING SCHOOL

Links:
    from: SET-UP SCREEN—TAXI CENTRAL DISPATCH
    to: SET-UP SCREEN—TAXI CENTRAL DISPATCH

Graphics:
Inside of taxi with subset of instruments available. See SCREEN 3c, TAXI GAME SCREEN—EXPERT HACK.

- Each storyboard page corresponds to one event in the script.
- Every visual element is identified. For example, the types of camera shots are described, such as if it is a close-up shot (CU). All on-location and set shots are discussed. Any special instructions to the camera operator or director are also written. Some common camera shots include:

  CU: A close-up shot has a small field of view compared to a relatively large image. *Field of view* refers to the whole shot as the user sees it. A CU of a person would show her or his head to just below the shoulders.

FIGURE 6-11   A description of the Taxi Game Screen shown at the bottom of the left column of the storyboard illustrated in Figure 6-8. Courtesy of Aurora Media.

SCREEN 3c: TAXI GAME SCREEN—EXPERT HACK

Links:
> from: SET-UP SCREEN—TAXI CENTRAL DISPATCH
>   INFORMATION CENTER
> to: INFORMATION CENTER

Graphics:

Inside view of taxi slightly futuristic (Jetsons) with familiar looking features—like METER, odometer, front windshield, steering wheel, driver, etc.

The passenger visible next to the taxi driver is a slightly bizarre silhouette that looks like an alien but turns out to just another weirdo hair-do or hat. Entrance and departure of passenger may be animated.

The view out the window is the QuickTime movie of Planetary Highway.

The METER has been enhanced to TRIP METER functions, which include elapsed time in days and years since the beginning of the mission, and a DESTINATION selector, which lists the planets and displays the DISTANCE to each selected. DISTANCE counts down (to zero) as taxi approaches destination on the highway. For mission with built-in time limits, the flag on top of the METER shows amount of time remaining. The ODOMETER shows total mileage traveled in this cab (i.e., in this game). It goes up to 10 trillion miles (after which time the cab is shot and you have to go back to Central Dispatch). The ODOMETER has a "gauge" that shows graphically how far you have driven this cab.

A TEXT WINDOW displays text messages from CENTRAL DISPATCH and "system messages."

A TITLE appears at the top of the screen announcing the mission (ex: Interplanetary High Jump Record).

Next to the TITLE are two SCORES:
Number of MISSIONS COMPLETED and TIPS earned.

MS: A medium shot contains what is known as a normal field of view with normal-sized images. A MS of a person would show her or his head to her or his thighs.

LS: A long shot is a large field of view with a small image. A LS of a person would capture her or his head down to her or his knees.

EXT: An exterior shot is shot outdoors.

INT: An interior shot is shot indoors.

- A storyboard will probably specify the camera movements. Basically, there are two kinds of camera movements: (1) only the camera lens is moved to change the view, such as in a *pan shot* of a photograph where the lens rotates horizontally over the photograph and (2) the whole camera itself is physically moved, such as in *truck shot* where the camera moves along side of a moving subject like a moving train. Following is a description of the various camera movements:

Pan: While the camera is held in a stationary position such as a tripod, the camera lens physically rotates horizontally across the field of view. A panoramic view is created.

Tilt: This is a vertical pan where the lens is pivoted up and down. This shot is typically used to capture views of tall objects like skyscrapers.

Zoom: A zoom shot is created with the lens. A *zoom-in* means that the field of view changes from a long or medium shot to a close-up. The image appears larger as the camera zooms in for a very close shot.

Crane: A crane is used to move the camera and camera operator up and down. While this is occurring, pans, tilts, and zooms can also be done.

Dolly: While the camera is locked in place, both the camera and tripod are moved toward or away from the subject. A *dolly* is a small cart on which the camera is mounted. The dolly can be either manually pulled or driven. *Dolly-out* is a shot where the cart is rolled away from the subject. *Dolly-in* is where the cart is moved toward the subject.

Truck: Trucking is similar to a dolly shot where the camera and tripod are mounted to a cart, but here the camera travels along side of a moving subject. Trucking is a popular technique used to capture the action of a moving train or car.

- A storyboard may specify the location for shooting, as well as any props, clothing, and actors. Special video effects and transitions may be entered, such as cuts, wipes, dissolves, and mosaics. When textual or graphic overlays are laid on top of the video, these are referred to as *overlays (OVRLs)*.

- A storyboard may note the beginning and ending times for each event. Each event has a starting and stopping time code, referred to as the *in* and *out points*, respectively. These points are written using SMPTE time code—Society of Motion Picture and Television Engineers. *SMPTE time code* is the standard in video production. It is used to keep track of the length of the video recording—to make sure that it is not too short or too long. Each time code is a series of eight digits separated by colons, as in 13:30:55:20, which is the equivalent of hours:minutes:seconds:frames, based on a 24-hour clock. One second of time in a videodisc is equal to 30 frames. These in and out time code numbers will be referred to when the tape is edited.

- The storyboard may refer to the corresponding page in the script where the audio is described.

Software products, such as IVD Toolkit for the Macintosh by Electronic Vision Inc., can aid in creating the storyboard. Storyboard pages can be printed out and distributed to key personnel for discussion. Revisions, deletions, and updates can be quickly made and a new version of the storyboard can be printed out. Figure 6–12 shows a printout from IVD Toolkit.

FIGURE 6-12   A printout of a storyboard page developed on the Macintosh using the IVD Toolkit by Electronic Vision Inc. With IVD Toolkit, each storyboard page can be directly linked to its script page as well as to its corresponding symbol on the flowchart.

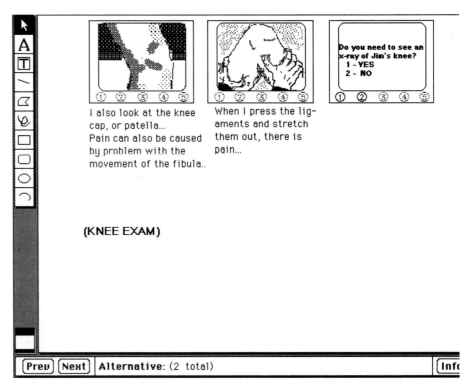

Creating the Production Script

Scriptwriting for an IVD is different from traditional scriptwriting for a television or film production. Some of the unique characteristics of an IVD include the following:

- An IVD is interactive—compared to the production of a linear video program. The user can make choices as she or he works through the IVD. Depending on the choices made by the user, a different story is seen and heard. Watching a VHS tape is considered linear because the user watches it from beginning to end with little if any interaction. Also, there is only one storyline in a VHS tape. The user can choose to go forward or backward in a tape, but cannot choose to see a different video event. On the other hand, because an IVD is interactive, the user can choose which events to watch. To accommodate this interactivity, the script is broken into separate events corresponding to the various points in the software where the user can make choices. For example, let's say the user is presented with a main menu in the software that provides for four options—A, B, C, and D. The user selects B from the main menu. At this point, the software then branches to that selection and shows the corresponding video event on the videodisc monitor. The main menu in this instance is considered a *branching point* because the user may select among two or more destinations (in this case, there are four optional paths). The script, as well as the storyboard, will indicate this branching point along with the four corresponding video events. Each event is an independent video recording that tells its own story with its own script.

- An IVD relies on the power of visual communication. Writing for an IVD requires a scriptwriter who has a strong sense of visualization because the script is written for an audience interested in the visuals as for demonstrations, examples, and simulations.

- The IVD should be personable. This attribute can be achieved in the audio by using everyday language with which the user is familiar, by having actors talk right into the camera (as in a cut-away shot), and by shooting scenes that look familiar to the viewer.

- Each event can have two or more audio tracks for it. Therefore, each will be accompanied by two or more audio scripts. A popular use of the dual audio channels is where one track is in English and the other in Spanish. The Bio Sci II science videodisc by Videodiscovery Inc. does this. Another use is to tell different accounts of the same story (that is, different narrations for the same content). For example, an IVD on the use of instructional strategies in the classroom could play the live, on-location dialog between a teacher and her or his students on audio track 1. Track 2 would play the narrated account of the teacher reflecting back on the classroom situation and what she or he was trying to achieve. The teacher would talk about what she or he was attempting to accomplish, what cued her or him into the individual needs of the students, and the effectiveness of the instructional techniques that were used. This second track could be interspersed with student excerpts related to their feelings about the instruction. Another use of dual audio tracks is exemplified in Burried Mirrors by Films Incorporated. This IVD teaches introductory Spanish at two levels of comprehension. The Spanish dialog on one track is spoken very distinctly and slowly. On the other track, it is spoken at a much faster speed, as in everyday conversation. Track 1 is aimed toward the beginning Spanish student, whereas track 2 is for the intermediate Spanish student. The audio tracks can address different levels of students.

Any revisions to the script usually require the approval of the scriptwriter. After all the revisions have been made, the script is handed over to the producer and director so that the video production can begin. At this point, the script becomes what is known as the *production script* or *shooting script* because it serves as a guide for the video production.

Creating a Flowchart for the Software Interface to the Videodisc

Generally, the instructional designers will design a software flowchart for the IVD following the script and storyboard. Software authors (programmers) also know how to do this and are sometimes recruited for this task.

As illustrated in Figure 6–13, a flowchart graphically depicts the logic flow of the software program. The flowchart depicted in Figure 6–13 was developed on the Macintosh using IVD Toolkit by Electronic Vision Inc. A

FIGURE 6-13   Using software on the Macintosh, such as the IVD Toolkit by Electronic Vision Inc., a detailed flowchart representing the flow of the interactive video program can be specified.

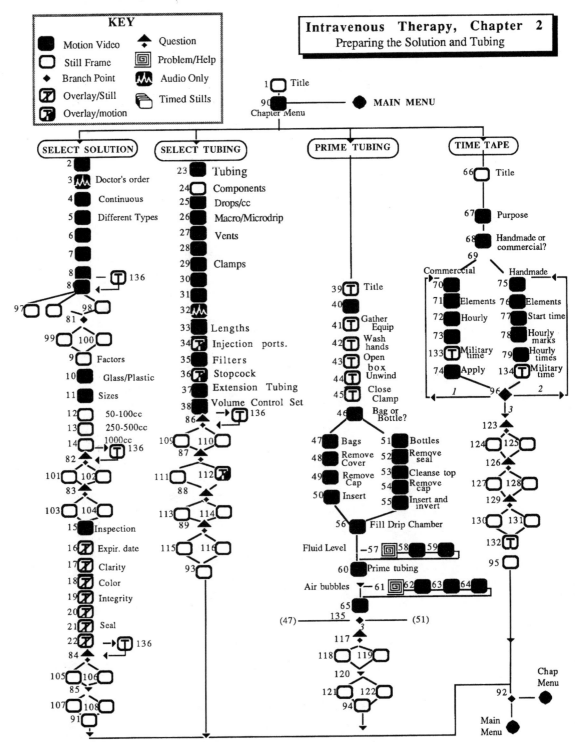

FIGURE 6-14   A flowchart developed with the use of the MacFlow software by Mainstay. This flowchart shows the process and activities involved in creating a flowchart. It is read from the top on down.

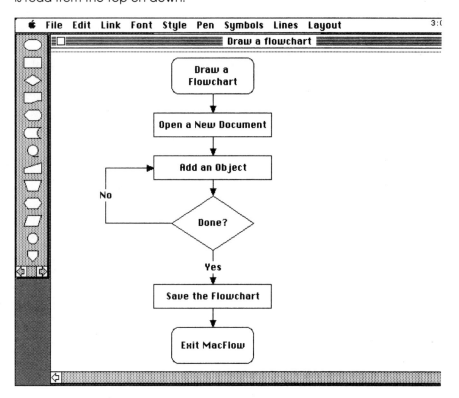

FIGURE 6-15   Some flowchart symbols with a description of their uses and meanings. This diagram was created on the Macintosh using MacFlow by Mainstay.

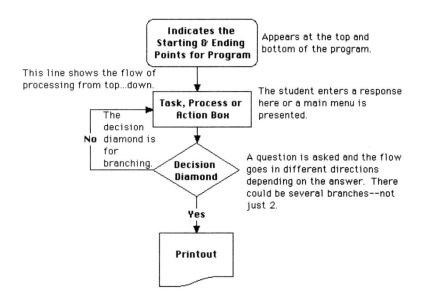

flowchart visually represents the branching and the overall flow and organization of the software. It is a map of the possible paths to take through the IVD software based on the choices, decisions, or answers given by the user. A flowchart defines all the nodes, menus, graphics, text, buttons, interfaces with videodisc events, subroutines, and the various kinds of acceptable user input. All areas for feedback are also indicated.

Flowcharts are read in a linear fashion from top to bottom. Arrows show the direction of the logic flow moving from top on down. Figure 6–14 illustrates another kind of flowchart developed with MacFlow by Mainstay. This flowchart is about the process for drawing a flowchart.

Macintosh software products, such as IVD Toolkit, MacFlow, Flow-Chart Express, TopDown, and Authorware Professional, make drawing flowcharts much easier than with paper and pencil. A flowcharting software product for the IBM is Authorware Professional for Windows. Generally, any one of these software products lets you select flowchart symbols from a palette of symbols, much in the same way that a draw and paint program works. You use your mouse to point and click on the desired symbol. Flowchart symbols can be quickly moved to any position within the flowchart with simple click and drag actions of the mouse. Symbols can be easily added, deleted, or moved. Figure 6–15 shows some flowchart symbols and their interpretations.

After the flowchart is created, it is handed over to the software authors, who will carefully follow the flowchart in programming the software interface to the videodisc.

Developing a Production Database

A *production database* is a written document listing all the audio/video elements described in the storyboard. It is a list of what needs to be shot and produced. Each element is listed in detail, including the location and type of shot, such as a close-up (CU), medium shot (MS), or long shot (LS).

The production database serves as a guide for the efficient scheduling of the video production. Instead of shooting visual elements in the same order listed in the storyboard or script, ordering of the video shots may be affected by the renting of video equipment, weather, location, and availability of actors. To keep costs down, shots occurring at the same location may be scheduled at the same time to minimize transportation of equipment. Later, during editing, the shots will be dispersed throughout the tape. A production database helps the video producer and project manager make sure that everything gets done in an efficient manner.

Producing Original Artwork, Computer Graphics, and Animations

The production database determines what artwork needs to be produced. Have the artists review all requests for artwork to determine the overall style, font style, font sizes, and color schemes.

Microcomputer animation software lets the artist input her or his design using a keyboard, light pen, electronic stylus, mouse, graphics tablet, digitizer, or graphics scanner. Using software, the artist can easily manipulate the image—enlarge, shrink, stretch, and copy.

The process of developing a computer animation is modeled after traditional cell animation techniques where the animator redraws the object at new locations in subsequent frames called *cells*. The computer screen replaces the cell. When the animation is played through, the object will appear to be in motion as it moves across the screen.

Animations can make real what is normally difficult or impossible to perceive. For example, with an animation on the human heart, the viewer can visually ride inside of a main artery surrounded by red and white blood cells. Inside the heart, the viewer can watch the force of the pumping heart. A very sophisticated computer animation of a blood cell can be seen in Figure 6–16 from the Bio Sci II Videodisc published by Videodiscovery Inc. This animation was first created on a computer, transferred to tape, and then mastered on the videodisc.

A computer animation can make an architect's drawing become life-like and life-size for the client. Using an animation, the viewer can walk through the lobby, see the elevators, offices, doors, and hallways from the perspective and scale of an averaged-sized human being walking through the building. By making the architectural model life-size, the client can realize what the skyscraper will eventually look and feel like before large amounts of money are spent to build it.

Animations can also re-create natural phenomena—such as hurricanes, earthquakes, and tornados—and can alter or emphasize certain

FIGURE 6-16   The Bio Sci II Videodisc presents an animation of a cell. Used by permission of Videodiscovery Inc., Seattle, WA., publishers of interactive video for science education.

aspects of reality to help in our understanding. Things can be slowed down, sped up, enlarged, and increased in velocity and momentum. Using an IVD, users can specify an earthquake's size and epicenter, then watch the visual effects played back as an animation. Most of us will only be able to travel to planets in vicarious manners made real through animations. For example, an interactive video will allow users to fly over a simulated Mars landscape, determine a specific route, and even change routes.

A well-executed animation can easily substitute for an expensive video production. Animations do not require paid actors, rental of props and costumes, or production crew. In addition, a computer animation is easier to modify than a video production. Also, many scientific and technical demonstrations can be done quite safely without the use of toxic chemicals and just as effectively with animations.

Conducting a Rehearsal

Before the video production begins, the talent will read aloud the script with the video producer, project manager, and director. Sometimes, the scriptwriters are at the rehearsal to help with any last-minute changes in the script. Rehearsals are a way of improving the scenes, dialog, and camera shots specified in the script. Afterwards, the camera crew will physically walk-through the script to determine the location of the camera and other equipment in getting the correct camera angles and shots.

Evaluating at the Development Stage

At the development stage, the key personnel read-through the script and storyboard. Their feedback is used in revising the script and storyboard. The camera crew will also do a physical walk-through of the script and storyboard to determine if the feasibility and quality of the camera shots. In addition, the instructional lessons detailed in the script can be practiced with testers from the target audience. An educator could be put in charge of this task. The various lessons could be presented to the testers and evaluated in terms of their overall effectiveness. Their feedback would be used to revise the script and improve the instructional effectiveness of the IVD.

Stage Four: Production

During production, a tape is created, edited, and dubbed, and the dub is sent out to be mastered into a videodisc by a company specializing in the mastering of videodiscs. Production involves the following:

- Shooting the video events
- Editing the tape
- Mastering the videodisc
- Authoring the software interface to the videodisc
- Replicating the videodisc

Shooting the Video

Video production begins when the script and storyboard are handed over to the director. The *director* is the key person in the video production who is responsible for making the script and storyboard become a reality on tape. The director is in charge of shooting all the video events.

The director will recruit a professional video production crew to work with her or him in shooting and editing the tape. The video production crew consists of two kinds of personnel—those who work on the set and those who are in the control room. Listed below are some of the key personnel for a typical video production:

Personnel on the Set

- Art Director: Works with artists in creating artworks, computer graphics, and animations; responsible for obtaining the props, clothing, and whatever else to make the sets look and feel right
- Camera Operator: Makes sure that the technical and aesthetic aspects of the shots follow the director's instructions and the script; reviews the production script to establish the type of shots, lighting, and camera angles
- Lighting Director: Creates the lighting for the sets, which establishes the mood (the mood should be consistent with the feeling projected in the script and the director's instructions)
- Gaffer: Hangs the lights for the video production
- Sound Person: Handles the recording equipment, such as holding the microphone over the talent and monitoring the recording level; makes sure that the proper microphones are used and that they are properly hidden when the scenes are shot; controls the peripheral noises caused by clothing, air conditioning, camera movements, and traffic
- Talent: Professional actors and narrators who are seen and heard in the video and audio production (they may appear on the camera as live talent or in voice-over narrations)

Personnel in the Control Room

Fiigure 6–17 illustrates a typical control room. This photograph was taken at California State University, Los Angeles (Creative Media Services).

- Audio Engineer: Monitors the quality of the audio production from the control room; makes sure that the volume and sound are recorded at a consistent level
- Script Supervisor: Makes sure that the script is followed, the dialog is accurately recorded, and that things like props and clothing stay constant between takes; is responsible for the continuity of the shots and that everything in the script gets done; numbers each shot and notes the good takes; describes each scene, describes the contents of the audio tracks, indicates the SMPTE time code in and out points, and highlights any technical problems (each tape and every shot is logged; this log will be used later during editing)
- Technical Director: Handles the switching of cameras and special effects from the control room upon the director's instructions

FIGURE 6–17   A typical control room, taken at California State University, Los Angeles. Courtesy of Creative Media Services.

- Video Engineer: Monitors the quality of the video production in the control room; makes sure a good, clean signal is received; checks the chroma and luminance levels to make sure they are of a high quality and consistent.

The director will start the shooting as soon as the script and production schedule are received. Before the first day of shooting, the sets should have been constructed, the props placed, the camera equipment hooked up to the electrical power, and the lighting set up. The director and talent should be ready to step onto the set, and the production crew should be ready to shoot. Figure 6–18 shows a typical video production in session on the set at California State University.

During shooting, a videolog is kept that lists all the good shots. Later, the director will go back over the videolog and select all the good takes.

Editing the Tape

Editing is a postproduction activity because it occurs after the shooting in a postproduction facility.

Off-Line Editing   An *off-line edit* is a rough draft tape that assembles all the good shots together. All the good takes, computer graphics, still frames, and any other elements are assembled together in the correct order and mixed with audio so that the director can assess the effective-

FIGURE 6-18   A video production in session on the set at California State Unversity. Courtesy of Creative Media Services.

ness of the scenes. Figure 6–19 shows an edit form that can be used in the edit suite to guide the editing. This edit form was generated with the IVD Toolkit on the Macintosh.

The off-line editing session uses a tape that has been prestripped with SMPTE time code. The SMPTE time code helps the editor in being precise about the sequencing of shots and the timing of video events. During the off-line edit, the editor will also identify any errors including technical errors, content problems, or missing elements.

Field Dominance   Since each videodisc frame in an IVD can be individually accessed, the clarity of the image when displayed in the still mode could look jittery or scrambled due to two different pictures being displayed simultaneously. Visual clarity is achieved during editing. Each video frame is made up of information coming from two interlacing fields—field 1 and field 2. Each field contains half of the visual information for a single video frame. To avoid having problems with jittering, the field dominance is set to either one of the two fields, 1 or 2, and then this same field dominance is maintained throughout the editing of the tape. A field dominance of field 1 means that field 1 is the first, followed by field 2 of the same time code location.

Window Dub   During the off-line editing session, a 1/2" VHS tape is dubbed from the off-line edit. *Dubbed* means the same as duplicated or copied. A window dub is special because it is shows the SMPTE time

FIGURE 6-19   An edit form such as this can aid the editor in making editing decisions. This edit form was made on the Macintosh with the IVD Toolkit by Electronic Vision, Inc.

· IVD TOOLKIT ·
EDIT FORM
Page 1

| Chapter 3 | Scene 6 | | Type Video |

Video	Audio 1	Audio 2
Close-up of the order	The elements of the order include Type of solution, amount of solution, and rate of infusion.	No, you must consult the Physician's orders to begin setting the rate

Video Timecode	Audio 1 Timecode	Audio 2 Timecode

Graphics	Branching
Chyron: Highlight and label the TYPE OF SOLUTION, AMOUNT OF SOLUTION, RATE OF INFUSION.	Next Scene If Review Flag=>c3:s80

Notes

code in a window at the bottom of the picture, as illustrated in Figure 6-20. The director will refer to the time code displayed in the window dub when making editing decisions. The time, which is separated by colons, stands for hour:minute:second:frame:field.

Edit Decision List   After the director has reviewed the window dub and has made her or his decisions, a list of all the video events that will eventually appear in the final video is made. This list, called the *edit decision list* (EDL), follows the exact instructions given by the director. It notes each video event that will be in the final tape and the corresponding in and out points. The in and out points are written using SMPTE

FIGURE 6–20   A window dub is a copy of the off-line edited tape with the time code displayed in a window, as shown at the bottom of this picture.

time code numbers, noting each scene's starting and ending time location on the off-line tape.

Following are some criteria that can be used in evaluating the off-line edit:

- Are there any errors in the instructional content, missing visuals, poor audio recordings, technical glitches, and any places where the visuals or audio are out of sequence or out of sync with each other?

- Does the narration sound believable, convincing, and natural? Or does it sound like its being read aloud? The audio has to be clear, concise, and free of any accoustic problems.

- Is the talent properly casted? Does the talent appear real and convincing?

- Are the lighting and chroma values consistent throughout the tape? Are there any takes containing glitches, such as shadows, reflections, or variations in color?

On-Line Editing   During the *on-line edit*, the final edited tape that will be used to base the videodisc on is created. This tape is referred to as a *premaster tape* because it is the one that is sent to the videodisc mastering company. This editing session follows the director's decisions provided in the EDL.

The on-line editing session is computer controlled. The editor enters in the numbers from the EDL into a computerized editing system that performs the edits, including special effects, text overlays, graphic overlays, titles, and digital video effects. Transitions between video sequences, such as dissolves, are also created at this time. At this time, the audio is layed down on both audio tracks.

Before starting the on-line edit, a videodisc mastering company should be consulted for their postproduction specifications. Videodisc mastering companies publish their technical requirements for setting up the master tape. Figure 6–21 shows the Post Production Guide from 3M listing the technical specs for mastering a videodisc. A typical specification would be that the SMPTE time code must be present throughout the tape from the beginning color bars to the end. This time code is used by the videodisc mastering company for accurate frame numbering, making each videodisc frame accessible.

There are a variety of desktop video editing and production systems for doing broadcast quality on-line editing with your personal computer. Video Toaster by NewTek Inc. is an entire television studio combined into

FIGURE 6–21   The Post Production Guide from 3M outlining their technical requirements for setting up the master tape for an IVD. Photo courtesy of 3M Prerecorded Optical Media.

one affordable desktop production system. By simply pointing with a mouse, the same video effects and graphics performed at television studios can be created on a desktop. On-line editing can be performed with Video Toaster when used with an editing controller. The most common use of Video Toaster is as a *video transition device*. It includes a broadcast-quality production switcher and digital video effects generator (DVE). Video Toaster can create special digital video effects generally performed on very expensive broadcast switchers. Some of the effects and transitions include zooms, warps, tiles, spins, splits, stretches, mosaics, cuts, fades, wipes, and character-generated titles. Video Toaster includes a quality character generator that comes with 32 fonts for generating title screens and 16.5 million colors for creating electronic art. More fonts can be added to the system. The Video Toaster production switcher shown in Figure 6–22 replaces expensive broadcast switchers. The Toaster can tumble and spin up to four live incoming video sources around the screen and add titles. It also features three-dimensional animation and 24-bit paint abilities.

The Video Toaster is available as a stand-alone workstation and as an add-in computer card that fits into the video slot of the Amiga 200 and 2500. The Video Toaster stand-alone workstation is pictured in Figure 6–23. The Toaster is also available for the Macintosh.

Another broadcast-quality desktop video production system is Video Explorer by Intelligent Resources Integrated Systems. As in Figure

FIGURE 6–22   With the Video Toaster Production Switcher, cuts, fades, and advanced animated and organic wipes can be performed between any of four live input video signals. Video Toaster a registered trademark of NewTek, Inc., based in Topeka, KS.

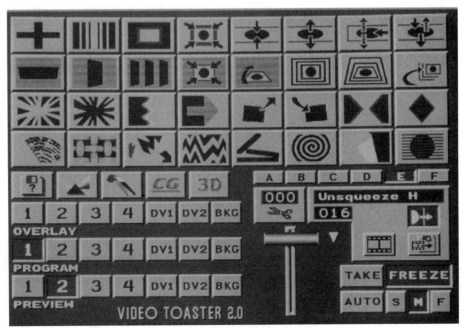

6–24, Video Explorer is a digital video processing card for the Macintosh that lets you have full control of the editing process frame by frame. When the Video Explorer is used with professional-level video equipment, broadcast-quality video can be produced. With it, you can control the luminance level, overlay titles, and graphics on live incoming video; combine multiple live incoming video signals; and perform a wide array of effects and transitions, including fades, wipes, dissolves, and special digital video effects. In addition, Video Explorer provides image capture, real-time video effects, animation, multimedia, paint, character generation, graphic overlays, anti-aliased titles, and a variety of other features.

MicroKey/1100 by Video Associates turns your MS/PC-DOS computer into a multimedia editing machine. Desktop video production and editing systems are a practical and affordable way for producing broadcast-quality, dazzling, and effective multimedia.

FIGURE 6–23   Broadcast quality video production can be done on your desktop with the Video Toaster Workstation by NewTek, Inc. Video Toaster is a registered trademark of NewTek Inc.

FIGURE 6-24   Video Explorer is a broadcast-quality video production system on a computer card for the Macintosh. Video Explorer is by Intelligent Resources Integrated Systems. Photo courtesy of Intelligent Resources Integrated Systems.

Mastering a Videodisc

Instead of sending a 1/2" VHS videotape out to a videodisc mastering, a D-2 (composite digital videotape), 1", or 3/4" U-matic tape is the more desirable format to send out. These formats are of a much higher quality than a 1/2" VHS tape. If you are working with a 1/2" VHS tape, you will need to transfer it (bump up) to one of the higher-quality formats. After the on-line edit tape is completed, make a dub of the final premaster tape. The dub is what is sent out to the videodisc mastering company instead of the source tape. Appendix D lists a variety of companies that master videodiscs. Before you begin your project, contact a videodisc mastering company for its specifications.

Draw Disc   At the videodisc mastering company, a laser beam recorder creates a *draw* (direct read after write) disc, which can be played back in any LaserVision videodisc player. The recorder uses a high-powered laser beam that burns millions of microscopic pits of information into the disc. When the draw disc is played, a lower-powered laser beam housed inside the videodisc player focuses on the pits in the surface of the videodisc. Differences in pits affect the reflection of the beam. It is this detection of differences that is converted into the audio and video signals and is what we see and hear played back on the video monitor. Figure 6-25 shows a draw disc. Optical Disc Corporation (ODC) is a recognized leader in the recording of draw discs.

A draw disc is the first disc made off the tape. It is used to evaluate the quality, sequence, and effectiveness of the content presented in the video events. All changes recommended as a result of testing the draw disc are edited back onto the master tape. Then another draw disc is recorded and sent out for review.

A draw disc is of a slightly lower visual quality and cost than the final videodisc. The costs to cut a one-sided CAV plastic draw disc can range from $150 to $450. A one-sided glass draw disc, which has a slightly higher video quality than the plastic draw disc, costs from $400 to $500 (CAV format). One limitation to the glass is that it is breakable. Figure 6-26 shows a draw disc being recorded from a backup tape with ODC's Model 610A Videodisc Recording System. After recording, the draw disc can be played back immediately on a standard LaserVision videodisc player.

FIGURE 6-25   A low-cost draw disc can be used to check the effectiveness and quality of the IVD program before it is mastered. Just after the draw disc is recorded, it can be played back immediately in a videodisc player. Photo courtesy of Optical Disc Corporation (ODC).

A plastic draw disc must be handled carefully because the surface can be easily scratched and it is susceptible to warping with changes in humidity. Also, with repeated use, the quality of the video and audio deteriorates, especially at the outer rim. A draw disc is a one-time-only disc that is not designed for replication. If you are planning on duplicating the disc, then a check disc is the way to go.

Check Disc   A *check disc* is the first disc replicated off the glass master disc. It is not as durable as a master disc, nor does it have the quality of a master disc. However, a check disc is a good way to review the accuracy and quality of the software interface as used in conjunction with the videodisc. Are the frame numbers listed in the software accurate? Are all the branching points working correctly with the videodisc? A check disc runs between $250 and $750.

Authoring the Software

While the video production crew was creating the video, the software authors were programming the software interface to the videodisc. Figures 6–27 and 6–28 show two screens in development for the interactive CD-ROM product called "Planetary Taxi." Although the digitized motion video is not displayed in these figures, you can see where it would be displayed in the center of the screen in the rectangular boxes

FIGURE 6–26　　A draw disc being recorded on Optical Disc Coroporation's Model 610A Videodisc Recording System. Photo courtesy of Optical Disc Corporation (ODC).

that currently are blank. (Both figures correspond directly to the storyboard shown in Figure 6–8.)

Today, there are many sophisticated and easy-to-use software authoring tools specifically for use with videodiscs that have built-in interfaces to videodisc players. Some of these authoring tools include Authorware Professional for Macintosh computers and MS/PC-DOS computers with Windows; the Videodisc ToolKit, which is available for Macintosh computers with HyperCard and MS/PC-DOS computers with Windows and ToolBook; and LinkWay for the MS/PC-DOS computers. These authoring tools are so user-friendly that even a nonprogrammer, such as a teacher or student, can use them to create customized lessons and multimedia presentations that work with videodiscs. Authoring tools are extensively discussed in both Chapters 4 and 5; Appendix C provides a listing of various authoring tools.

The software authors will convert the in and out points listed in the EDL to videodisc frame numbers that are used by the software program. Frame numbers on a videodisc run sequentially from 1 to 54,000. Frame 1 on a videodisc is located at the inner rim of the disc, and frame 54,000 is at the outer rim. Each in and out point time code in the EDL can be converted to a frame number using the following formula:

$$(\text{Minutes} \times 1800) + (\text{Seconds} \times 30) + \text{Frames} = \text{Frame Number}$$

Having converted all the SMPTE time codes into frame numbers, the software authors will start inputting the frame numbers into the software

FIGURE 6-27   A computer screen in development for the CD-ROM entitled "Planetary Taxi." (This screen corresponds directly to the storyboard drawing illustrated in Figure 6-8.) Eventually, the digitized video will be displayed in the empty white space in the center of the screen. Screen printout courtesy of Aurora Media.

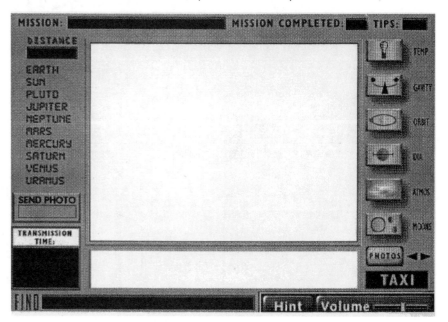

FIGURE 6-28   Another screen in development for the CD-ROM product entitled "Planetary Taxi." Later in development, the digitized video will be displayed in the rectangular black box in the center of the screen. (Refer to Figure 6-8 to note how closely this resembles the original storyboard drawing). Screen printout courtesy of Aurora Media.

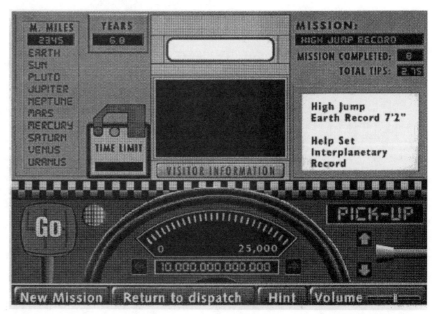

program. They do not have to wait for the draw disc to return to begin their calculations and programming. Then, when the draw disc does return, they can test out their software program and make any minor adjustments for frame numbers that have been incorrectly entered.

Replicating the Videodisc

Once all the revisions have been made to the master tape and the check or draw disc has been thoroughly reviewed and approved, it is time to duplicate the disc. During the setup, the signals from your tape are synchronized with the laser beam recorder. Then a very thick polished glass master coated with photoresist is loaded into the recorder. A high-powered laser beam changes the photoresist surface of the glass master following the signals from the tape you provided. Through this process, the glass master is etched with the information coming from your tape. Each side of the glass master can be etched with some 14.5 billion pits of information. The glass master is then plated with nickel to create a stamper disc, which is mounted into the stamper. The stamper is the reverse image of the glass master. It is used to stamp out the information onto clear plastic videodiscs. Next, a thin reflective aluminum layer is applied to each plastic disc. Finally, the entire disc is sealed with a clear protective lacquer coating and the center hole is punched out. At each step in the process, technical experts closely check the quality of the product, as illustrated in Figure 6–29.

Leading videodisc mastering facilities include Pioneer, Sony, and 3M. Generally, setup charges for creating a one-sided CAV master disc range from $1800 to $2100, with plastic replicas at $7 to $18 a disc, depending on the facility.

Evaluating at the Production Stage

The finished IVD should be reviewed by the producer, the instructional designers, and the testers from the target audience. Following are some criteria to use in evaluating the finished IVD:

*   Critique the IVD as compared to the original treatment. Does it work as it was originally conceived?
*   How well does the intended audience perform after having completed the lesson presented in the IVD? Where do they have problems?
*   Are the software directions, menus, and instructional content clear?
*   Does the IVD meet the instructional needs of the audience?

Based on the feedback, revisions to the software and videodisc will be discussed and considered for revision. If it is cost effective to make the necessary revisions, then do so. Otherwise, develop other instructional media to fill any instructional gaps. Other media that can enhance the learning include printed manuals, videotapes, additions and enhancements to the software, and stand-up classroom training.

FIGURE 6–29 A technical expert checking the quality of a disc being mastered at the 3M Optical Recording Department. Photo courtesy of 3M Prerecorded Optical Media.

Stage Five: Evaluation

Evaluation is an ongoing activity occurring throughout the development of the IVD. There are two kinds of evaluation that are performed at different points in the IVD project—formative and summative evaluation.

Formative Evaluation

Formative evaluation occurs during the development of the IVD. It is called formative because it happens as the IVD is being formed or made. Typically, formative evaluation is of a qualitative nature—surveying, observing, interviewing users, conducting task analyses, testing lessons with the target users, doing a read-through of the script, doing a walk-through of the script by the camera crew, checking out the accuracy of the frame numbers in the draw disc, and testing out the software with the check disc. At various stages of creation, the various IVD project deliverables—such as the treatment, script, storyboard, flowchart, draw disc, and check disc—can be assessed by the instructional designers, representative users from the target audience, educators, video producer, director, scriptwriters, SMEs, and project manager.

Summative Evaluation

Summative evaluation is a postproduction activity occurring after the software and the draw or check disc are made. It is called summative evaluation because it happens at the very end of the IVD project after the video production and when the software and disc are completed. It is an evaluation of the total sum of parts. Summative evaluation typically takes the form of a quantitative study, such as a statistical analysis assessing the effectiveness of the instructional content with the intended audience. The evaluation could also be qualitatively done or be a combination of quantitative and qualitative methodologies.

At the completion of the IVD, the learning outcomes of the audience should be compared to the original objectives to see if the targeted audience actually did accomplish what the IVD was intended for. Was the training effective? Did the users learn the necessary skills and knowledge to perform the desired tasks? Did they fulfill the objectives? Were their needs met by the lesson presented in the IVD?

Results from the summative evaluation are gathered and analyzed, and conclusions are made. Based on the conclusions, the IVD is ready for implementation in the classroom or perhaps further revision.

Implementation

Implementation means that the IVD is ready for use by the target audience at the intended location. The implementation process should account for users who may have varying degrees of technological proficiency. Some expert users may have extensive experience with IVDs, whereas novice users may never have worked with or even seen one before. A properly planned IVD will account for the varying levels of computer literacy by offering on-line help in the software, as well as verbal and visual instructions in the videodisc. Even beginners can get around in the IVD using context-sensitive help screens, tutorials, and videodisc sequences explaining and demonstrating the use of the IVD. Additionally, a brief user's manual might be desirable, describing step by step how to install the software and set up the videodisc for the first time. If necessary, some classroom instruction may also take place, showing teachers how to effectively integrate the IVD into their curriculum and classroom. The instruction might be provided by a salesperson representing the IVD product, by a consultant such as a teacher specializing in IVDs, or by school district personnel such as an instructional technologist.

Conclusion

Nothing can be more exciting for those who work with educational technology than the design, development, and production of an IVD. Its a merging of two media worlds—computer-assisted instruction and multimedia. It combines the power and interactivity of a computer with the high-quality visuals and audio of a video. An IVD is a blend of digital data in the computer software and analog data in the videodisc. It is interactive, user driven, colorful, moving, and dynamic.

The use of an IVD for instructional applications is increasing exponentially on a daily basis. There is a real need for educators to be involved in the creation of commercially produced IVDs. Educators can bring to the project a knowledge of sound instructional design principles and teaching experience. Teachers know what makes learning effective and how to motivate a variety of students to learn. The varied backgrounds of educators can only enhance the educational effectiveness of the IVD being produced. Educators can be involved in the planning, design, development, and testing of the IVD. If you are a visual thinker with experience in developing interactive software programs, then you will be well suited for the role of the instructional designer in creating an IVD. If you have experience in education, are familiar with video production, and are an excellent writer, then you are prepared to enter the field of scriptwriting for an IVD. In addition, you might also be called on to develop any ancillary printed materials to accompany the IVD, such as activity manuals and worksheets, as well as to conduct instructional seminars on how to use an IVD effectively in the classroom.

To develop an IVD, consider spending as much time in the planning and preparation as you would for the video production itself and the editing. An effective IVD can be attributed to a well-conceived and developed production plan in addition to an experienced and creative team. Ultimately, what starts off on paper becomes reality in the videodisc. There is a real need for having more educators involved in the development of interactive video products for education. Educators know from their own professional backgrounds, what motivates children to learn, what instructional strategies are effective, how to provide quality reinforcement, and how to evaluate the educational successfulness of the lessons learned.

To learn more about the making a videodisc, you might want to consider attending a conference that focuses on interactive multimedia. Appendix B lists a variety of organizations that you can join, conferences concentrating on interactive video, and books and journals on the use and creation of interactive video for education.

We hope that you have enjoyed learning about the process of making an IVD and that perhaps you can play a part in the creation of one someday. Have fun making your IVD.

Suggested Learning Extensions

1. Contact a company that specializes in the development of interactive video products. Take a field trip there and summarize the experience in terms of photographs, a written report, an audiotape recording, or a videotape.

2. Contact a company that masters videodiscs. Take a field trip there and summarize the experience in terms of photographs, a written report, an audiotape recording, or a videotape.

3. Conduct an interview with an individual who is significantly involved with interactive video, such as a commerical software developer, a president or manager of a company, or a sales representative. Develop questions before going to the interview. Document the interview with photographs, videotape, or a written report.

4. Create a flowchart for a proposed interactive video product consisting of 10 cards/pages. Do this either manually on paper or using flowchart software such as MacFlow.

5. Create a storyboard for a proposed interactive video product consisting of five storyboard screens. Do this either manually with paper and pencil or with a software program such as the Interactive Videodisc Design Toolkit.

6. Invent your own interactive video product. Write a treatment describing this product.

Chapter References and Additional Readings

AEC Management Systems, Inc. (1989). *Fasttrack schedule 1.5.* 20524 Amethyst Lane, Germantown, MD 20874. (703) 450-1980.

Allen, B. S. (1990). Graduate training for interactive multimedia designers. In B. Branyan-Broadbent & R. K. Wood (Eds.), *Educational media & technology yearbook* (vol. 16), pp. 139–155.

Anderson, C. J., & Veljkov, M. D. (1990). *Creating interactive multimedia.* Glenview, IL.: Scott, Foresman.

Apple Computer, Inc. *Macintosh.* 20525 Mariani Avenue, Cupertino, CA 95014. (408) 252-2775 or (408) 996-1010.

Asymetrix Corporation. (1991). *ToolBook version 1.5.* 110-110th Avenue, N.E., Suite 717, Bellevue, WA 98004. (206) 637-1500.

Aurora Media. (1992). *Planetary taxi.* 4 Mohawk Avenue, Corte Madera, CA 94925.

Awardy, J. W., & Gayeski, D. M. (1989). *Using video: Interactive and linear designs.* Englewood Cliffs, NJ: Educational Technology Publications.

Barron, A., & Fisher, H. (March 1993). Affordable videodisc production. *Tech Trends, 38*(2), 15–21.

Bergman, R. E., & Moore, T. V. (1901). *Managing interactive video/ multimedia projects.* Englewood Cliffs, NJ: Educational Technology Publications.

Claris Corporation. (1991). *HyperCard*. 5201 Patrick Henry Drive, Box 58168, Santa Clara, CA 95052-8168. (800) 628-2100. FAX: (408) 987-3950.

Claris Corporation. (1991). *MacProject pro*. 5201 Patrick Henry Drive, Box 58168, Santa Clara, CA 95052-8168. (800) 628-2100. FAX: (408) 987-3950.

Commodore-Amiga, Inc. (1991). *AmigaVision*. (215) 431-9440 or (800) 662-6442.

Computer Associates International, Inc. (1992). *Superproject for windows*. One Computer Associates Plaza, Islandia, NY 11788-7000.

DeBloois, M. L. (1982). *Videodisc/microcomputer courseware design*. Englewood Cliffs, NJ: Educational Technology Publications.

Edmark Corporation. *Touchwindow*. P.O. Box 3218, Redmond, WA 98073-3218. (800) 426-0856. FAX: (206) 746-3962.

Educational Technology Publications, Inc. (1989). *Interactive video*. Englewood Cliffs, NJ: Educational Technology Publications.

Electronic Vision, Inc. (1991). *Interactive video design toolkit*. 28 Station Street, Athens, OH. 45701. (614) 592-2433. FAX: (614) 592-2650.

Elographics. *E274-13 Accutouch screen*. 41752 Christy Street, Fremont, CA 94538. (415) 651-2340.

Films Incorporated Video. (1993). *Buried mirrors*. 5547 North Ravenswood Avenue, Chicago, IL 60640-1199. (800) 323-4222, Ext. 43.

Floyd, S. (1991). *The IBM multimedia handbook*. New York: Brady Publishing.

Gagné, R. M., Briggs, L. J., & Wager, W. W. (1988). *Principles of instructional design*. New York: Holt, Rinehart and Winston.

Greenfield, E. (February 1991). Center creates interactive discs with desktop video system. *T.H.E. Journal, 18*(7), 50–52.

IBM Corporate Headquarters. Old Orchard Rd., Armonk, NY 10504. FAX: (914) 765-5099.

IBM Corporation. *LinkWay 2.01*. P.O. Box 2150 (H05K1), Atlanta, GA 30301-2150. (800) 627-0920.

Intelligent Resources Integrated Systems. (1991). *Video explorer*. 3030 Salt Creek Lane, Suite 100, Arlington Heights, IL. 60005-5000. (708) 705-9388 or (708) 670-9388. FAX: (708) 670-0585.

Iuppa, N. V., & Anderson, K. (1988). *Advanced interactive video design*. White Plains, NY: Knowledge Industry Publications.

Kaetron. (1992). *Flowchart express*. Available from MacWarehouse, P.O. Box 3013, 1720 Oak Street, Lakewood, NJ 08701-3013.

Kaetron. (1992). *Topdown flowcharter 3.0*. Available from MacWarehouse, P.O. Box 3013, 1720 Oak Street, Lakewood, NJ 08701-3013.

LaserEdit, Inc. *An ODC videodisc recording facility*. 540 N. Hollywood Way, Burbank, CA 91505. (818) 842-0777.

Macromedia. (1991). *Authorware professional*. 600 Townsend St., San Francisco, CA 94103. (800) 288-0572 or (415) 442-0200.

Macromedia. (1991). *Authorware professional for windows.* 600 Townsend St., San Francisco, CA 94103. (800) 288-0572 or (415) 442-0200.

Mainstay. (1990). *MacFlow ver. 3.5.* 5311-B Derry Avenue, Agoura Hills, CA 91301-9863. (818) 991-6540. FAX: (818) 991-4587.

Mainstay. (1990). *MacSchedule 2.5.* 5311-B Derry Avenue, Agoura Hills, CA 91301-9863. (818) 991-6540. FAX: (818) 991-4587.

Merrill, M. D. (1983). Components display theory. In C. M. Reigeluth (Ed.), *Instructional design theories and models.* Hillsdale, NJ: Lawrence Erlbaum.

Microsoft Corporation. (1991). *Microsoft project 1.1.* One Microsoft Way, Redmond, WA 98052-6399. (800) 541-1261 or (800) 227-4679.

Microsoft Corporation. (1991). *Microsoft project for windows 1.0.* One Microsoft Way, Redmond, WA 98052-6399. (800) 541-1261 or (800) 227-4679.

Microsoft Corporation. (1991). *Microsoft windows 3.1 environment with multimedia extensions.* One Microsoft Way, Redmond, WA 98052-6399. (800) 541-1261 or (800) 227-4679.

Multimedia Computing Corp. (1990). *Interactive videodiscs.* Santa Clara, CA: Multimedia Computing Corp.

NewTek Incorporated. (1991). *Video toaster system 2.0.* 215 S.E. Eighth Street, Topeka, KS 66603. (612) 881-2862, (800) 368-5441, or (913) 354-1146. FAX: 354-1584.

Optical Disc Corporation. 12150 Mora Drive, Santa Fe Springs, CA 90670. (310) 946-3050. FAX: (310) 946-6030.

Perlmutter, M. (1991). *Producer's guide to interactive videodiscs.* White Plains, NY: Knowledge Industry Publications.

Pioneer Communications of America. 600 E. Crescent Ave., Upper Saddle River, NJ 07458.

Pioneer Communications of America. Multimedia Systems Division. 915 E. 230th Street, Carson, CA 90745. (213) 513-1016 or (313) 567-9810. FAX: (310) 522-8699.

Scholastic Software. (1990). *Interactive NOVA: Animal pathfinders.* 730 Broadway, New York, NY 10003. (212) 505-6006.

Schwier, R. (1987). *Interactive video.* Englewood Cliffs, NJ: Educational Technology Publications.

Sony Video Communications. 9 West 57th Street, New York, NY 10019.

Souter, G. A. (1988). *The disconnection: How to interface computers and video.* White Plains, NY: Knowledge Industry Publications.

Swain, D. V., & Swain, J. R. (1991). *Scripting for the new AV technologies.* Boston: Focal Press.

Symantec Corporation. *On target for windows* 10201 Torre Avenue, Cupertino, CA 95014-2132.

Symantec Corporation. *Time line for windows.* 10201 Torre Avenue, Cupertino, CA 95014-2132.

3M Optical Recording Department. 3M Center Building 223-5N-01, St. Paul, MN 55144-1000. (231) 726-6350 or (213) 235-5567.

van Nostran, W. J. (1989). *The scriptwriter's handbook.* White Plains, NY: Knowledge Industry Publications.

Video Associates Labs. *Microkey/1100.* 4926 Spicewood Springs Road, Austin, TX 78759. (512) 346-5781 or (800) 331-0547.

Videodiscovery Inc. *Bio Sci II and life cycles.* 1700 Westlake Ave. N., Suite 600, Seattle, WA 98109-3012. (206) 285-5400 or (800) 548-3472.

Voyager Company, The. (1991). *Videodisc toolkit.* Santa Monica, CA: The Voyager Company. (213) 451-1383. FAX: (310) 394-2156.

Appendix A
Sources for Educational Videodiscs

ABC News InterActive. *Vote 88, in the Holy Land, Martin Luther King, and AIDS.* 7 West 66th Street, New York, NY 10023. (212) 887-2467.

Access Network. *English for life and work.* 295 Midparkway SE, Calgary, Canada T2X 2A8. (403) 256-1100.

Active Learning Media. *Videodiscs for science, English/language arts, and guidance.* Barr Films, 12801 Schabarum Ave., P.O. Box 7878, Irwindale, CA 91706-7878. (800) 234-7878 or (818) 338-7878.

Agency for Instructional Technology. *Attributes for successful employability, introduction to sign language, and workplace readiness.* Box A, 1111 W. 17th Street, Bloomington, IN 47402-0120. (800) 457-4509.

AIMS Media. Over 150 titles. 6901 Woodley Avenue, Van Nuys, CA 91406-4878. (800) 367-2467.

American Chemical Society. *Doing chemistry.* 1155 Sixteenth Street, N.W., Washington, DC 20036.

Annenberg/CPB Collection. *The mechanical universe...and beyond.* (800)-LEARNER.

Applied Learning. *Mathematics for business and reading for business.* (708) 369-3000.

AVS Video and Sound Ltc. 11304 142nd Street, Edmonton Alberta Canada. (403) 451-4616.

Barr Films. *Active learning media catalog.* 12801 Schabarum Ave., P.O. Box 7878, Irwindale, CA 91706-7878. (800) 234-7878.

Bloomsburg Foundation. *Attributes for successful employability.* Carver Hall, Bloomsburg, PA. (717) 389-4806.

Britannica Videodiscs. 310 Michigan Avenue, Chicago, IL 60604. (800) 554-9862.

CEL Educational Resources. *The video encyclopedia of the 20th century.* 477 Madison Avenue, New York, NY 10022. (800) 235-3339.

Churchill Media. 12210 Nebraska Avenue, Los Angeles, CA 90025. (800) 334-7830.

Comsell, Inc. 500 Tech Parkway, Atlanta, GA 30313. (404) 872-2500.

Coronet/MTI. 108 Wilmont Road, Deerfiedl, IL 60015. (800) 621-2131.

Dave's Video. 13511 Ventura Blvd., Sherman Oaks, CA 91423. (800) 736-1659 or (818) 906-DISC.

Davidson & Associates, Inc. *English express and the great paper chase.* P.O. Box 2961, 3135 Kashiwa Street, Torrance, CA 90509. (800) 545-7677 or (213) 534-4070.

Deltak Training Corporation. *Fundamental study skills.* 1751 Diehl Road, Naperville, IL 60540. (312) 369-3000.

Discovery Channel. *Treasures of a lost voyage: Vols. I and II & invention: Mastering sound.* 8201 Corporate Drive, Suite 1200, Landover, MD 20785. (301) 577-1999 Ext. 5443.

Edudisc, Inc. *Materials and discs on how to make IVDs.* 1400 Tyne Blvd., Nashville, TN 37215 (615) 378-2506.

Electronic Vision. *AIDS education videodisc.* 28 Station Street, Athens, OH 45701. (614) 592-2433.

Emerging Technology Consultants Inc. *The videodisc compendium for education and training—A sourcebook for educational videodiscs.* 2819 Hamline Avenue North, St. Paul, MN 55113. (612) 639-3973. FAX: (612) 639-0110.

Evergreen Laser Disc, Inc. *Mist-modular investigations into science technology.* 2819 Hamline Avenue N., St. Paul, MN 55113. (612) 639-1418.

Falcon Software, Inc. *Exploring chemistry: Interactive videodisc laboratory in general chemistry.* (603) 764-5788.

Ferranti Educational Systems, Inc. *Essential teaching skills and interactive mathematics.* (717) 898-0890.

Films Incorporated Video. 5547 North Ravenswood Avenue, Chicago, IL 60640-1199. (800) 323-4222 Ext. 43. FAX: (312) 878-0416.

Floyd Design. *Hurricane Hugo.* (800) 344-6219.

Grand Plains National (GPN). *Andrew Wyeth: The Helga pictures & The Annenberg/CPB project, music videodisc.* Box 80669, Lincoln, NE 68501-0669. (800) 228-4630.

Grolier Electronic Publishing Division. 95 Madison Avenue, New York, NY 10016. (212) 696-9750.

Hart, Inc. 320 New Stock Road, Ashville, NC 28804. (800) 654-8012.

Health EduTech. 435 Alberto Way, Suite 7, Los Gatos, CA 95030. (408) 354-4584.

Hoffman. *Laser learning and reading in the content area.* 1863 Business Center Drive, Duarte, CA 91010. (800) 826-8377 or (818) 359-0977.

Houghton Mifflin. *American history, Western civilization, and non-European history.* One Beacon Street, Boston, MA 02108. (617)725-5000.

IBM Corporation. *Principals of the alphabetic literacy system (PALS).* 4111 Northside Parkway, Atlanta, GA 30327. (800) 627-0920 or (404) 988-2351.

Instructional Resources Corporation. *The world history videodisc: Non-European history.* 1819 Bay Ridge Avenue, Annapolis, MD 21403. (800) 922-1711.

Intellimation. P.O. Box 1922, Santa Barbara, CA 93116-1922. (800)-3-INTELL.

Interactive Media Corp. 165 West 46th Street, Suite 710, New York, NY 10036. (212) 382-0313.

Interactive Training Corporation. *English for industry.* 4401 Ford Avenue, Suite 200, Alexandria, VA 22302. (703) 824-2048.

Interactive Videodiscs. 2151 Michaelson Drive, Suite 145, Irvine, CA 92715. (714) 995-1950.

John Wiley & Sons. 605 Third Avenue, New York, NY 10158.

LaserDisc Corporation of America. (1988). *Encyclopedia of animals volume, reptiles and amphibians.* 200 West Grand Avenue, Montvale, NJ 07645.

Laser Learning Technologies. 3114 37th Place South, Seattle, WA 98144. (800) 722-3505 or (206) 722-3002.

Laser's Edge. 20929 Ventura Blvd., Woodland Hills, CA 91364. (818)70-LASER.

Maryland Interactive Technologies. *The business disc.* 11767 Bonita Avenue, Owings Mills, MD 21117. (301) 337-4117.

MCA Non-Theatrical. 70 Universal City, Universal City, CA 91606. (818) 777-4315.

MECC. 3490 Lexington Ave. North, St. Paul MN 55126. (612) 481-3670.

Media Learning Systems. *Earth & Space, PALS,* and a variety of videodiscs for other subject areas. 1492 W. Colorado Blvd., Pasadena, CA 91105. (800) 321-5936, (800) 451-2959 in California, or (818) 449-0006.

Miami-Dade Community College. *Interactive math: Probability and statistics.* 11011 SW 104 Street, Miami, FL 33176. (305) 347-2158.

Minnesota Educational Computing Consortium (MECC). *The presenter.* 3490 Lexington Avenue North, St. Paul, MN 55126. (800) 228-3504 Ext. 527.

Modern Solutions/Modern. *TIP-aaids & tip-dart.* (212) 838-6877.

National Education Training Group (NETG). *Videodiscs for training in a variety of subject areas including driver's education, programming, communication, and business management.* Corporate Headquarters, 1751 West Diehl Road, Naperville, IL 60563-9099. (800) 225-3063 or (708) 369-3000. FAX: (708) 983-4541.

National Geographic Society Educational Services. Dept. 5413, Washington, D.C. 20036. (800) 368-2728.

Nebraska Videodisc Group. P.O. Box 83111, Lincoln, NE 68501.

North American Philips. P.O. Box 6950, Knoxville, TN 37914.

Optical Data Corporation. *Windows on science, the living textbook, multimedia libraries, & space disc.* 30 Technology Drive, Warren, NJ 07059. (800) 524-2481 or (908) 668-0022.

Optical Programming Assoc. 445 Park Avenue, New York, NY 10022. (212) 605-2755.

Pioneer LDCA, Inc., 2265 East 220th Street, Long Beach, CA 90810. (213) 835-6177.

Pyramid Film & Video. 2801 Colorado Ave., Santa Monica, CA 90404. (310) 828-7577.

Scholastic Inc. *Interactive Nova multimedia science library.* 2931 East McCarty Street, P.O. Box 7502, Jefferson City, MO 65102-9968. (800) 541-5513.

SETS. 15717 Crabbs Branch Way, Rockville, MD 20l855-2634. (800) 422-7387.

Silver Burdett & Ginn. (1992). *Science horizons videodiscs.* Product Manager, Science, Silver Burdett & Ginn, 250 James Street, Morristown, NY 07960-1918.

Simon Fraser University. Burnaby British Columbia, Canada 25A1S6. (604) 291-4418.

Social Studies School Service. A variety of subject areas in addition to social studies. 10200 Jefferson Boulevard, Room 10, P.O. Box 802, Culver City, CA 90232-0802. (800) 421-4246 or (310) 839-2436. FAX: (310) 839-2249.

Starship Industries. 605 Utterback Store Road, Great Falls, VA 22066. (702) 430-8692.

Systems Impact, Inc. *Mastering fractions, mastering decimals and per cents, mastering rations and word problem strategies, mastering equations, roots, and exponents, understanding chemistry and energy, & earth science.* 4400 MacArthur Blvd. NW, Suite 203, Washington, DC 20007. (800) 822-4636 or (202) 342-9369.

Technology Resources Center of the U.S. Department of Education. 80 F Street, N.W., Washington, DC.

TELL Systems. *A good beginning (TESOL).* 650 E. Windward Circle, Tucson, AZ 85704. (602) 297-0754.

Texas Learning Technology Group (TLTG). P.O. Box 2947, Austin, TX 78769. (512) 467-0222.

TVOntario U.S. Office. 143 West Franklin Street, Suite 206, Chapel Hill, NC 27516. (800) 331-9566.

Universal Color Slide Co. *Videodiscs for art.* 8450 South Tamiami Trail, Sarasota, FL 34238-2936. (800) 326-1367. FAX: (800) 487-0250.

University of Delaware. Newark, DE 19716. (302) 451-8161.

Verne's Magnavox. 15266 Goldenwest Blvd., Westminister, CA 92683. (714) 898-9561.

Videodiscovery, Inc. *Bio sci II, life cycles, the cell biology videodisc, our environment, the Smithsonian laserdisc collection, & exotic plants.* 1700 Westlake Ave. N., Suite 600, Seattle, WA 98109-3012. (206) 285-5400 or (800) 548-3472.

Voyager Company, The. *Regard for the planet, the Vincent Van Gogh revisited, the National Gallery of Art, the first emperor, & the Louvre.* 1351 Pacific Coast Hwy., Santa Monica, CA 90401. (310) 451-1383 or (800) 446-2001.

VPI/AC Video Incorporated. *Videodiscs for art.* 381 Park Avenue South, Suite 621, New York, NY 10016. (212) 685-5522. FAX: (212) 685-5486.

Wiley and Sons. 605 Third Avenue, New York, NY 10158. (212) 850-6000.

Wings for Learning. 1600 Green Hills Road, P.O. Box 660002, Scotts Valley, CA 95067-0002. (800) 321-7511.

Wisconsin Foundation for VTAE, Inc. *Interactive modumath.* (608) 831-6313.

Yale University Press. *Perseus 1.0.* 92A Yale Station, New Haven, CT 06520. (203) 432-0912. FAX: (203) 432-2394.

Zenger Video. A variety of subject areas. 10200 Jefferson Blvd., Room 902, P.O. Box 802, Culver City, CA 90232-0802. (800) 421-4246 or (310) 839-2436. FAX: (310) 839-2249.

Ztek Co. Over 300 titles. P.O. Box 952, Lexington, KY 40555. (800) 247-1603 or (502) 584-8505.

Appendix B
Organizations, Conferences, and Publications on Newer Media: CD-ROMS and Videodiscs

Organizations and Conferences

Association for the Development of Computer Based Instruction (ADCIS). ADCIS sponsors an annual international conference and a publication. Miller Hall 409, Western Washington University, Bellingham, WA 98225.

Association for Educational Communications & Technology (AECT). AECT sponsors an annual international conference and several publications. 1126 16th Street, N.W., Washington, DC 20036.

CD-ROM Conference. Sponsored by Microsoft. (206) 867-3341 or (206) 882-8080.

EDUCOM (Educational Computing). (609) 520-3343.

Institute for Graphic Communication, Inc. (IGC) 375 Commonwealth Avenue, Boston, MA 02115.

Institute for the Transfer of Technology to Education. National School Boards Association, 1680 Duke Street, Alexandria, VA 22314.

Interactive Video Industry Association. P.O. Box 5, Falls Church, VA 22046. (703) 534-1019.

International Communications Industry Association. 3150 Spring Street, Fairfax, VA 22031.

International Interactive Communications Society (IICS). IICS has local chapters, meetings, newletters, as well as national meetings and publications. 2298 Valerie Court, Campbell, CA 95008-3723. (408) 866-7941.

International Society for Technology in Education (ISTE). ISTE sponsors several annual conferences, journals, and books. NECC is an ISTE-sponsored event. University of Oregon, 1787 Agate Street, Eugene, OR 97403-9905.

National Demonstration Lab (NDL). The NDL conducts several in-house teacher training seminars on interactive video as well as being a source for review and selection of educational videodiscs. Smithsonian Institute, Arts and Industries Building, Room 1130, Washington, DC 20056.

Nebraska Videodisc Design/Production Group. This organization conducts several annual professional seminars on videodiscs with a broad list of topics ranging from how to use a videodisc to how to make one. P.O. Box 83111, Lincoln, NE 68501. (402) 472-3611.

NECC (National Educational Computing Conference). This annual national conference is sponsored by ISTE. See ISTE.

Optical Data Corporation. 30 Technology Drive, Box 4919, Warren, NJ 07060. (800) 524-2481, (201) 668-0022. FAX: (201) 668-1322.

Optical Information Systems Conference. Meckler Publishing Corporation, Westport, CN (203) 226-6967.

Society for Applied Learning Technology (SALT). SALT sponsors several annual national conferences and a newsletter. 50 Culpeper St., Warrenton, VA 22186. (800) 457-6812, (703) 347-0055.

Technology Resources Center. U.S. Department of Education, 80 F Street, N.W., Research Library, Washington, DC 20208-5725.

University of Nebraska. The Videodisc Design/Production Group sponsors workshops. KUON-TV/University of Nebraska-Lincoln, P.O. Box 83111, Lincoln, NE 68501-3111. (402) 472-3611.

Publications

Academic Computing. Academic Computing Publications, Inc., 200 West Virginia, McKinney, TX 75069.

AmigaNews. Scholastic Inc., 730 Broadway, New York, NY 10003.

Archives and Museum Informatics. Archives & Museum Informatics, 5600 Northumberland Street, Pittsburgh, PA 15217. (412) 421-4638.

CBT Directions. Weingarten Publications, Circulation, 38 Chauncy Street, Boston, MA 02111. (617) 542-0146.

CD-I World. 49 Bayview, Suite 200 (P.O. Box 1358), Camden, ME 04843. (207) 236-8524.

CD-ROM Professional. 11 Tannery Lane, Weston, CT 06883.

CD-ROM Review. CW Communications, Peterborough, NH. (800) 258-5473 or (603) 924-9471.

Classroom Computer Learning. Technology on Campus, 2451 East River Road, Dayton, OH 45439.

Computing Teacher. Journal of the International Society for Technology in Education (ISTE), University of Oregon, 1787 Agate Street, Eugene, OR 97403-9905.

CUE Newsletter. Computer Using Educators, Inc., P.O. Box 2087, Menlo Park, CA 94026.

Curriculum Product News. Six River Bend Center, 911 Hope Street, Stamford, CT 06907-0949.

Educational Technology Abstracts. Carfax Publishing Company, P.O. Box 25, Abingdon, Oxfordshire, OX14 3UE, United Kingdom. 1-0235-30444.

Educational Technology Journal. 720 Palisade Avenue, Englewood Cliffs, NJ 07632.

Electronic Learning. 730 Broadway, New York, NY 10003.

HyperAge. HyperAge Communications, Inc., Sunnyvale, CA. (212) 601-2832.

HyperLink Magazine. Publisher's Guild, Inc., Eugene, OR. (503) 484-5157.

Hypermedia. Taylor Graham Publishing, 500 Chesham House, 150 Regent Street, London, W1R 5FA, United Kingdom.

HyperNexus—Journal of Hypermedia and Multimedia Studies. ISTE, University of Oregon, 1787 Agate Street, Eugene, OR 97403-9905.

IACE Journal. International Association for Computers in Education, 2130 17th Street, N.W., Washington, DC 20036.

IICS Reporter. P.O. BoxThe International Council for Computers in Education, University of Oregon, 1787 Agate Street, Eugene, OR 97403-9950.

InCider/A+. 80 Elm St., Perborough, NH 03458. (603) 924-0100.

Instruction Delivery Systems. Interactive Instruction Development, 50 Culpepper Street, Warrenton, VA 22186.

Interact. International Interactive Communications Society, College of Communications, California State University-Chico, Chico, CA 95929-0504.

International Council for Computers in Education, University of Oregon, 1787 Agate Street, Eugene, OR 97403-9950.

Journal of Computing in Higher Education. Paideia Publishers, P.O. Box 343, Ashfield, MA 01330.

Journal of Educational Multimedia and Hypermedia. Association for the Advancement of Computing in Education. P.O. Box 2966, Charlottesville, VA 22902. (804) 973-3987.

Journal of Educational Technology Systems. Society for Applied Learning Technology, 50 Culpepper Street, Warrenton, VA 22186.

Journal of Technology and Teacher Education. Association for the Advancement of Computing in Education. P.O. Box 2966, Charlottesville, VA 22902. (804) 973-3987.

Media & Methods. 1429 Walnut Street, Philadelphia, PA 19102.

MedicalDisc Reporter. 5219 Acadcia Ave., Bethesda, MD 20814.

Multimedia & Videodisc Monitor. P.O. Box 26, Falls Church, VA 22040. (703) 241-1799.

MusDisc News. University of Delaware, Department of Music, Newark, DE 19716. (302) 451-2577.

NewMedia Magazine. Editorial Department, 901 Mariner's Island Blvd., Suite 365, San Mateo, CA 94404. (415) 573-5170.

Optical Information Systems Magazine. Meckler Publications, Westport, CN. (203) 226-6967.

Presentation Products Magazine. P.O. Box 1142, Skokie, IL 60076-8142.

SIGVIM Newsletter. The International Council for Computers in Education, University of Oregon, 1787 Agate Street, Eugene, OR 97403-9950.

Syllabus for the Macintosh. P.O. Box 2716, Sunnyvale, CA 94087-0716. (408) 257-9416.

Tech Trends. The Association for Educational Communications & Technology (AECT). 1025 Vermont Avenue, NW, Suite 820, Washington, D.C. 20005. (202) 347-7834.

T.H.E. Journal. 80 E. Northwest Highway, Suite 822, Palatine, IL 60067.

The Quick Time Forum. Meckler Corporation, 11 Ferry Lane West, Westport, CT 06880. (203) 226-6967.

Training. 50 South Ninth Street, Minneapolis, MN 55402.

Video Computing. Indiatlantic, FL. (305) 777-1607.

Videodiscs in Museums: A Project and Resource Directory by Roberta H. Binder. A profile of 102 US museums, 29 international sites, and 41 national parks using videodiscs. Available from Future Systems Inc. (703) 241-1799 or (800) 323-DISC. FAX: (703) 532-0529.

Video Technology Newsletter. Vidmar Communications. 1680 Vine Street, Hollywood, CA 90028.

Books

Avanced Interactive Video Design. (1988). Nicholas V. Iuppa & Karl Anderson. Knowledge Industry Publications, Inc., 701 Westchester Ave., White Plains, NY 10604.

The Complete Interactive Video Courseware Directory. Convergent Technology Association. 97 Devonshire Drive, New Hyde Park, NY 11040. (516) 248-5984.

Creating Interactive Multimedia. Carol J. Anderson & Mark D. Veljkov. (1990). Scott, Foresman Macintosh Computer Books, 1900 E. Lake Avenue, Glenview, IL 60025.

Directory of Multimedia Equipment, Software and Services. International Communications Industries Association, 3150 Spring Street, Fairfax, VA 22031-2399. (703) 273-7200. FAX: (703) 278-8082.

The DISConnection: How to Interface Computers and Video. (1988). Gerald A. Souter. Knowledge Industry Publications, Inc., 701 Westchester Avenue, White Plains, NY 10604.

Effectiveness and Cost of Interactive Videodisc Instruction in Defense Training and Education. (July 1990). J. D. Fletcher. Institute for Defense Analyses, 1801 N. Beauregard Street, Alexandria, VA 22311-1772. IDA Paper P-2372.

The IBM Multimedia Handbook. (1991). Steve Floyd. Brady Publishing, 15 Columbus Circle, New York, NY 10023.

Interactive Video. (1987). Richard Schwier. Educational Technology Publications, Englewood Cliffs, NJ 07632.

Interactive Video. (1989). The Educational Technology Anthology Series, Volume 1. Educational Technology Publications, Englewood Cliffs, NJ 07632.

Making Movies on Your Macintosh. (1992). Robert Hone. Prima Publishing. Available from booksellers nationwide.

Managing Interactive Video/Multimedia Projects. (1990). Robert E. Bergman & Thomas V. Moore. Educational Technology Publications, Englewood Cliffs, NJ 07632.

The Power of Multimedia—A Guide to Interactive Technology in Education and Business. (1990). Interactive Video Industry Association, 800 K Street, N.W., Suite 440, Washington, D.C. 20001.

Producer's Guide to Interactive Videodiscs. (1991). Martin Perlmutter. Knowledge Industry Publications, Inc., 701 Westchester Avenue, White Plains, NY 10604.

The Videodisc Compendium for Education and Training. (1993). A complete sourcebook listing thousands of videodiscs, CD-ROMs, and multimedia software authoring tools for education and training. Emerging Technology Consultants, Distribution Center, P.O. Box 120444, St. Paul, MN 55112. (612) 639-3973. FAX: (612) 639-0110.

Using Video: Interactive and Linear Designs. (1989). Joseph W. Arwady & Diane M. Gayeski. Educational Technology Publications, Englewood Cliffs, NJ 07632.

Videodisc/Microcomputer Courseware Design. (1982). Michael L. De-Bloois. Educational Technology Publications, Englewood Cliffs, NJ 07632.

Appendix C
Directory of Authoring Tools

Act III Ver. 2.0—for MS/PC-DOS machines.
> Informatics Group, Inc., 80 Shield Street, West Hartford, CT 06110. (203) 953-4040.

Adapt—for MS/PC-DOS machines.
> Loral Aerospace Corporation, 7150 Standard Dr., Building 4, Hanover, MD 21076. (301) 796-2198.

Adroit—for MS/PC-DOS machines.
> Computer Associates, 400 Oak St., Garden City, NY 11530. (516) 227-3300 or (201) 874-9000.

AIP Coursemaster—for MS/PC-DOS machines.
> Am. Inds. Publications, P.O. Box 2831, Durham, NC 27705. (919) 286-2199.

AIS-II PC—for MS/PC-DOS machines.
> McDonnell Douglas Training Systems, 2450 S. Peoria St., Suite 400, Aurora, CA 80014. (303) 671-4800.

AmigaVision 1.2—for Amiga computers.
> Commodore, 1200 Wilson Dr., West Chester, PA 19380. (215) 431-9100.

Applause—for MS/PC-DOS machines.
> Ashton-Tate, 20101 Hamilton Ave., Torrance, CA 90502-1341. (800) 437-4329, (213) 538-7725, or (213) 329-8000.

ASAP!—for MS/PC-DOS machines.
> Ashton Interactive Training, P.O. Box 1067, Vestal, NY 13851. (607) 748-4015.

Ask-Me 2000—for MS/PC-DOS machines.
> Ask-Me Information Center, 112 Roberts Street, Suite 14, Fargo, ND 58102. (800) 678-5511 or (701) 293-1004.

Audio Visual Connection—for MS/PC-DOS machines.
> IBM Corp, 4111 Northside Parkway, Atlanta, GA 30327. (800) 627-0920.

Authology: MultiMedia—for 386 MS/PC-DOS machines.
> CEIT Systems, 4800 Great American Pkwy, Suite 200, Santa Clara, CA 95054. (408) 986-1101 or (408) 943-9797.

Authority—for MS/PC-DOS machines.
> Spectrum Interactive, 9 Oak Park Drive, Bedford, MA 01730. (617) 271-9500.

AuthorPlus Color—versions are available for Apple II computers and for MS/PC-DOS machines.

Daines Associates, Box 75962, St. Paul, MN 55175. (612) 298-1104.

Authorware Professional—versions are available for MS/PC-DOS machines with Windows 3.0 or later and for Macintosh computers.
　　Macromedia, 600 Townsend St., San Francisco, CA 94103. (800) 288-0572 or (415) 442-0200.

AutoTrainer—for MS/PC-DOS machines.
　　Grey Management Consulting Associates, 730 Gay St., Westwood, MA 02090. (617) 890-4670.

AVC (AudioVisual Connection)—for MS/PC-DOS machines.
　　IBM Corporation. 4111 Northside Parkway, HO4L1, Atlanta, GA 30327. (800) 426-9402, (800) 627-0920 or (404) 238-3245. AVC is available from local IBM offices or through IBM resellers.

Bar'n'Coder—for Macintosh computers.
　　The Pioneer Corp., 600 E. Crescent Ave., Upper Saddle River, NJ 07458. (800) LASER-ON.

Cadenza—for MS/PC-DOS machines.
　　Inspiration, Inc., 6 High View Drive, High Bridge, NJ 08829. (908) 638-4900.

CAN-8—for MS/PC-DOS machines.
　　Homecom Learning Sys. Inc., 150 Bloor St. W., #307, Toronto, M5S 2X9, Ont, Canada. (416) 969-7155.

CAST—for MS/PC-DOS machines.
　　Master Class Corporation, 2697 International Parkway, #201, Viriginia Beach, VA 23452. (804) 427-5090.

CDI Tools—for Macintosh II computers.
　　Interactive Support Group, Inc., 21032 Devonshire St., Suite 209, Chatsworth, CA 91311. (818) 709-7387.

CDS/Genesis—for MS/PC-DOS machines.
　　Interactive Technologies Corp., 9625 Black Mtn. Rd., Ste 315, San Diego, CA 92126. (619) 693-1020.

Challenger!—for MS/PC-DOS machines with Windows 3.0 or later.
　　SASI, 1980 Dominion Way, #203, Colorado Springs, CO 80918. (719) 599-8251.

CLAS-CBT—versions are available for Amiga and for MS/PC-DOS machines.
　　Touch Technologies, 9990 Mesa Rim Rd. #220, San Diego, CA 92121. (619) 743-0494.

Course Builder V4.0—for Macintosh computers.
　　TeleRobotics International, Inc. 7325 Oak Ridge Highway, Suite #104, Knoxville, TN 37931. (615) 690-5600.

CourseMaster—for MS/PC-DOS machines.
　　InterDigital, Inc., Water Street, Lebanon, NJ 08833. (908) 832-2463.

CoursePlus & CoursePlus Two—for MS/PC-DOS machines.
　　Softwords, 4252 Commerce Circle, Victoria, BC, Canada V8Z 4M2. (604) 727-6522.

CourseWriter—for MS/PC-DOS machines.
　　DKW Systems Inc., 9919 105th St., #730, Edmonton, T5K 1B1, Alta, Canada. (403) 426-1551.

CSR Trainer 4000—for MS/PC-DOS machines.
 Computer Sys Research Inc., 40 Darling Dr., Avon, CT 06001. (800)
 922-1190.

Dan Bricklin's Demo II—for MS/PC-DOS machines.
 Software Garden Inc., P.O. Box 373, Newton Highlands, MA 02161.
 (617) 332-2240.

Desktop Studio—for MS/PC-DOS machines.
 Wonder Corp., 51 Winchester St., Newton Highlands, MA 02161. (617)
 965-8400.

Drake—for MS/PC-DOS machines.
 Drake Training & Technologies, 8800 Queen Ave. South, Bloomington, MN. 55431. (612) 921-6807.

Dynamite on Course—for MS/PC-DOS machines.
 Softwords Ltd., #235 560 Johnson St., Victoria, BC V8R 2B9. (604) 381-
 5502.

Educator—for MS/PC-DOS machines.
 Applied Learning, 9 Oak Park Dr., Bedford, MA 01730. (617) 271-0500.

Electronic Publishing System (EPS)—for MS/PC-DOS computers.
 Intellisance Corporation, 1995 Lundy Ave., San Jose, CA 95131. (408)
 432-0430 or (800) 982-1213.

Examiner—for MS/PC-DOS machines.
 Technovision, Inc., 5155 Spectrum Way, Unit 31, Mississauga, Ont,
 Canada L4W 5A1. (416) 625-DISC.

Exemplar—for MS/PC-DOS machines.
 BehaviorTech, 5215 N. O'Connor Blvd., Ste. 2550, Irving, TX 75039.
 (214) 402-9394.

Fast Pitch—for Macintosh computers.
 Objectic Systems, Inc., P.O. Box 58292 Renton, WA 98058. (206) 271-
 6864.

Foundation 2.7—for Amiga computers.
 Impulse Inc., Minneapolis, MN. (800) 328-0184.

GUIDE—versions are available for Macintosh computers and for MS/PC-
 DOS machines.
 OWL International, Inc., 2800 156th Ave. S.E., Bellevue, WA 98007.
 (206) 747-3203.

Hollywood 1.0—for MS/PC-DOS machines with Windows.
 IBM Corporation, Desktop Software Application Systems Division, 472
 Wheelers Farms Road, Milford, CT 06460. (404) 956-4000.

HyperCard—versions are available for Macintosh and Apple IIGS computers.
 Claris Corporation, 5201 Patrick Henry Dr., Santa Clara, CA 95052.
 (408) 727-8227.

HyperCASE—for MS/PC DOS 3.0 or higher machines.
 Interactive Image Technologies, 908 Niagara Falls Blvd., North
 Tonawanda, NY 14120. (416) 361-0333.

Hyperdoc 2.1—for MS/PC DOS machines.
 Hyperdoc, Inc., One Almaden Blvd., #620, San Jose, CA 95113. (408)
 292-7970.

HyperStudio GS 3.0—versions are available for Macintosh and Apple IIGS computers.
   Roger Wagner Publishing, Inc., 1050 Pioneer Way, Suite P, El Cajon, CA 92020. (619) 442-0524, (619) 442-0522, or (800) 421-6526.

HyperWriter 3.0!—for MS/PC DOS 3.0 or higher machines.
   Nitergaid, Inc., 2490 Black Rock Trpk., #337, Fairfield, CT 06430. (203) 380-1280.

IconAuthor—for MS/PC-DOS machines with Windows 3.0 or higher.
   Aimtech Corp., 20 Trafalgar Sq., Nashua, NH 03063. (800) 289-2884 or (603) 883-0220.

I.De.A.S.—for MS/PC-DOS machines.
   OmniCom Associates, 407 Coddington Rd., Ithaca, NY 14850. (607) 272-7700.

IDI Author—for Macintosh computers.
   Tandberg Educational Inc., Instructional Design International, 1775 Church St., NW, Washington, DC 20036. (202) 332-5353 or (914) 277-3320.

IMAGES—for MS/PC DOS computers.
   Computer Knowledge International, 1300 Weathervane Lane, #210, Akron, OH 44313. (216) 836-1866 or (216) 836-1872.

IMRI—for MS/PC-DOS and Macintosh machines.
   Armpwotz, 488 Green Glen Way, Mill Valley, CA 94941. (415) 383-2878.

IMSMATT 2000—for MS/PC-DOS machines.
   IMSMATT Corp., 500 N. Washington St., #101, Falls Church, VA 22046. (703) 533-7500.

InfoWindows Presentation System Version 1.0 (IWPS)—for IBM computers. IBM has discontinued its marketing and support of IWPS.
   IBM Education System, 301 Windy Ridge Pky, Atlanta, GA 30327. (404) 988-2344.

Infowriter Pro—for MS/PC-DOS machines.
   Infowriter, 7323 E. 59th St., Tulsa, OK 74145. (918) 663-0218.

Insight—versions are available for Apple II computers and for MS/PC-DOS machines.
   Whitney Educational Services, 415 S. Eldorado St., San Mateo, CA 94402. (415) 340-9822.

Instructor—for Apple II computers.
   BCD Associates, Inc., 7510 N. Broadway Ext., #205, Oklahoma City, OK 73116. (405) 843-4574.

Interact—for MS/PC-DOS machines.
   Ashton Interactive Training Co., P.O. Box 1067, Vestal, NY 13851. (607) 748-4015.

Interactive DiskCourse—for Macintosh II computers.
   Key Learning Centers, 21S Huckleberry Dr., Norwalk, CT 06850. (203) 847-2368.

Interactive Virtual Video—for MS/PC-DOS machines.
   V_Graph Inc., Box 105, 1275 Westown Thorton Rd., Westown, PA 19395. (215) 399-1521.

InterFlex—for MS/PC-DOS machines.

Catharon Productions, Inc., Rt. 1, Box 8, Ghent, NY 12075. (518) 392-9003.

IV-D—for MS/PC-DOS machines.

Computer Sciences Corp., 813 Diligence Drive, #110, Newport News, VA 23606. (804) 873-1024.

IWPS—for MS/PC-DOS machines.

IBM Corp, 4111 Northside Pkwy., Atlanta, GA 30327. (800)627-0920.

KAware Disk Publisher—for MS/PC-DOS machines.

Knowledge Access International, 2685 Marini Way, Suite 1305, Mountain View, CA 94043. (415) 969-0606.

KSS Author—for MS/PC-DOS machines.

Comware Inc., 4225 Malsbary Road, Cincinnati, OH 45242. (513) 791-4224.

The Laserdisc Controller 2.0—for MS/PC DOS 2.1 or higher machines.

Vidcomp Distributors. (517) 799-4139.

Laserworks—for Apple II computers.

Teaching Technologies, P.O. Box 3808, San Luis Obispo, CA 93403.

LessonCard—for Macintosh computers.

School Vision, 240 Cypress St., Abilene, TX 79601. (800) 299-6709.

LessonMaker—for Macintosh computers.

Optical Data Corp., 30 Technology Drive, Warren, NJ 07059. (800) 524-2481.

Leverage Language Authoring Sys.—for MS/PC-DOS machines.

Creative Learning Systems, 7901 4th St North, Suite 207, St. Petersburg, FL 33702. (813) 579-4597.

LinkWay Live!—for MS/PC DOS 2.1 or higher machines.

IBM Corporation. P.O. Box 2150 (H05K1), Atlanta, GA 30301-2150 or from IBM Corporation, 4111 Northside Pkwy., Atlanta, GA 30327. (404) 238-3245, (800) 627-0920, (800) 426-9402, or (800) IBM-2468.

LinkWay Toolkit—for MS/PC DOS 2.1 or higher machines.

A toolkit of various multimedia buttons, such as interface buttons to control a videodisc player.

Washington Computer Services, Bellingham, WA. (206) 734-8248.

LinkWay Version 2.01—for MS/PC DOS 2.1 or higher machines.

IBM Corporation. P.O. Box 2150 (H05K1), Atlanta, GA 30301-2150 or from IBM Corporation, 4111 Northside Pkwy., Atlanta, GA 30327. (404) 238-3245, (800) 627-0920, (800) 426-9402, or (800) IBM-2468. LinkWay is also available from local IBM offices or through IBM resellers.

Linx Industrial and Linx Lite—for Macintosh computers.

Warren-Forthought, 1212 North Velasco, Angleton, TX 77515. (409) 849-1239.

LS/1—for MS/PC-DOS machines.

IBM Corporation, 4111 Northside Parkway, H04L1, Atlanta, GA 30327. (800) 426-9402.

MacPresents—for Macintosh computers.

Intellimation, Santa Barbara, CA 9333116. (800) 346-8355.

MacroMind Director 3.0—for Macintosh computers.
> MacroMind, 600 Townsend St., San Francisco, CA 94103. (800) 288-0572 or (415) 442-0200.

MacVideo Interactive—for Macintosh II computers.
> Edudisc, Inc., 1400 Tyne Blvd., Nashville, TN 37215. (615) 373-2506.

MediaMaker—for Macintosh II computers.
> Macromedia, (800) 288-0572 or (415) 442-0200.

MediaText—for Macintosh computers and MS/PC DOS 2.1 or higher machines.
> Wings for Learning, 1600 Green Hills Rd., Scotts Valley, CA 95067. (800) 321-7511 or (408) 438-5502.

Mentor/MacVideo—for Macintosh computers.
> Edudisc, Inc., 1400 Tyne Blvd., Nashville, TN 37215-4416. (615) 373-2506.

MESA—for MS/PC-DOS machines.
> Interactive Tech. Inc., P.O. Box 948, Springdale, AR 72765. (501) 442-0301.

Microinstructor—for MS/PC-DOS machines.
> Mosby Co., 11830 Westline Inds Dr., St. Louis, MO 63146. (800) 325-4177.

Multimedia Presentation Generator (MPG)—for MS/PC-DOS machines.
> IBM Corporation. P.O. Box 2150 (H05K1), Atlanta, GA 30301-2150. (800) 627-0920.

NATAL—for MS/PC-DOS machines.
> Softwords, 4252 Commerce Circle, Victoria, BC, Canada V87 4M2. (604) 727-6522.

Nexus—for MS/PC-DOS machines.
> Rush Order, 3216 Ash, Palo Alto, CA 94306. (800) 522-5939.

Oasys 2.0—for MS/PC-DOS machines.
> Online Computer Systems, Inc., 20251 Century Boulevard, Germantown, MD 20874. (301) 428-3700 or (800) 922-9204.

Pareto—for MS/PC-DOS machines.
> Information Proc. Assn., 5218 Craigmont, Memphis, TN 38134. (901) 522-0242.

PCD3—for MS/PC-DOS machines.
> Control Data Corp., 8100 34th Ave. S., Minneapolis, MN 55440. (612) 921-6904.

PC Interact—for MS/PC-DOS machines.
> Ridgewood Industries, Inc., P.O. Box 409, Glenview, IL 60025. (708) 724-9273.

PCS—for MS/PC-DOS machines.
> Sage Software, 1700 NW 167th Pl., Beaverton, OR 97006. (800) 537-7800.

PC Train—for MS/PC-DOS machines.
> Eng. Research Assoc., 6425 N. Pensacola Blvd., Pensacola, FL 32505. (904) 476-1750.

Persuasion 2.0—versions are available for Macintosh computers and for MS/PC-DOS machines for Windows.

Aldus Corporation, 411 First Avenue South, Seattle, WA 98104. (206) 622-5500.

Phoenix Micro—for MS/PC-DOS machines.
Goal Systems International, 7965 North High St., Columbus, OH 43235. (614) 888-1775 or (800) 848-4640.

PIDAS—for MS/PC-DOS machines.
Professional Train Sys., 430 10th St., Ste S-108, Atlanta, GA 30318. (404) 872-9700.

Plus 1.0—versions are available for Macintosh computers and for MS/PC-DOS machines with Windows.
Spinnaker Software, 201 Broadway, Cambridge, MA 02139. (617) 494-1200, (617) 494-9148, or (800) 323-8088, ex. 328.

Podium—for MS/PC DOS 2.1 machines and for Windows.
The Instructional Technology Center, 305 Willard Hall Education Buidling, University of Delaware, Newark, DE 19716-1128. (302) 831-8164 FAX: (302) 831-2089.

PowerPoint 3.0—versions are available for Macintosh computers and for MS/PC-DOS machines with Windows.
Microsoft Sales and Service, One Microsoft Way, Redmond, WA 98052-6399. (800) 426-9400.

Presenter—for Apple II machines.
Minnesota Educational Computing Corporation (MECC), 3490 Lexington Avenue North, St. Paul, MN 55126.

PROPI—for MS/PC-DOS machines.
ASYS Computer Systems, Inc., 104 Viewcrest, Bellingham, WA 98225. (206) 734-2553.

PTP/1—for MS/PC-DOS machines.
Software & Edu Assn., 3888 Riviera Dr., #301, San Diego, CA 92109. (619) 270-4570.

Quest Authoring System 4.0—for MS/PC-DOS machines with DOS 2.1 or higher.
Allen Communications, 5225 Wiley Post Way, Salt Lake City, UT 84116. (800) 325-7850 or (801) 537-7800.

SABER—for MS/PC-DOS machines.
Pinnacle Courseware Inc., 814 Blossom Hill Rd., Ste 215, San Jose, CA 95123. (408) 972-8383.

Sage—for 80286/80386 PC
WICAT: The Learning Improvement Company, 1875 S. State St., Orem, UT 84058. (800) 759-4228, ext. 305.

SAM for Windows—for MS/PC-DOS machines with Windows 3.0 or higher.
Technology Applications Group, 1700 West Big Beaver Rd., Suite 265, Troy, MI 48084. (313) 649-5200.

Scholar/Teach—for MS/PC-DOS machines.
Boeing Computer Ser., 665 Andover Park West, Tukwila, WA 98188. (206) 575-7793.

Scrypt—for MS/PC-DOS machines.
New Media Graphics, 780 Boston Rd., Billerica, MA 01820. (617) 663-0666.

Shelley—for MS/PC-DOS machines.
>ComTrain Inc., 152 Mill St., Grass Valley, CA 95945. (916) 273-0845.

Showcase—for MS/PC-DOS computers.
>Optical Disk & Video Systems, 1142 Manhattan Ave., Suite CP27, Manhattan Beach, CA 90266. (213) 318-0506.

Simulation Construction Kit—for Apple II computers.
>Hartley Courseware, Inc., 133 Bridge St., Dimondale, MI 48821. (517) 646-6458.

SOCRATIC—for MS/PC-DOS machines.
>Solutions Unlimited, P.O. Box 140, Edgecomb, ME 04556. (207) 882-6222.

Spinnaker Plus—for Macintosh computers and computers operating OS/2 or Windows 3.0.
>Spinnaker Software, Cambridge, MA (617) 494-1200.

Storyboard Live!—for MS/PC-DOS computers.
>IBM Corporation,Desktop Software, Application Systems Division, 472 Wheelers Farms Road, Milford, CT 06460. (800) IBM-7699 or (404) 956-4000.

Study Guide II—for Apple II computers.
>Minnesota Educational Computing Corporation (MECC), 3490 Lexington Avenue North, St. Paul, MN 55126.

Summit Authoring System—for MS/PC-DOS computers.
>Conceptual Systems, Inc., 1010 Wayne Ave., 14th Floor, Silver Spring, MD 20910. (301) 589-1800.

SuperCard—for Macintosh computers.
>Silicon Beach Software, Inc., P.O. Box 261430, San Diego, CA 92126. (619) 695-6956.

Syllabus—versions are available for Macintosh computers and for MS/PC-DOS machines with Windows.
>Goal Systems International, 26 Landsdowne, Suite 125, Cambridge, MA 02139. (617) 621-9974.

tbt Author—for MS/PC-DOS machines.
>HyperGraphics Corporation, 308 N. Carroll Blvd., Denton, TX 76201. (800) 438-6537 or (817) 565-0004.

Teachers Aide—for MS/PC-DOS machines.
>Selection Sys Inc., 2731 77th St. SE, Mercer Island, WA 98040. (206) 236-2700.

TenCORE Producer—for MS/PC-DOS machines.
>Computer Teaching Corporation, 1713 S. State St., Champaign, IL 61820. (217) 352-6363.

TIE—for MS/PC-DOS machines with Windows.
>Global Info. Systems, 1800 Woodfield Dr., Savoy, IL 61874-9505. (217) 352-1165.

ToolBook 1.5—for MS/PC DOS 3.1 or higher machines with Windows 3.0 or higher.
>Asymetrix Corp., 110-110th Avenue N.E. Suite 717, Bellevue, WA. (800) 756-6971, (206) 637-1600, (206) 637-1500, or (206) 462-0501.

Trainer 4000—for MS/PC-DOS machines.
  Computer Systems Research, Avon Park South, P.O. Box 45, Avon, CT 06001. (203) 678-1212.

Trillian Concurrent—for MS/PC-DOS machines.
  Trillian Computer Corp., 405 Alberto Way, MS/1, Los Gatos, CA 95030. (408) 358-2761.

Tutor-Tech—for Apple II series of computers.
  Techware Corporation, P.O. Box 151085, Altamonte Springs, FL 32715. (407) 695-9000, (407) 695-9000 or (800) 34-REACH.

Unison Author Language—for MS/PC-DOS 2.0 or higher machines.
  Courseware Applications, Inc., 481 Devonshire Drive, Champaign, IL 61820. (217) 359-1878.

Video Builder—for Macintosh computers.
  Telerobotics International Inc. (615) 690-5600.

Videodisc ShowMaker—for Macintosh computers
  Intellimation, Santa Barbara, CA 93116. (800)-346-8355.

VideoDiscWriter—for Macintosh computers.
  Whitney Educational Services, 18 Eleventh Ave., San Mateo, CA 94401. (415) 341-5818.

VideoLesson Writer—for Apple II computers.
  Whitney Educational Services, 415 S. Eldorado Street, San Mateo, CA 94402.

VideoMaker—for Macintosh computers.
  Intellimation, Santa Barbara, CA. (800) 3-INTELL.

VIDKIT II—for MS/PC-DOS machines.
  Videodiscovery, 1515 Dexter Ave. N., Seattle, WA 98109. (800) 548-3472 or (206) 285-5400.

The Voyager Videodisc ToolKit—for MS/PC DOS 2.1 or higher machines with Windows 3.1 with Multimedia Extensions.
  The Voyager Company, 1351 Pacific Coast Hwy., Santa Monica, CA 90401 (310) 451-1383 or (800) 446-2001.

The Voyager Videodisc ToolKit ver. 2.2—for Macintosh computers with HyperCard 2.1.
  The Voyager Company, 1351 Pacific Coast Hwy., Santa Monica, CA 90401 (310) 451-1383 or (800) 446-2001.

Appendix D
Sources for Videodisc Mastering Companies

Optical Disc Corporation (ODC) Facilities for Recording Draw and Check Discs

Crawford Communications. 535 Plasamour Drive, Atlanta, GA 30324. (800) 831-8027 or (404) 876-7149.

Dinner+Allied. 620 Third Street, San Francisco, CA 94107. (415) 777-1700.

Disc Manufacturing, Inc. 1120 Cosby Way, Anaheim, CA 92806. (714) 630-6700.

EditDroid Los Angeles. A Division of LucasArts, 3000 West Olympic Blvd., Suite 1550, Santa Monica, CA 90404. (310) 315-4880 or (310) 315-5050.

Editworks. 1776B Century Blvd., Atlanta, GA 30345. (404) 325-2289.

Henninger Video. Arlington, VA. (703) 243-3444.

Image PreMastering Services. Mendota Heights, MN. (612) 454-9622.

Kimball Audio-Video. 6221 N. O'Conner, Suite 100, Six Dallas Communications Complex, Irving, TX 75039. (214) 869-0117.

L.A. LaserArts International Ltd. Vancouver, Canada. (604) 739-1136.

Laser Disc Recording Center, Inc. Cambridge, MA. (617) 354-7628.

Laser Edit. 540 N. Hollywood Way, Burbank, CA 91505. (818) 842-1111.

Laser Video. Chicago, IL (312) 467-9006.

Legal Medical Presentation Systems. Richardson, TX. (214) 918-9390.

Magnetic North. 70 Richmond Street East, Suite 100, Toronto, Ontario, Canada M5C 1N8. (416) 365-7622.

Magno Sound & Video. 729 7th Avenue, 9th Floor, New York, NY 10019. (212) 302-2505.

Optical Disc Corporation. 12150 Mora Drive, Santa Fe Springs, CA 90670. (800) 350-3500 or (310) 946-3050.

Optimus. 161 E. Grand Avenue, Chicago, IL 60611. (312) 321-0880.

Pacific Video. Hollywood, CA (213) 462-6256.

Pioneer Corporate Offices. 600 East Crescent Ave., Upper Saddle River, NJ 07458. (800)-LASER ON.

The Post Group. 6335 Homewood Avenue, Hollywood, CA 90028 (213) 462-2300.

The Post Group at the Disney/MGM Studio, Roy O. Disney Production Center, Lake Buena Vista, FL 32830. (407) 560-5600.

Stokes Slide Services. Austin, TX. (512) 458-2201.

Technidisc, Inc. 2250 Meijer Drive, Troy, MI 48084-7111. (800) 321-9610.

Telstar Editing. 29 W. 38th Street, New York, NY 10018. (212) 730-1000.

3M Optical Recording Department. 1425 Parkway Drive, Menomonie WI 54751. (715) 235-5567.

3M Optical Recording Department. 223-5S Center, St. Paul, MN 55144-1000. (715) 235-5567 FAX: (715) 235-0500.

Videodisc Mastering Companies for Producing Videodiscs in Quantities

Pioneer Communications of America. Multimedia Systems Division. 915 E. 230th Street, Carson, CA 90745. (213) 513-1016.

Sony Multimedia Systems Division. Montvale, NY. (201) 930-6034.

3M Optical Recording Department. 3M Center, St. Paul, MN 55144-1000. (612) 733-1110.

Index